Troy Heffernan

Bourdieu and Higher Education

Life in the Modern University

Troy Heffernan
School of Education
La Trobe University
Bundoora, VIC, Australia

ISBN 978-981-16-8223-0   ISBN 978-981-16-8221-6 (eBook)
https://doi.org/10.1007/978-981-16-8221-6

© The Editor(s) (if applicable) and The Author(s), under exclusive license to Springer Nature Singapore Pte Ltd. 2022
This work is subject to copyright. All rights are solely and exclusively licensed by the Publisher, whether the whole or part of the material is concerned, specifically the rights of translation, reprinting, reuse of illustrations, recitation, broadcasting, reproduction on microfilms or in any other physical way, and transmission or information storage and retrieval, electronic adaptation, computer software, or by similar or dissimilar methodology now known or hereafter developed.
The use of general descriptive names, registered names, trademarks, service marks, etc. in this publication does not imply, even in the absence of a specific statement, that such names are exempt from the relevant protective laws and regulations and therefore free for general use.
The publisher, the authors and the editors are safe to assume that the advice and information in this book are believed to be true and accurate at the date of publication. Neither the publisher nor the authors or the editors give a warranty, expressed or implied, with respect to the material contained herein or for any errors or omissions that may have been made. The publisher remains neutral with regard to jurisdictional claims in published maps and institutional affiliations.

This Springer imprint is published by the registered company Springer Nature Singapore Pte Ltd.
The registered company address is: 152 Beach Road, #21-01/04 Gateway East, Singapore 189721, Singapore

Foreword

Bourdieu wrote a lot about education. He wrote about schools, universities and the relationships between the two. He wanted to understand and change the contribution that education made to the production and reproduction of the inequitable status quo. He was particularly concerned at the ways in which privilege was transferred from generation to generation via education, despite the promise made by successive French governments to educate all children and young people equally well, and to reward their meritorious efforts. Bourdieu took up and took on: the hierarchy of disciplines; systems of codification which elevated some knowledges over others; the selective use of languages; and the promotion of particular ways of being a scholar and doing scholarship. He was particularly concerned with sorting and selection processes, not only formal examinations but also the ways in which cultural and social networks of the like-minded excluded and included, promoted and ignored, feted and vilified.

Bourdieu saved some of his most cutting analyses for his own field of sociology which, he argued, was the discipline positioned to understand, explain and critique social and academic injustices. But he saw social scientists as too often blinded by their own internal truths, codes of conduct and values; they were thus ignorant of the ways in which they both benefited from, and were complicit in, inequitable educational and social outcomes.

It is salutary to revisit Bourdieu's writings about the logics of scholarly practice. How little some of this has changed. Many of us smile wryly at Bourdieu's description of academic celebrities who gain "symbolic capital of renown partly independent of recognition within the institution" (Bourdieu 1988, p. 112) and "consecrated heretics" who are "free to choose their own lecture topics for the benefit of a small number of future specialists" only because their colleagues are compelled to teach a largely prescribed syllabus to very large numbers (p. 107). And Bourdieu's critique of the sociological "armchair left", confusing "revolutions in the order of words as radical revolutions in the order of things" (Bourdieu 2000, p. 2), still has strong traction.

However, the universities of postwar France are not the same as today's higher education institutions. In the UK and Australia, where this book is set, universities typically educate a far more numerous and diverse range of students. University websites signal global aspirations and networks, flows of international student populations and modernising managements. And universities are now part of assemblages which signify and materialise the global reach and status of the nation state. They contribute significantly to national GDP. They educate and credential mobile elites, both in country and offshore, via branch campuses. Nevertheless, universities are often tethered to national funding regimes and policy priorities which delimit how much and what they can do. And the higher education landscape across the world is far from equitable, stitched firmly into the economic, political and cultural global positioning of various state and supra-state organisations.

But broad historical patterning holds tight. Higher education is still a powerful engine of social, economic and cultural (re)production. It is still organised according to the logics of hierarchy, even if the measures of distinction are now made visible and legitimated through quantified, rather than being clouded by allusion to the illusion of history and tradition as they were in Bourdieu's France. The realisation of the status quo has nonetheless shifted.

One powerful example of change lies in Bourdieu's analysis of academic work as *skhole*. Bourdieu defines *skhole* as scholastic leisure, time that is "liberated from practical occupations and preoccupations" (Bourdieu, 2000, p. 13) in order to think, contemplate and speculate. Scholars are, he says, educated through a long apprenticeship to value and see as a necessity the provision of time free from immediate demands and pressures; they/we are disposed to see time for thinking as the essence of academic life. While this value may still be prevalent in the academy today, it is hard to imagine today's universities as "scholastic enclosures" where isolated scholars beaver away in a "studious atmosphere withdrawn from the hubbub of the world" (p. 14). Today's casualised academics are likely to view with grim cynicism Bourdieu's articulation of the logics of academic practices-free speech and independent thought borne of the privilege of secure tenure and unfettered hours and weeks to read and write. These days, lecturers struggling with hefty workloads, fragile tenure and temporary contracts yearn for Bourdieu's description of a university where it was apparently possible to be ignorant of the social and economic conditions that supported a life of unencumbered reflective scholarship. Even more secure and established academics might think cynically about the competitive funding regimes which govern who is able to "withdraw from the world in order to think it" (Bourdieu 2000, p. 49), as they are variously subject to publication targets, public engagement and impact rubrics, and a variety of quality and productivity audits.

The example of *skhole* alone is sufficient warning that it is not particularly helpful to transfer the published results of Bourdieu's analyses to contemporary higher education institutions and systems. Rather, it is more generative to work with his theoretical and onto-methodological approach to address the specificities of location, cultural traditions, disciplines and contemporary practices and logics.

Bourdieu orients researchers to ask questions and pursue lines of inquiry which have social, economic and cultural justice as their driver. He offers inter-related points (field, positions and capitals) and methods through which everyday practices and equity-based problems can be explored. Bourdieu advocated using his "toolkit" creatively and thoughtfully. He made no claims that his analysis of, for example, the

French real estate system, housing market and the wider French economy (Bourdieu 2005) would hold in other locations and at other times. He did suggest that the mode of inquiry he used could be adapted to examine other economies, as can be seen in his later collaborative research in *The Weight of the World* (Bourdieu et al. 1999), which is explicitly presented as a methodological and textual exploration.

Bringing Bourdieu to an empirical study of higher education thus requires an historically, culturally and geographically located research design, and deep reflexivity on the part of the researcher. In the case of *skhole* then, which Bourdieu argued was a deeply held truth and moral virtue of and in the French academy, it could be interesting for current critical higher education researchers to consider whether, where, for whom and how the belief in the necessity and value of scholarly time holds, and what troubles and benefits it brings. And, drawing on debates about "fast" and "slow" academic work (Leibowitz and Bozalek 2018; Seeber and Berg 2016; Taylor 2020; Vostal 2019), which show the academy now marked by intensified working conditions, wedded to the exploitation of precarious academic labour and deeply embedded in neoliberalist management and public relations practices (Fleming 2021; Hil 2012; Slaughter and Leslie 1997; Smyth 2017), researchers might find Bourdieu a helpful companion. Working in conversation with Bourdieu not only allows an investigation to go deeper into the situated specifics of this line of thinking, but also to critically evaluate its premises and its generalisations.

Thinking and researching with Bourdieu demands deep engagement with his writings. That is precisely what Troy Heffernan has done. This book not only reports on three research projects, but also offers an elaborated example of what it means to engage with Bourdieusian theory in research. It is, in this sense, a profoundly pedagogical text.

Bourdieu said that it was important to begin any study through an examination of the field. Heffernan begins this book in exactly this way. Drawing on an extensive literatures survey, he develops an explanation of the higher education field. His first empirical step is thus also an explanation of key Bourdieusian ideas. All Bourdieusian scholars need to do precisely this—to engage with Bourdieu's conceptual "tool kit" and to see what it means in the specific context in which fieldwork is to be conducted. Bringing Bourdieu to research is not a superficial answer seeking a problem. Thinking with and through Bourdieu means asking, for example: what is this field; what are its logics, narratives and teleologies, rewards and practices; how did the field come to be like this; what points of tension and struggle exist; what positions and agents are in the field; how is the field connected to wider social, economic and cultural structures and patterns; what lines of change exist and might come to exist. Through thinking with and through distinct, grounded examples, Bourdieu's theory comes to be both embedded and embodied as a way of approaching and generating new understandings.

In partnership with Bourdieu, Heffernan offers a picture of a higher education field in flux, with modern universities looking, being and working very differently than they did relatively recently. The book speaks of, and to, a massified higher education field, to which many more have access, but where changing logics dictate how strong hierarchies of privilege are maintained. Despite moves to be more open to more students, Heffernan argues, universities are subject to financial pressures and a press for global prestige which support agents and positions with both advantaged social capitals and dispositions and newer corporate capitals and dispositions. Heffernan does not suggest that this is an homogenous picture, but rather that the corporatisation and marketisation of higher education play out differently in different institutions dependent in part on their place in university status hierarchies. There are also, he suggests, variations in practices in different disciplines. Heffernan invites us to consider these differences, their consequences and possibilities of and for further change.

The second half of the book takes three positions in the higher education field—(1) the job(s) at the top, the Chancellory, (2) the middle layer, the Dean or head of school and (3) the teaching and researching academic. Using interview and documents as his material, Heffernan examines the varying logics of practice of each position and the relational tensions between them. The data affords analysis of the dispositions necessary for success and survival in each position as well as identification of ongoing changes in the value of particular capitals. Heffernan shows, for instance, that while research capitals may be important in the career pathway from academic to dean, it is entrepreneurial and managerial capitals that matter more for survival in the Chancellory. While some of this explanation is familiar, the distance generated by the Bourdieusian sociological analysis contextualises everyday tensions and makes comprehensible the minutiae of administrative processes and the ambitions and directions taken by senior leaders. Heffernan's explanation of how these leader actions and middle management mediations create the patterning of everyday scholarly life is perhaps some source of small comfort to today's jobbing academics—it's not just me, my school or faculty, my university.

This book contributes to the growing field of critical university studies, as well as to Bourdieusian educational sociology. Those interested in understanding life inside the contemporary university will find the work reported here of value. Those who also want to work with Bourdieu's theoretical approach will also find this an accessible and highly instructive text. I enjoyed reading the book for both of these reasons, and I hope that you do too.

September 2021
Pat Thomson
Professor of Education
The University of Nottingham
Nottingham, UK

References

Bourdieu P (1988) Homo academicus (trans: Collier P). Stanford University Press, Stanford, California
Bourdieu P (2000) Pascalian meditations (trans: Nice R). Polity Press, Oxford
Bourdieu P (2005) The social structures of the economy. Polity, Cambridge

Bourdieu P et al (1999) The weight of the world. Social suffering in contemporary societies (trans: Ferguson PP). Stanford University Press, Stanford, California
Fleming P (2021) Dark academia. How universities die. Pluto Press, London
Hil R (2012) Whackademia. An insider's account of the troubled university. NewSouth, Sydney
Leibowitz B, Bozalek V (2018) Towards a slow scholarship of teaching and learning in the South. Teach High Edu 23(8):981–994
Seeber BK, Berg M (2016) The slow professor. Challenging the culture of speed in the academy. University of Toronto Press, Toronto
Slaughter S, Leslie L (1997) Academic capitalism: politics, policies and the entrepreneurial university. John Hopkins University Press, Baltimore
Smyth J (2017) The toxic university. Zombie leadership, academic rock stars and neoliberal ideology. Palgrave Macmillan, London
Taylor CA (2020) Slow singularities for collective mattering: new material feminist praxis in the accelerated academy. Irish Edu Stud 39(2):255–272
Vostal F (2019) Slowing down modernity: a critique. Time Soc 28(3):1039–1060

Contents

1	**Introduction**	1
	References	6

Part I Bourdieu's Key Theories for Examining Higher Education

2	**Introducing Bourdieu and Higher Education**	9
	Bourdieu in Context	10
	Bourdieu's History	11
	Theory and Bourdieu	11
	Bourdieu on Theory	14
	Bourdieu on Methods and Methodology	15
	Bourdieu on Statistics	16
	Bourdieu on Quantitative and Qualitative Analysis	16
	Theory of Practice	20
	Bourdieu on Education	22
	Summary	25
	References	25
3	**Habitus**	27
	Defining Habitus	28
	Habitus on a Personal Level	32
	Habitus and Its Relationship with Field and Capital	34
	Well-Informed Habitus	37
	Distinction	38
	Hexis	39
	Conditioning	40
	Knowledge and Labouring Classes	43
	Summary	45
	References	46

4	**Field**	49
	Defining Field	50
	Field Trajectory	53
	Status in Academia	61
	Field Theory	63
	Summary	64
	References	64
5	**Capital**	67
	Bourdieu on Capital	68
	Economic Capital: A Starting Point	68
	Economic, Cultural, and Social Capital	69
	Capital Attracts Capital	72
	Reproduction	73
	Increasing Status in a Field	75
	Education is Capital	78
	Summary	81
	References	81

Part II Life in the Modern University

6	**The End of the Ivory Tower**	85
	The Doxa of the Ivory Tower	86
	Incremental Shifts Are Lost in Translation	90
	Summary	94
	References	94
7	**Vice-Chancellors and Presidents: Surveying National and International Academic Markets**	97
	The Changing Field of Senior Leadership	98
	Leaders' Views of Their Roles in the Modern University	100
	Summary	105
	References	106
8	**Deans: The Faculty's New Managers**	109
	The Pressures of Being Dean	111
	Summary	117
	References	118
9	**Academics: The Business of Teaching and Research**	121
	Academic Work in the Modern University	124
	Networks and Success	130
	Summary	132
	References	132

10	**Shifting Borders in the Modern University**	135
	Why Shifting Borders Matter	136
	Who Does (and Does not) Benefit from These Shifting Borders?	137
	Shifting Borders in a Context of Change	140
	The Fields of the Modern University	141
	Where Leaders Find Themselves	145
	Vice-Chancellors and Presidents Looking Outward	146
	The New Fields of Deans	148
	Academics in Their Own Field	150
	Summary	155
	References	155

Conclusion New Directions in the Modern University 157

References 163

Chapter 1
Introduction

Abstract The introduction positions the book within the field of higher education research and explores why Pierre Bourdieu provides relevant theories to examine the changing space of higher education. This chapter also provides some historical context that discusses how things have unfolded in the sector to bring us to the current day, and highlights some of the major issues that will be addressed, answered, and analysed throughout the book.

This book examines how and why universities are changing, what this means for the sector today and in the future, and the dangers within and outside the sector of these changes not being acknowledged. This investigation takes place primarily through a Bourdieusian lens. None of these focus areas or choices regarding theoretical lenses have occurred by chance or in isolation. A brief account of how I came to higher education research and an explanation of why these are pressing issues makes my intentions and the purpose of this book clear. These reasons serve to highlight to those not in the higher education or Bourdieusian research fields why this book is not only about the advancement of knowledge, it is also relevant to anyone working within, or who has an interest in, higher education.

My introduction into academia did not begin in education research, or even the social sciences, but rather in the humanities, and more precisely early modern British history. My choice to study England's queens, kings, and society was relatively uncomplicated. In my view, the seeds of modern-day life in terms of society, business, and education are present in the sixteenth and seventeenth centuries and provide clear connections to the world we know today. At the same time, I enjoyed studying history at school, and university was a natural extension of that learning environment. Thus, with an interest in history and enjoying research, reading, and writing, pursuing a career in academia seemed like a plausible, though far from straightforward, career path.

Making those decisions and hoping to complete the transition from *going to* university, to *working in* a university was where I first began to encounter hurdles; and I suggest these are issues that continue to cause issues for higher education as a sector. I liked history, and I enjoyed school, but why did I believe that I knew what it would be like to work in a university?

© The Author(s), under exclusive license to Springer Nature Singapore Pte Ltd. 2022
T. Heffernan, *Bourdieu and Higher Education*,
https://doi.org/10.1007/978-981-16-8221-6_1

In reality, I, like most people, had no idea. My ideas about university life came from books, and popular culture. While I do not necessarily think many people believe life in a university directly reflects the portrayals they see in popular culture, I for one assumed there would be some semblance of similarity in the sense that working at a university meant giving lectures in theatres, talking about those topics in tutorial groups, grading papers, and doing research—writing books and journal articles. As we will soon explore in this book, this notion of what people *think* working in a university entails, is what Bourdieu would call the doxa of higher education. It is this view of universities, the doxa, that is connected to the far-reaching, long-lasting belief that life in the university is about teaching, engaging in debate, and doing research in offices overflowing with books and eclectic trinkets. Thus, it is necessary to establish early on that very little of this idealistic view remains in the modern university.

Even when I went to university as a student, my perceptions of higher education did not change much because the people I saw working in the university were teaching lectures, talking about those topics in tutorials, or doing research in offices that were filled with books and papers—or so I gathered from walking past offices with open doors. I was not naive enough to think this was all they did, but it was what was *visible*. When you are trying to fill in the blank spaces to make connections with the information you have, you tend not to deviate much from what appears to be the straightest path; and in this instance, the straightest path was one from teaching to research.

So, with an undergraduate and master's degree, I began my doctorate in history. Not long after, I was given the opportunity to begin working in a university. The clarity that formed around the reality of higher education compared with my perceptions occurred almost from the moment I taught my first class and began talking with colleagues. Students were considered to be like customers, and as such, there was an element of a transactional approach that meant there was at least some student expectation that if they paid their tuition and completed the work (somewhat regardless of quality level) they would at least receive a passing grade.

At the same time, the reality of research became clearer. People researched in a field and were working on papers that contributed to their wider body of work, but the discussions in meetings and in the corridors were mostly about publication metrics. It was good that a research idea was published, but the measure of how good that research idea was fell significantly more on the prestige of the journal that published the work than the ideas themselves. It was also about volume of production. One article in a good journal was a great achievement, but it was not enough for promotion. To achieve promotion, you needed two, three, four (the more the better) articles per year for several years to show consistency and growth. The research also had to be in areas that might lead to funding. Everyone knew funding was hard to get, and you would be lucky to get it (especially in the humanities compared to, for example, the sciences), but you had to try. Even if you were not successful, being considered 'competitive' for funding meant you were also building a strong profile to represent yourself and the university positively.

Entering this environment in a professional sense (as an academic and colleague rather than a student), and seeing the true reality of what life in a university was like on a day-to-day basis, really caught my attention and it began to trouble my long-held perceptions. As much as I enjoyed researching about and teaching history, the questions surrounding the issues impacting on my colleagues, students, the university—and the wider sector—continued to mount, and I made the decision to shift my research focus from history to higher education equity, policy, leadership, and administration.

Jump forward six or seven years, and these questions are now my focus and role as an academic. Over the past several years I have examined issues surrounding university funding models, the impact of university ranking tables, and the repercussions of prestige and research excellence being measured in this way. I have also investigated what the job market looks like to new academics, and questioned the role of merit-based achievements in securing employment, gaining promotion, and receiving grants. Much of my current work is about the equity of these systems and questioning just how much equity truly exists in a sector that so readily advertises itself as a place that values, protects, and fosters the success of staff and students from diverse and inclusive backgrounds. Much of this research indicates a shift of higher education towards business models, corporate practices, and subsequently, the university needing to be managed rather than led.

This shifting notion of university leadership and administration has led to a pathway within my research focusing on university leaders (from vice-chancellors and university presidents to faculty deans) discussing how their role has evolved now that they are closer to CEOs and managers than what their role once entailed—acting as the senior academics who led faculty and university research and teaching trajectories. These groups have also spoken about the emotional toll leadership has had on them. Few people became academics with aspirations of being business managers, and participants have spoken about the hostile work environments leadership and management roles can create among academics and other staff members.

My research with academics has shown not only that they are working in systems where merit can be subverted quite easily, year-by-year their worth to a faculty and institution becomes less about the quality of their research, and more about how this research (and the subsequent publications and achieved funding) appear on spreadsheets. Academics are also responding differently to these pressures as some in the later stages of their career have not coped well with the change in university systems, while others have accepted that things have shifted significantly since they began their careers. New academics also speak of operating in this new environment differently. Some are attempting to hold onto the idealistic ways of the past that they never experienced because that was the version of academia they thought they were entering. On the other hand, some new academics, who have never known anything but the new business-like version of academia, have taken a hyper-competitive, metrics-driven approach. This approach may not fit the traditional view of academia, but it fits within any occupation following a business model such as law or finance.

Throughout this research, clear themes have emerged. This book is largely the culmination of my existing research and tying together the causes of these changes, and the far-reaching impacts that affect people from the vice-chancellors and presidents of some of the world's most prestigious universities, to new beginning casual employees at small regional universities. The global nature of higher education goes far beyond policy borrowing. Academic migration of students and staff means universities are often competing internationally. At the same time, ranking tables mean universities must compete nationally and internationally, whether they want to or not. Additionally, being that performance metrics (such as Google Scholar, ResearchGate etc.) make it possible for virtually instant assessments of an academic's work or comparison to another, academics are also forced to operate in a global sphere. Nonetheless, it is necessary to consider that higher education's international reach often has limitations. For example, this book builds on studies conducted in Australia, Canada, and England, with participants from these locations plus New Zealand, the United States, Ireland, Scotland, and Wales among many others. There is subsequently a significant global reach to this work, but of course, that reach is also within the bounds of locations and universities that speak English, and subsequently are predominantly white. While this is a limitation, and a repercussion of my own monolingualism and working in Australia, there are some broader aspects to be considered. Primarily, university and university policy may be spread throughout the world, but most people would consider Oxford, Cambridge, or the United States' Ivy League colleges as the pinnacle of higher education. This leaves every other university in the world, regardless of their location, language, or the cultural background of their staff or students, to either model themselves after and look to compete with what is happening in England and the United States, or choose to operate in a very location or country-specific sphere with less influence from the white, English speaking higher education sector. Many universities and university systems opt for the latter, but most (and for the reasons this book explores), choose the former due to the influence the world's ancient and famous universities hold.

Thus, this book looks at how the changes to the sector are global in nature. Issues impacting on one university can alter how another operates. A government in one country might change a policy to their university funding model, but universities in that country must adapt because they know they will be judged against universities internationally and no allowance will be given for funding changes within a single country when these judgements are made. The sector has also changed globally. For the most part this means less funding, greater expectations, a demand for higher returns on investments, and ultimately a pressure on individuals to streamline their work processes or risk working more for less. All these factors were also part of the equation prior to 2020 and the onset of the COVID-19 pandemic which has had significant implications to the global higher education sector. As this book will discuss, the pandemic was unpredictable, but how governments reacted and what the consequences were to higher education were entirely predictable as we have seen funding shrink, student numbers fall, and universities having to budget accordingly.

This book argues that these changes have been incremental in nature and started decades ago. These small changes mean sometimes people (particularly those outside of the sector) are not aware of the full repercussions of how far universities have moved beyond the perceptions created decades and even centuries ago. At the same time, the university remains steeped in history and traditions, and even though roles and tasks inside them are changing, titles remain the same, so it is understandable that people assume a faculty dean or vice-chancellor perform the same tasks they do today as they did twenty, fifty, even one hundred years ago. However, the changes go beyond these positions. This book highlights that every role, position, level of management, and requirement in the university is different today than it was at the start of the twenty-first century, let alone in the 1960s, 1970s, and 1980s.

As we have now entered the third decade of the twenty-first century, this book accepts that universities are still about teaching and research, but a revision of the myriad smaller factors within higher education leadership and administration that researchers have studied in the past is necessary. Perhaps more crucially, this book also examines how these changes have combined to form an almost entirely reshaped higher education sector where every level of the management and academic hierarchy is now focused on different tasks than they were only a few decades ago, and being guided by new and evolving motivations.

The major contribution of the work is two-fold. First, it combines the many individual areas of research that I have conducted regarding the changing university to provide an in-depth analysis of how these individual components have reshaped the university and the higher education sector in the twenty-first century and more recent years. The book determines that in most situations, we need to rethink the traditional notion of the university as an institution rarely influenced by governments, business, or society whose role was to create and disseminate knowledge. A much better starting point in the twenty-first century is to view the university as a corporation that employs business-like practices in the pursuit of educating students with customer-like expectations and conducting financially viable research.

The second contribution is that the book both acts as an introduction to Pierre Bourdieu, for scholars with a new interest, or policymakers, administrators, and a wider audience who may not be familiar with his theories. It uses these ideas to understand what has happened in the sector, and how we have ended up where we are today. Bourdieu's relevance to higher education and the insights examining the data through his theories provides is of particular use when it comes to understanding structures, roles, and how people fit within these ecosystems. The issues this book discusses could be examined via the works of many other philosophers such as Jean-François Lyotard and Michel Foucault (as many other researchers have done), but this book nonetheless focuses on Bourdieu for several reasons. Bourdieu, an academic who is primarily known for his theories, warned against using theory without justifiable reasons when he stated that:

> Let me say outright and very forcefully that I never 'theorize', if by that we mean engage in the kind of conceptual gobbledygook (laïus) that is good for textbooks and which, through an extraordinary misconstrual of the logic of science, passes for Theory in much of Anglo-American social science (Wacquant 1989, p. 50).

In addition to Bourdieu's suggestion that theory should not be applied for theory's sake, this book (and my work more widely) has been influenced by one of my favourite quotes from Pat Thomson who pointed out that:

> Bourdieu's conceptual frame must be brought into conversation with particular data and used to make sense of a particular research question and to guide its empirical investigation. Bourdieu cannot be draped over data like a tablecloth (Thomson 2017, p. 114).

Not only are Thomson's words a good piece of advice that can be extended to the use of theory more generally, they reflect my own experience with theory and higher education. As I touched on earlier, my interest in higher education in part originated from entering the field and seeing that things were not as I expected them to be, and seeing the changes that had been and were taking place. These changes, the new pressures on universities and those people working within them, were numerous and clearly related and influenced by each other, but exactly how they related and influenced each other was unclear to me. For me, and as I hope this book makes clear, it was Bourdieu who needed to be brought into the conversation with the data for it to make more sense. Bourdieu's theories allow for an understanding of these issues which can aid in informing readers of why life in the modern university is the way it is. It also informs readers of what can be done to perhaps help people adjust to a new way of academic life because it is unlikely to return to the idealised version of life in the university that has existed in previous decades—I say 'idealised' because I, like essentially all researchers discussing the *ivory tower* and notions of what life in the university used to be like, know we are working with idealised memories or perceptions. That is to say, universities were pleasant places to be for those who fit the mould, and were significantly less desirable (or even accessible) places to be for those who did not which routinely included women, people of colour, people of different nationalities, or people with disabilities. These issues and their impacts are far from solved in many instances.

The book looks at these issues through a Bourdieusian lens that is primarily focused on his notions of *capital, habitus, cultural trajectory, field,* and *doxa*. As Bourdieu was an academic and has written extensively about higher education, he provides a valuable lens by which to interpret the data within this book. These aspects will be of interest to readers as they have previously been surveyed through similar lenses on many occasions, but they have been assessments that focused on individual topics rather than providing a full analysis of how differing issues have influenced each other, as this book does.

For readers familiar with Bourdieu, the book provides a detailed example of how his theories can be applied to a whole sector. For unfamiliar readers, the work acts as an introduction to Bourdieu that demonstrates how his theories can be applied to higher education, but also why his ideas can help stakeholders better understand the mechanics of life in the modern university.

References

Thomson P (2017) Educational leadership and Pierre Bourdieu. Routledge, Abingdon
Wacquant L (1989) Towards a reflexive sociology: a workshop with Pierre Bourdieu. Sociol Theor 7(1):26–63. https://doi.org/10.2307/202061

Part I
Bourdieu's Key Theories for Examining Higher Education

Chapter 2
Introducing Bourdieu and Higher Education

Abstract This chapter provides a brief history and introduction of Bourdieu as an academic and philosopher. The chapter outlines what motivated Bourdieu's work, and discusses how his theories have been applied to many evaluations of society and the mechanics of class and cultural trajectory. The chapter also outlines how and why Bourdieu designed and refined these theories in academic settings, and used academia as the setting by which to demonstrate practical applications of his work. The chapter concludes with an overview of Bourdieu's own views of higher education, while also taking into account the period and setting in which his views were shaped.

This chapter provides a brief history of Pierre Bourdieu as an academic and philosopher, and how his work has been taken up by researchers. It includes some discussion of how Bourdieu's life influenced and led to the formation and revision of several of his major concepts. These are important discussion points because it is relevant that though Bourdieu's concepts can be applied to situations outside of education, he was nonetheless an academic working in a university, regularly dealing with administration, leaders, academics, and students, and this impacted and guided his thinking. This chapter provides basic information so that the concepts can be further explored as they are used to provide advanced analysis of the relevant issues in later chapters.

This chapter's discussion is aimed primarily at examining these points in a way that connects them to higher education; though the theories can be, and have been, used to analyse an untold number of fields inside and outside of educational settings. For me, it has been through seeing how Bourdieu's (and other philosophers') theories have been applied to scenarios that I am familiar with that I have most successfully come to understand these theoretical notions. This book is aimed at anyone with an interest in higher education because, as was discussed in the previous chapter, this is a book about the changing nature of higher education, with an examination through a Bourdieusian lens. Thus, the following explanations and examples of Bourdieu's work are intended to make this book accessible for readers with an interest in higher education whether they be students, academics, policymakers, or people who have an interest in universities—regardless of their knowledge of Bourdieu. At the same time though, Bourdieusian scholars will find Bourdieu's theories applied to new datasets and areas of analysis to further explore the continuing changes affecting the modern university.

Bourdieu in Context

Works concerning Bourdieu's ideas more widely in terms of theory, or being applied to education as a whole, tend to devote considerable time to surveying Bourdieu's own history. They often examine his personal and professional life to put his own motivations and the potential limitations and complications of his work into context without providing the detail that might be found in a biography. Some good examples of this can be found in Grenfell (2014), Grenfell and James (1998), Webb et al. (2002), while Schirato and Roberts' (2018) account includes a detailed analysis of critiques of Bourdieu's work before and after his death in January 2002. These overviews of Bourdieu's life are important because if a researcher wants to use or build upon Bourdieu's views about higher education, the issues that shaped Bourdieu's views will often be a relevant part of the discussion. Bourdieu was not creating theories in the abstract. Rather, his work was shaped and formed by what he saw and experienced. However, it cannot be ignored that depending on circumstance, it has been noted that sometimes the experiences Bourdieu used to inform his theories did not always translate like-for-like into other areas. Therefore, it has been noted that a significant divide exists between the French university system in which Bourdieu worked, compared to the systems of Great Britain, North America, Australia, and New Zealand (Harker et al. 1990). The same is true of some of Bourdieu's ideas around class and power, and their lack of consideration of the impact of gender or race (Thomson 2017), and I will add sexual identity, disability, and social class as it pertains to the university sector. This is because Bourdieu worked in France from the late-1950s until 2002 and these notions do not always represent the ideas of the 2020s and beyond.

These critiques have been considered heavily in this book, as well as in my and other Bourdieusian researchers' work. Importantly, in this book, Bourdieu's work is the starting point of the analysis rather than the focal point of these discussions. Thus, my objective in this book as it pertains to critiques of Bourdieu's ideas, and highlighting what may have been missing factors in some of his concepts, is to highlight that the critiques exist, point out where some considerations are missing, and direct the audience to works that focus more heavily on those topics. Some aspects of his life can be discussed to frame why certain topics were of particular interest to him, and the environments and groups he was working with and around as he formed and refined his theories. Ultimately, the topics discussed within this book use Bourdieu's notions of the later-twentieth century to begin the discussion and assessment of topics that continue into the twenty-first century.

Bourdieu's History

Bourdieu was born in 1930 in a poor part of rural France, and it was through academic success from a young age that he became one of the most influential philosophers and academics of the twentieth century. Growing up poor and becoming an influential philosopher was not usually what happened to people who grew up in areas like him, and he was acutely aware that he was the exception to the rule (Bourdieu 2007). Most of his work thus highlighted the fact that most children from a poor background, such as a lower-class farming community, would in a significant majority of cases never have the opportunity (or possess the family *capital* or *habitus,* as we will soon get to) to go to the right schools, or have the support to do well enough in schools, to have the option of attaining the academic opportunities and success that he had. Bourdieu knew this, and was open about most people not likely ever having the same luck and opportunities that he had, and wrote of himself having 'miraculous social mobility' because of it (Bourdieu 2007, p. 5).

Bourdieu's academic achievements at the school-level led him to the École Normale Supérieure in Paris in 1951 where he studied philosophy—at that time one of the most academically revered disciplines (Schirato and Roberts 2018) which seems worth noting considering the less-prestigious connotations surrounding the humanities in the twenty-first century. After completing his studies in 1955, Bourdieu completed his military service in Algeria during which time he wrote Sociologie de l'Algérie (The Algerians) which was published in 1958. After his military service, he took up a position at the University of Algiers from 1958 to 1960, before returning to Paris and the Centre de Sociologie Européenne (Schirato and Roberts 2018).

Thus, after completing his schooling in 1954, it was only during Bourdieu's period of military service that he was not operating in, or very closely associated with, universities and academic environments. As a result, all his theories were being formed, refined, the people he collaborated with, and the papers and books that defined his career and place in sociological research, took place with the backdrop of university life, other academics, administrators, and students. This helps explain Bourdieu's own interest in education and higher education, the social interactions that shaped much of his work, and why many of his theories can be applied to issues away from education, but educational settings were nonetheless an area he surveyed regularly (Bourdieu 2007; Grenfell 2014) and explains why his work can be used to explore so many issues within higher education from the sector as a whole, to every rung of the administrator, academic, and student ladder within an institution.

Theory and Bourdieu

Before addressing Bourdieu and his theories, it is necessary to mention theory's place in educational research because it has changed significantly over the last seventy years, and Bourdieu played a major role in that change. These changes have primarily related to educational theory separating itself from 'theory' as it is known and used in the sciences. This meant theory in educational research up until the 1950s was mostly used as a tool that related to hypotheses and their development and testing (O'Connor 1957). Grenfell and James (1998) determined that due to education being a practical activity, early theories derived from new and evolving methodologies, and pedagogies were judged on their theoretical merits and then applied to the classroom and teaching methods. Thus, if the theory worked in a theoretical sense, it was applied to the practical setting because it had to work, because the scientific methodologies on which it was based said it would.

During the 1960s a shift occurred in how theory was being used and applied in educational research. Paul Hirst is frequently cited as the philosopher to first discuss these changes (Grenfell and James 1998). Hirst's (1966) starting point was no different to O'Connor's (1957) the decade before. Traditionally, educational theory had followed the same rules as in the sciences; theory was used to verify ideas surrounding changes to teaching and learning techniques. In the sciences, Hirst saw theory as being the interconnect between a hypothesis (or hypotheses) and the results. In surveying the differences of theory in education to the sciences, Hirst again followed O'Connor's (1957) argument and concluded that theory (in the 1960s) continued to be used in education as something that would result in a successful practical application, but it was Hirst's final thoughts that acted as a springboard to Bourdieu's work (among many other theorists) and remains relevant today and in this book.

Hirst argued that theory in educational research was also about finding ways to organise knowledge so that we might better understand practical activities, and therefore also make better informed recommendations on how to address current problems (Hirst 1966), or 'make choices to affect and determine that activity in the first place' (Grenfell and James 1998, p. 8). The theories Bourdieu was forming, and refining, were primarily about this notion of finding ways to organise knowledge so we could better make sense of it and understand what was happening. His work around habitus, capital, and field can help us to understand what is happening in any given situation today, why much of what led to that situation is predictable, and why that predictability will continue into the future. Thus, while O'Connor was focused on theoretical changes to improve pedagogy, Hirst and Bourdieu (among many others since) have examined classrooms and the practical aspects of education, using this information to create theories to understand what is taking place.

As was stated earlier, there is also no shortage of researchers arguing that Bourdieu got some points wrong. They suggest he failed to notice the importance of issues such as not allowing for how different the French systems that governed much of the society he was familiar with were compared to the rest of the Westernised world when he was making general conclusions. This is particularly the case given that Bourdieu wrote not just about education systems, but also governments, journalism, art, real estate, and other forms of media among many other topics (Thomson 2017). In these instances, the common criticism is that Bourdieu may have been correct about many scenarios concerning these topics, but he failed to acknowledge some determining factors that many consider highly relevant to the field (Webb et al, 2002).

It also cannot be denied that areas of social science research have moved on since the latter-half of the twentieth century when Bourdieu completed his work, and this can cause issues that must be acknowledged. A clear example of this relates to Bourdieu's views on cultural and economic capital. Bourdieu (2005) wrote at length about social capital being tied to economic capital, and the notion of a person's capital rising or falling with their economic status. However, in doing so, he did not always address ideas around systemic oppression and the difficulty of someone changing their economic status, or realising it was even an option to do so; as we would today with ideas that have changed due to several more decades of social science research (Thomson 2017). The same is true concerning Bourdieu's views relating to women, gender, and marginalised groups. Bourdieu often wrote of occurrences relating to a non-descript agent or agents (people) but these groups frequently exhibited the traits of white men and thus the analysis rarely considered the implications surrounding being a woman, a person of colour, having a disability, or coming from a marginalised group. When Bourdieu did discuss gender or women in the field, it is perhaps unsurprising that he exhibited notions familiar to approaches to gender of the period, which are not always relevant today, and has led to many of his conclusions needing to be reassessed and revaluated to consider current understandings of the differences and prejudices different groups can face when being discussed using Bourdieu's theories (Reay 2004a; Webb et al. 2002).

A note of caution can also apply to researchers studying the catalogue of Bourdieu's works and applications of his theories. Grenfell (2014) and Webb et al. (2002) highlighted that some discrepancies exist with Bourdieu's work and the timing of which it was transcribed into English. They noted instances of some works, and more famous works, being transcribed into English at the time of their original (or near to their original) publication which ensured that researchers working in the English language were working with Bourdieu's current thoughts. However, on many occasions, Bourdieu's lesser-known papers, or his own critiques or revisions of his own work, were not transcribed into English immediately, and often it was decades later, which resulted in English language scholars sometimes working with Bourdieusian ideas that Bourdieu had already altered. This is less of an issue today as Bourdieu's prominence ensures essentially all his works are translated into English, and those that are not (should any exist) can easily be translated into English using modern technology. However, the circumstance of reading older articles or books that work with Bourdieu's theories must nonetheless be read with the knowledge that, depending on the topic and languages the researcher was familiar with, they may be working with slightly different notions of Bourdieu's work that have since been revised by Bourdieu himself.

Finally, it cannot be ignored that scholars have noted a risk of Bourdieu (but indeed any theorist) being applied to a dataset not because it adds a necessary avenue of analysis to improve knowledge, but simply because it adds another lens by which to examine already established information. This criticism is what led Thomson to highlight that theory cannot be draped over data like a 'tablecloth' (2017, p. 114). Thomson also pointed out that Reay (2004b) argued, specifically regarding Bourdieu, that just because his theories can be applied to a dataset, does not mean they should or that they will produce new results or understandings. I would suggest often the temptation or reasoning for educational researchers to apply Bourdieu's notions to their work originates from him working so often within the educational field because certainly the ways in which his work can be applied are numerous. However, as Thomson and Reay suggested, the question must be, even though Bourdieu's work (or any theory) *can* be applied, what does it add to the analysis? This is perhaps particularly the case when producing research for audiences such as administrators, policymakers, or researchers not overly familiar with educational theorists or theory. For these audiences, I would suggest that the effort required to become familiar with the notions or mechanics of a theory need to at least be transactionally equal to what the use of theory adds to the analysis and findings—a suggestion that has remained at the forefront as I wrote this book.

Bourdieu on Theory

Bourdieu's own views can also tell us much about his motivations for research areas, methodologies, and how his theories formed. Bourdieu by the later part of his career was aware that his popularity and that of his theories were leading to his ideas being applied to great swathes of research which led him to conclude that he, and those using his work, should never theorise for theory's sake and that the application of his theories should only occur as 'a response to an actual practical context' (Wacquant 1989, p. 50). These words were largely a reiteration of how he wrote about his work almost thirty years earlier in 1962 when he said that he hoped to connect 'people to the meanings of actions' (Bourdieu 1962, p. 109), or as Grenfell (2014) summarised, Bourdieu was on 'a mission to explain the social, political, and cultural practices that surrounded him' (p. 15).

Bourdieu also knew that different groups of researchers would look at his work using their own academic gaze. That is to say, a researcher focused on making a theoretical contribution to scholarship might work with Bourdieu's ideas solely for the purpose of furthering theoretical ideas. Conversely, a researcher using Bourdieu's theories to understand a practical situation may do so without making any contribution of how those theories are considered. However, Bourdieu argued his work was never supposed to be used in such a siloed way and to do so was to misrepresent his efforts. Webb et al. (2002) highlight an interview where Bourdieu was asked if his work had culminated in 'a set of thinking tools […] of wide, if not universal, applicability' (2002, p. 47.). Bourdieu agreed with the notion of his work resulting in 'thinking tools' but clarified that 'these tools are only visible through the results they yield' and argues that they were never intended to be solely 'thinking tools'. Instead, he said that:

> The ground for these tools […] lies in research, in the practical problems and puzzles encountered and generated in the effort to construct a phenomenally diverse set of objects in such a way that they can be treated, thought of, comparatively (Bourdieu and Wacquant 1992, p. 160).

It is difficult to ignore how many reviews of Bourdieu's work (and how it has been used) exist, and subsequently how much Bourdieu had to defend his work (particularly towards the latter-half of his career when he had gained global popularity) regarding the issue of whether his work is just theory, and whether it was leading to practical applications or increasingly niche philosophical and theoretical discussions. Certainly, this is rarely the case in educational research as a significant majority of analyses using Bourdieu's work use it to enable practical advances. Yet, arguably the negativity around theory and theoretical advances, rather than practical, lies in the fact that it is not directly contributing to societal change, but is helping to understand the philosophies underlying social circumstances. As a final example of Bourdieu being mindful of how his work was sometimes perceived, he succinctly concluded 'There is no doubt a theory in my work, or, better, a set of thinking tools visible through the results they yield, but it is not built as such' (Wacquant 1989, p. 50). Nonetheless, twenty-five years later, and many years after Bourdieu's death, warnings of the temptation to use Bourdieu as the centrepiece of the research continue. Grenfell concluded in his 2014 book:

> Do not make Bourdieu more interesting than the research to which his ideas are being applied. Really, the life and times of a French intellectual who lived in the second half of the twentieth century are incidental to the use to which the ideas can be applied (p. 227).

Perhaps the greatest irony to the immense focus on Bourdieu's theories, how they are used, and if they contribute to society, is that this discussion occurs despite the hundreds, perhaps thousands, of journal articles and books that have only used his work to better understand and organise knowledge for the purpose of making informed recommendations. Additionally, Bourdieu's own work rarely focused on pure theory, it almost always explored these concepts through practical applications or datasets because it was the practical situations that Bourdieu was trying to understand as wholly understanding a scenario is the first step to making informed recommendations on how to improve the situation. Bourdieu's attempts at this are perhaps nowhere more evident than in his work surrounding education.

Bourdieu on Methods and Methodology

A focus on this area is necessary because just as we earlier saw Bourdieu step in and be part of the changes to educational research that O'Connor and Hirst began, Bourdieu had to be strategic in how he implemented and discussed his methods as they aided in (along with many other theorists) reshaping social science practices. Grenfell (2014) summarised this situation by noting that 'Bourdieu's discussions of knowledge and scientific method have been elements of a strategy to give himself the power to practice what he has preached' (p. 37). However, the philosophical changes O'Connor and Hirst discussed were about major changes to educational research, and those changes were going to result in new methodological approaches entering the field. In some instances, Bourdieu was in the right place at the right time to be working in a field as it reached a change-point.

Bourdieu was part of the change from educational research being about devising theories and methods to improve pedagogy, to focusing on how we think about people, situations, and how these experiences can mix in *generally* predictable ways and have predictable results. I have placed emphasis on the word *generally* as that was what his methods were about. He was bringing scientific thought, and views on scientific methods, to the knowledge surrounding the social sciences which can be very different from how methods are approached in the hard sciences. Bourdieu was shaping philosophies and tools for understanding people and groups despite the infinite variabilities of these groups; a practice that inevitably meant some separation from the methods and knowledge associated with traditional scientific views were necessary.

Bourdieu on Statistics

Bourdieu's views and use of statistics is indicative of his approach to hard conclusions and why they can be problematic in social science research. Bourdieu used statistics regularly in his work and did so for most of his career. Statistics were most often used to map findings so that analysis could occur, or the statistics surrounding an event or phenomena provided the catalyst for investigation. What is important to note is that though he used statistics extensively, they were part of the analysis or instigated the analysis (Wuggenig and Mnich 1994). What Bourdieu was cautious of is how statistics were used in other fields, in his view, to 'crush methodological rivals' because they represented facts about a given situation (Grenfell 2014, p. 24). Bourdieu's argument is that statistics (and other hard-lined scientific methodologies) might reveal what is happening with the data, but people are more complicated than data. Due to this, these approaches do not reveal *why* data has been found or *how* findings relate to one another; it is the role of the social scientist to make these conclusions (Wuggenig and Mnich 1994) and it is this approach that Bourdieu takes to all methodologies; he is rarely dismissive of them, but he is cautious of how they are used.

Bourdieu on Quantitative and Qualitative Analysis

Bourdieu's concern regarding methodologies and methods that explain what has happened, with less concern to why it has happened, extends to his general views on the merits and uses of quantitative and qualitative analysis. Exploring even a basic definition of quantitative analysis highlights its potential issues to researchers, regardless of Bourdieu's views. Quantitative analysis in its broadest sense is numeric research, it is analysis that occurs to data which is quantifiable. However, as Punch

(2013) highlights, 'information about the world does not occur naturally in the form of numbers' (p. 85). Punch's point is that there are no numbers assigned to, for example, people's actions, decisions, or histories. Quantitative researchers subsequently endeavour to 'impose the structure of the number system' to data where it does not naturally fit, but for the purpose of hoping this process helps analyse and understand the data (Punch 2013, p. 85).

It should not be unsurprising then that Bourdieu expressed caution around quantitative analysis, but as with his views surrounding statistics (itself an integral component of quantitative analysis) he nonetheless used quantitative methodologies regularly. As a system of methodologies, however, his hesitations were not simply that quantitative analysis is more about the 'what', and less about the 'how' and 'why' of a dataset. Bourdieu regularly spoke about the danger of the unopposed position held by quantitative analyses as they had 'ruled virtually unchallenged since the 1940s' (Bourdieu and Wacquant 1992, p. 31). More specifically, Bourdieu was concerned by the instrumental positivism with which quantitative methodologies had been regarded. Positivism is primarily the belief system which suggests that only that what can be scientifically proven (such as via mathematics) can be recognised as knowledge; a philosophy of thought which is in turn directly opposed to concepts of metaphysics such as what is 'being', 'knowing', 'feeling'.

For a scholar whose work centred around understanding why issues such as class, race, upbringing, and education had an impact (and a largely predictable impact at that), he knew he was dealing with issues, questions, and answers that did not easily fit within positivism's parameters. Another problem Bourdieu saw was a long history of positivist quantitative approaches being applied by governments to regulate people. He saw this as tests being designed and applied to measure physical and mental health, intelligence in schooling, and even more abstract constructs such as how 'employable' or 'reliable' someone might be (Webb et al. 2002). Not only did Bourdieu question the validity of a process that applied a number to an individual or group's attributes to determine their worth on an artificially created scale of value, he was also cautious of what this meant for research. His fear was that research focusing on dissecting these areas, and the researchers spending their time creating tests to provide these measures, did little to advance theories of understanding or provide steps or scaffolding to create further avenues of research to benefit comprehension of the issue. Methodologically speaking, this type of research might attribute a number to a finding, but it does little to advance knowledge (Webb et al. 2002).

Bourdieu helped counter his concerns around quantitative methodologies by bridging some of what he saw as quantitative research's gaps and shortcomings, by intertwining qualitative analyses. If quantitative data is about presenting issues in numerical forms, qualitative data is about empirical research and understanding issues through words. Denzin and Lincoln (2011) highlight that these words can come from many sources, but the most common examples are interview transcripts, survey answers, field notes, historical documents, and personal experiences through diary or journal entries. Bourdieu's intention was to produce work that originated from using the most prudent methodology to gain the information he needed.

Bourdieu knew this system was problematic. His early work took shape as qualitative methodologies began to increase in popularity. However, these methodologies in the 1950s, 1960s, and 1970s still face much of the same criticism in the twenty-first century (though perhaps to a lesser degree) as they did during Bourdieu's formative years. This circumstance is primarily because unlike the scientific certainty surrounding quantitative methodologies, qualitative methodologies include an element of researcher judgement that cannot be scientifically or mathematically proven, and thus, ensure a level of scepticism will always surround the results in the view of some researchers. Nonetheless, Bourdieu maintained that quantitative methodologies may explain what is happening, but not why: for that, qualitative methodologies are required. However, he was every bit as cautious of working solely via qualitative methods as he was quantitative (Bourdieu and Wacquant 1992).

Bourdieu was working with qualitative data to produce theories and dissect the issues he saw in society, but often the formation of those theories involved quantitative analyses as the data was analysed to reach his final results (Bourdieu and Wacquant 1992). He even saw his theories as sometimes bringing quantitative qualities to empirical work. Bourdieu was critical of, for example, the notion of lived experiences as a dataset, because lived experiences without a methodological tool with which to analyse the data is just a narrative of experiences. He saw habitus, capital, and field as tools which would make sense of that data. To paraphrase a collection of his ideas, he saw 'the myth of genesis as being to the theory of evolution, as lived experiences are to the notion of habitus' (Bourdieu and Wacquant 1992, pp. 132–133). That is to say, the former of each example may explain a situation, but it is the latter that brings scientific reasoning to the data. Thus, Bourdieu may have been trying to find a middle ground between quantitative and qualitative methodologies as he formed and refined his theories, but he is nonetheless a qualitative researcher.

As Bourdieu conducted his own work by balancing his use of quantitative and qualitative research, he also advocated for other social science researchers (not just sociologists) to do the same for the reasons outlined above in this section. However, he was aware that in encouraging researchers to select what research tools would best fit their approach to generate data and its analysis, he was also supporting a method that increased the potential variances in their data and analysis due to their selection of research tools.

This scenario was nonetheless far from the only instance where Bourdieu knew personal preferences and selections, which may be based on prejudice or predictions of the data, and can be intentional or subconscious choices, can influence data. His answer to these issues was his insistence that researchers employ a reflexive sociology (Bourdieu 1990). No shortage of books, chapters, and articles about reflexivity and its importance have been published by Bourdieu (such as the above reference, *In Other Words: Essays Towards a Reflexive Sociology*) and by many other scholars discussing the practice.

Bourdieu was calling for researchers to be aware of their personal assumptions, biases, and circumstances at all stages of the research design, data collection, data analysis, and reporting of studies and findings. Or more precisely, consider and correct for all the biases that can enter and augment social science research. Bourdieu wrote of research and theory about being a 'principle of vision and division' (Bourdieu, 1990, p. 18) because while researchers begin with a vision of what their research will look like, to get to the final point, their vision must be divided into the sections of research design, data collection, and analysis to create that vision. It is nonetheless the processes of division that requires a reflexive approach. Ultimately, he argued that no piece of social science research would be completely free of personal interest; at its core, one might suggest that a researcher conducting research already has a vested interested in the work because conducting the research at all is a core part of their job (Bourdieu 1990). However, Bourdieu suggested that if researchers actively work to minimise their biases, and outlay to their audience the biases that may have impacted on their research design and analysis, then the necessary steps have been taken and their audience will be aware of the issues that may have impacted on the work (Bourdieu 2004).

Bourdieu's views on reflexivity emphasises a need for researchers to be cautious of why and how they are designing and carrying out studies, analysing the data, and subsequently be considerate of the decisions they are making from a technical standpoint. However, Webb et al. (2002) make an additional point about social science researchers (and in fact any researcher) who has a selection of methodological tools available to them. They suggest that researchers in (for example) medicine or the hard sciences may only have one methodology available to them, that is to say, 'to test ABC, the methodology is XYZ'. This scenario ensures they are often limited in what approaches they can employ to gain their required result. The social scientist rarely has this option. Instead, they must select the methodological tools they anticipate will work best with participants to generate the required data; data that the researcher may or may not be able to predict.

These are the reasons that Webb et al. (2002) highlight Bourdieu's suggestion that elements of social science research are in fact skills that are not too dissimilar from an art or a craft. They summarise Bourdieu's views by stating that social science research:

> is an art in that it brings the unseen things in society, or the things that are disguised, to light. It is a craft in that it involves the skilful making of a product; the research activity and its outcomes (Webb et al. 2002, p. 72).

The basis for many of these suggestions originates from the debate surrounding quantitative and qualitative methodologies, and qualitative researchers often continuing to stand in the shadow of their quantitative counterparts. Bourdieu's point that because social science research is practical research, it is a skill, it can be honed, and experience can count in knowing how best to create a research design that can generate data from the myriad social issues that surround us.

Theory of Practice

Bourdieu knew, however, that despite what he saw as clear reasoning for a need for researchers to use qualitative methods to, for example, understand why the results of quantitative research were occurring, the need for these clear reasons to be explained via theory was essential. This is where his *theory of practice* begins to take shape. Theory of practice was something that Bourdieu worked on and refined throughout his career, and though its purpose and process evolved over several decades, the function it played remained the same.

His theory of practice began with little connection to education; it began while he examined the social differences of the various classes he saw around him after he left Paris for his military service in Algeria during the late-1950s. Thus, Bourdieu had data that suggested that different things were likely to happen in life to people born into different class structures, but there were few clear theories to explain why these social differences were occurring. On his return to Paris, he began refining his theory of practice as it related to education, which in itself is a social tool, and thus how one can use it, and what they get from it, is inextricably tied to class (as Bourdieu tells us through such theories as habitus, capital, and field).

In thinking about what Bourdieu was attempting to do, it is important to remember that he was also working on the forefront of philosophical changes in educational research. In the 1950s, education research was still about creating, testing, and implementing theories with direct, quantifiable, practical, and pedagogical benefits (O'Connor 1957). In the 1960s, Hirst saw educational research as not just being about designing and testing theories for practical improvement, but also understanding why those changes worked, with what demographics of students, and what subject areas. In Hirst's view (1966), understanding the mechanics behind the results would allow for more informed recommendations and further research to be completed. Thus, it was during this time of change to approaches in educational research that Bourdieu also realised the importance of investigating what was happening behind the data's results.

His theory of practice was about bringing a theory to this need in areas of research far beyond just educational research. The theory needed to be solid enough in its reasoning to justify its selection when a number of research tools exist, while at the same time, it had to be general enough to be applied to social situations covering a wide variety of research areas, individuals, groups, and many other classifications. Grenfell and James (1998) suggest that Bourdieu's theory of practice had two goals. The first was to determine the logic behind social activities, and the second was to do this while also reforming research practices to further aid in this endeavour.

Theory of practice is ultimately about understanding culture and society because the way society organises itself, or is organised by those with the power to shape such a structure, is highly determinant of the choices and trajectories of the individuals and groups within society. An oversimplified example of what this looks like in practice would be to think about one child being born into a middle-class family with educated and working professional parents, and another child born into a working-class family where one parent may be unemployed and the other works part-time in low-skilled employment. One could argue that if these children are born in a country with free education, then they have the same opportunities and both could grow up to attend university or learn a trade, and secure solid employment and financial security in their adult lives. Bourdieu's work and his theory of practice is largely dedicated to highlighting that though technically some data may suggest these children have the same opportunity to 'succeed', the child from the working-class family will have to overcome a long line of societally-imposed barriers to reach that point, while the middle-class child will have the gate opened at each barrier to enable them to pass through. Therefore, while the working-class child can overcome those barriers, and the middle-class child may choose not to walk through the open gates, Bourdieu's work and his theory of practice tells us that society has encouraged and made 'success' easier and statistically far more likely for the middle-class child, and because of that, the middle-class child is more likely to succeed.

Bourdieu went to great lengths to illuminate to what extent culture, and understanding culture's place in society, was the first step to understanding why his work (and social science research more broadly) was so important to dissecting the barriers society placed in front of some, but not others. As he saw it, society is essentially the collective term for a group of people, but it is their culture that is their knowledge, language, ideas, and values. Bourdieu also knew that culture could be used for multiple purposes. The first is its structural tradition as it is the shared culture of communication and knowledge that allows the structure of a society to form and grow. The second is its functionalist tradition that Bourdieu suggests means that as the culture of language and communication within a society grows, ideologies soon form which can be used to shape politics and direct social order (Bourdieu 1968).

Bourdieu also knew that cultures existed within cultures, and because of this *cultural trajectory* matters and it is trajectory that most often dictates an individual's or group's path forward within their society. Bourdieu believed this because he knew his cultural trajectory as the child of a poor farming family in a disadvantaged region of France was to grow up and become an adult who worked as a farmer or completed other manual tasks in a poor farming community. To use the above example of the working-class and middle-class children, their cultural trajectory is that the working-class child may find employment difficult and likely be limited to unskilled tasks, whereas the middle-class child will likely gain a trade, attend university, have fewer employment difficulties and have a successful career that results in financial stability, secure housing, and the ability to pay medical bills, etc. As has been touched on, cultural trajectories are not set in stone and unshakeable, Bourdieu's point was that societies and their cultures simply make cultural trajectory the most likely path to follow.

This is what much of Bourdieu's work is primarily about. His notions of habitus, capital, and field (among many others) explain why cultures form, why cultures exist within cultures, why cultural trajectory is real, and why breaking away from one's cultural trajectory can also have significant implications. He viewed himself as having the wrong cultural trajectory; the poor farming child did not always fit within France's elite universities and philosophical circles, and at the same time, he became a student and academic at France's elite universities and global philosophical circles who no longer fit so well within his poor farming community (Bourdieu and Wacquant 1992). This is another avenue of his research and one that has been studied at length by scholars because it is one thing to enable people to change their cultural trajectory, but it is another to realise that there will be social consequences to this change.

Bourdieu on Education

When so much of Bourdieu's work was born out of developing his theory of practice and the implications of cultural trajectory in shaping the paths of groups and individuals, it should not be a surprise that a sizeable portion of his work was either about education, or featured education as a primary component in explaining society's structures and rules. This is largely because education (in terms of compulsory schooling) is one of the first societal structures a child experiences outside of the home, and at the same time, schools tend to amplify what structures the child was already born into. Therefore, Bourdieu often spoke of the myth of merit in education, because hard work would not see the most dedicated student rise to the top of the class. Before children have even walked into a classroom, the likelihood of them being about to complete the 'hard work' that would enable them to rise to the top of the class has in most cases already been dictated by the habitus and capital of their family (Bourdieu 1977, 1988). Bourdieu's work on schooling is extensive and continues to be used as a theoretical lens by which to examine structures and social implication of compulsory education; I would suggest relevant works by Diane Reay and Pat Thomson are an excellent starting point for anyone interested in exploring these topics further.

Bourdieu, however, had a deep-seated interest in higher education that stemmed primarily from his own experiences of not fitting the mould of French academia, and it was from that standpoint that he examined everything he saw occurring within universities. In *Homo Academicus* (1988), his primary study of higher education (I say 'primary' because Bourdieu also published many journal articles and book chapters about or including discussions regarding higher education as a sector, universities, and what went on inside them) he likened this experience to being in a zoo looking at unusual animals he would not otherwise have come across. Webb et al. (2002) interpreted this by suggesting that Bourdieu found it strange that academics whose work usually included studying other people, were far less inclined to study themselves. However, I would add that the idea of the zoo also refers back to Bourdieu's own position as in outsider in the field. Thus, for academics whose cultural trajectory fit with elite universities and researching philosophy, pursuing this career and completing this work did not seem out of the ordinary so was perhaps not deemed worth reflecting upon. For Bourdieu though, this was not the case. What went on in universities was so far removed from his cultural trajectory that seeing the inner workings of university life could be compared to being at a zoo and peering in on animals you would never normally see. This positioning gave Bourdieu many insights into higher education. A brief discussion of some of these demonstrate the base from which several of his ideas originated from (which are heavily focused upon in this book), but others which are not but nonetheless paint a picture of the perspectives he held.

It is worth noting that much of Bourdieu's work on higher education relates to the French systems of higher education during the 1950s onwards, and sometimes his points only relate to that system; which is a criticism of his work being applied to global higher education systems (Webb et al. 2002). However, if one keeps this aspect in mind, the impact of his focus is less of an issue. For example, universities are often considered places of liberal thought and freedom, but Bourdieu (1988) questioned if this was true for academics whose cultural trajectories did not fit with higher education. Amongst this group, which of course included himself, he saw quite a conservative approach and academics from working-class backgrounds being unwilling to speak out against their institution or the system. Bourdieu refers to these people as *oblates* (in the church, a term sometimes used to describe lay people with high levels of dedication). He saw these academics as being afraid or not willing to speak out against the institution because they felt an obligation, or even loyalty, to the university and system of higher education. Oblates felt this way because universities had allowed them to enter a setting where they knew they did not naturally fit, and subsequently they were less likely to speak out against a system where they benefitted from the training, a career, and experiences they may not have otherwise had available to them (Bourdieu 1988).

Bourdieu extends this discussion to focus on university choice of academics (and students). He suggests that for those whose cultural trajectory is not to attend and work at a university, a great deal of their choice in what university they attend is removed. Without connections, experience, or the availability of insider knowledge, these groups can apply to certain universities, but in these instances the university holds complete power over who is and is not allowed into their system. This connects strongly with Bourdieu's notion of oblates because if someone with no power or choice in a matter is granted access to a university, they are quite likely going to feel a sense of gratitude, and later loyalty and obligation, to that institution.

Bourdieu takes this discussion one step further in *Homo Academicus* and examines where academics are likely to be employed based on their beliefs and a university's political stance. This discussion might be decidedly 1960s French and not specifically related to the Westernised world of the twenty-first century, but he also considered institutions on what activities they pursued in terms of research and teaching priorities. Bourdieu could not have planned for what higher education has turned into during the twenty-first century when he was collecting data and writing *Homo Academicus* up until its publication in the late-1980s, but certainly the early evidence of its shift as a global sector was already underway. Esson and Ertl (2016) argued that the traditional 'elite' system of higher education (for example, Oxford and Cambridge in England, the Ivy League in the US, and the similarly select groups of universities in other areas) was built upon during the early twentieth century as the Red Brick universities in England and the public college system in the US began to take shape, but it was the massification of the university system in the 1960s that changed the trajectory of higher education. The shift away from the small, elite system of universities saw competition for students, academics, and funding increase (Esson and Ertl 2016). Institutions having to engage in competition driven by consumer influences resulted in them needing to form marketing strategies, be present in the media, and gave rise to the importance of ranking table positions (Heffernan and Heffernan 2018) The need for universities to adopt business-like practices that significantly contravene the notions of the ivory tower, and perhaps Bourdieu's French ideals, were somewhat evident in 1988 when *Homo Academicus* was published. Thus, 'types' of universities had already formed and can be related to his notion of choice.

That a 'type' of university exists fits nicely with his argument that even when people do hold a cultural trajectory to attend and work in universities, they may have more choice in where they attend then those without that cultural trajectory. However, much of their choice is still determined by the institution's focus and the academic's ability to fit within that focus. For example, an academic with a career progression centred around teaching-focused universities may find it difficult to 'choose' to move to a research-focused institution because their time spent in a teaching-focused university has meant more of their time was spent teaching than researching; and it is the research record that the research-focused university values most. Bourdieu's point is that choice in universities were limited in 1988 when he wrote *Homo Academicus*, and I suggest they remain limited today. Choice, in terms of someone electing to move to a university, may almost be non-existent. However, one could argue that someone having the choice to apply for a position, and have a realistic chance of securing that position, depends greatly on their cultural trajectory, and career trajectory, pairing with the values of the institution.

Grenfell (2014) takes this notion one step further and suggests that Bourdieu felt in most circumstances people knew they were on a certain career path which may have been related to their 'cultural trajectory', but I would suggest it has to do with their 'career trajectory' (if we think about issues of cultural trajectory transferring into career prospects). Grenfell's point is that choice is thus even more limited when it comes to higher education because people, even those already in the academy, do not have choice; they are simply working within the spaces in which they fit. For these reasons, Bourdieu talks about choice in *Homo Academicus* primarily to discuss the lack of it in higher education.

This discussion also provides an example of Bourdieu's theories being designed in the French setting of the late-twentieth-century not necessarily fitting in the modern Westernised world. Bourdieu's point is that people have choice in so far as they can make selections based on their trajectory, but his example is that this 'leads the best qualified applicants towards the most [...] prestigious position' (Bourdieu 1988, pp. 93–94). The suggestion here is that merit will be rewarded. The best student in school will attend the best universities, the best universities create the best researchers, and the best academics will be located at the most prestigious universities. That might be the expectation in an ideological merit-based system, but at the same time, Bourdieu had already spent more than a decade in 1988 outlining how merit equalling success in essentially all forms of education was a myth (1977,

1988). Instead, he argued, that capital was the primary reason for academic success and though capital could stem from the quality of one's work, it also (and increasingly so) is a by-product of wealth and social advantage, and social connections. Thus, someone's university choices may once have been determined by the quality of their work and if it warranted them being offered a position at a prestigious university. However, it is important to note that career trajectory is now known to partly be determined by, or altered by, the power and influence of those they can befriend with enough capital in the field to influence hiring practices (Heffernan 2020).

Summary

In examining this brief look at Bourdieu's views on higher education it is clear he saw the absurdity of the system. His love of learning and scholarly talents led him to leave his family's farm to become an academic of global standing and whose popularity in France elevated him to a level of fame that far surpassed that of a successful academic. At the same time, he knew that every prize he received or keynote presentation he was asked to give took him away from his work, which often seemed nonsensical to him. It was these complexities and contradictions that fill higher education that motivated Bourdieu to spend so much of his time focused on this field or working on theories that also applied to it. As this book moves forward, the discussions begin to turn away from Bourdieu as an individual and much more towards his theories and how they can be used to understand many elements within universities and the sector. However, understanding the scaffolding behind the philosopher plays a key role in interpreting the perspective from which he examined education, class, and society.

References

Bourdieu P (1962) Célibat et condition paysanne. Etudes Rurales 5(6):32–136. https://doi.org/10.3406/rural.1962.1011
Bourdieu P (1990) In other words: essays towards a reflexive sociology. Stanford University Press, Stanford
Bourdieu P (2005) The social structures of the economy. Polity, Cambridge
Bourdieu P, Wacquant L (1992) An invitation to reflexive sociology. Polity Press, Cambridge
Bourdieu P (1977) Outline of a theory of practice (trans: Nice R). Cambridge University Press, Cambridge
Bourdieu P (1988) Homo Academicus (trans: Collier P). Polity
Bourdieu P (1998) On television and journalism (trans: Parkhurst Ferguson P). Pluto Press, London
Bourdieu P (2004) Science of science and reflexivity (trans: Nice R). Polity, Cambridge
Bourdieu P (2007) Sketch for a self-analysis (trans: Nice R). Polity, Cambridge
Denzin N, Lincoln Y (2011) The SAGE handbook of qualitative research. SAGE, California

Esson J, Ertl H (2016) No point worrying? Potential undergraduates, study-related debt, and the financial allure of higher education. Stud High Educ 41(7):1265–1280. https://doi.org/10.1080/03075079.2014.968542

Grenfell M (2014) Pierre Bourdieu: key concepts. Routledge, Abingdon

Grenfell M, James D (1998) Bourdieu and education: acts of practical theory. Routledge, Abingdon

Harker R, Mahar C, Wilkes C (eds) (1990) An Introduction to the Work of Pierre Bourdieu. Macmillan

Heffernan T (2020) There's no career in academia without networks': academic networks and career trajectory. High Educ Res Dev. https://doi.org/10.1080/07294360.2020.1799948

Heffernan T, Heffernan A (2018) Language games: University responses to ranking metrics. High Educ Q 72(1):29–39. https://doi.org/10.1111/hequ.12139

Hirst P (1966) Educational theory. In: Tibble J (ed) The Study of education. Routledge and Kegan Paul, London, pp 29–58

O'Connor D (1957) An introduction to the philosophy of education. Routledge and Kegan Paul, London

Punch K (2014) Introduction to social research: quantitative and qualitative approaches. SAGE, California

Reay D (2004) 'It's all becoming a habitus': beyond the habitual use of habitus in educational research. Br J Sociol Educ 25(4):431–444. https://doi.org/10.1080/0142569042000236934

Reay D (2004) Gendering Bourdieu's concepts of capitals? Emotional capital, women and social class. Sociol Rev 52(2):57–74. https://doi.org/10.1111/j.1467-954x.2005.00524.x

Schirato T, Roberts M (2018) Bourdieu: a critical introduction. Allen & Unwin

Thomson P (2017) Educational leadership and Pierre Bourdieu. Routledge, Abingdon

Wacquant L (1989) Towards a reflexive sociology: a workshop with Pierre Bourdieu. Sociol Theory 7(1):26–63. https://doi.org/10.2307/202061

Webb J, Schirato T, Danaher G (2002) Understanding Bourdieu. Sage, London

Wuggenig U, Mnich P (1994) Explorations in social space: Gender, age, class fractions and photographical choices of objects. In: Greenacre M, Blasius J (eds) Correspondence analysis in the social sciences. Academic Press, London, pp 302–323

Chapter 3
Habitus

Abstract This chapter explores the Bourdieusian concept of habitus. The chapter examines how habitus is the combination of the elements and aspects of someone's life that they are born into, raised in, and surrounded by throughout their life that shape them as an individual. It examines how someone's history, and their family's history, creates a cultural trajectory that predisposes them to having a certain type of life, having interests similar to those with similar habitus, and how habitus can tell researchers a lot about someone's life, current situation, and future. The chapter also provides a solid grounding for those unfamiliar with Bourdieu's concepts, and provides the first step as future chapters explore capital and field, and how these three concepts work together to provide distinct ways to think about the higher education sector.

The next chapters explore Bourdieu's key theories and relate them to higher education settings and scenarios. The primary focus is on habitus (and later) capital, and field as these are Bourdieu's greatest tools in understanding why people and social groups act the way they do and how they interact with one another. However, in examining the changing structures of the university and higher education, these are also the tools that help interpret how changes relating to policy, funding, and student choice (among many other wider issues) have reshaped and redefined what so many people and groups do within the university as priorities and values have changed. Thus, this book examines how dramatically universities have changed within the last several decades, but as it is primarily focused on the repercussions to those working within universities, or who aspire to working in a university, Bourdieu's theories help understand what the new environment means to individuals and their work. An exploration of the new university enables us to make clear how and why people are being assessed on new measures that researchers know are different to those ten years ago or twenty years ago, let alone sixty years ago; and that certainly differs from what the ideological picture of walking around the green grass of the quadrangle discussing philosophy. I am quite sure most people, or at least those intending to work at a university, know scenarios such as that are no longer realistic (if they ever were), but Bourdieu's theories help understand why these changes away from that reality or perception have occurred, and what counts as success in the twenty-first century.

© The Author(s), under exclusive license to Springer Nature Singapore Pte Ltd. 2022
T. Heffernan, *Bourdieu and Higher Education*,
https://doi.org/10.1007/978-981-16-8221-6_3

This chapter primarily focuses on habitus but many other of Bourdieu's theories also feature as part of the discussion. These explanations and explorations of the theories also do not occur in a binary way to higher education. An attempt has been made to relate the theories to higher education settings to establish the footings for the later detailed analyses about different aspects of the modern university. However, one of the brilliant parts of Bourdieu's work is the ease with which his theories can be transferred and applied across different situations. I would suggest that learning and working with Bourdieu is a two-step process. The first: to understand the concept of the theory, and the second: being able to apply the theory to situations where it fits. The next chapters will explore these theories and apply them to a higher education setting in a way that allows readers to then consider and apply the theories being discussed in understanding aspects of their own life and work, because these notions are highly transferrable.

Defining Habitus

Bourdieu goes into detail about the origins of 'habitus' as a word and a concept, and he is the first to acknowledge that he neither came up with the word or its meaning (Bourdieu 1993). Nonetheless, the use of habitus as a word and concept in sociological and educational research today is almost always tied to Bourdieu's evolution of the term and ideas so it is fair to think of habitus as a Bourdieusian concept.

As with many philosophical concepts, habitus can be defined rather simply or can be explored in much greater depth. Bourdieu spoke about habitus often and by understanding his work, it is possible to break habitus down into quite simple terms. At its core, habitus is the elements and aspects of someone's life that they are born into, raised in, and surrounded by throughout their life that shape them as an individual. It is their life-situations, characteristics and beliefs—and fact that these are predictors of someone's life and experiences (Bourdieu 1994). Or as Bourdieu puts it, habitus is the combination of properties that form the *structured* and *structuring structures* of an individual.

The easiest way to think about habitus and structured and structuring structures is to examine it via a simple example with clearly identified structures and structuring components. Let us take the idea of a thirty-year-old man who was born into an English aristocratic family and attended Eton and then Oxford and now works as a surgeon. The first point is that Bourdieu suggests habitus is an extension of understanding cultural trajectory, and means people in society, and researchers, can make predictions about the individual's character without knowing them. To take our example, without knowing the person, we know their habitus will be of someone who is a member of the aristocracy and attended elite schools. This will be evident through many smaller cues such as their dress, how they carry themselves, how they speak, their pastimes, their career, their career prospects, and where their children attend school—to name only a few.

Defining Habitus

On the surface, these claims may appear to be based on stereotypes, but in fact they begin with cultural trajectory. If a child is born into a family where the last ten generations of their male family members have attended Eton and Oxford, it is more than likely that the new generation will (or their family will, to be precise) possess the wealth and connections to ensure an eleventh generation begins life with Eton and Oxford which then prepares them for a certain career trajectory. To best understand cultural trajectory and habitus is where structured and structuring structures becomes a relevant thinking tool. Habitus is thus:

> *Structured* by past events that influence past and present circumstances. Being born into a wealthy family with a history of attending an elite school and university means there is a structure in place that suggests a child will attend those schools (or ones very similar to them), and go on to a career that is likely to be held by an individual with such structures behind them.
>
> If habitus provides a structure to the present, it is also *structuring* as it influences the future. If someone is born into generational wealth, then it is very likely they will become another generation of wealth for the family and this occurs not by chance, but because (as with the structure), the family has the money, connections, knowledge, and ability to attend schools and universities, and associate with the 'right' people to open the 'right' doors. To revert to the example, even without knowing the details, it is very much in the habitus of someone being born into the English aristocracy and attending Oxford that they would go on to have a professional career. Thus, the *structuring* is about knowing and acknowledging that a trajectory is linear and whatever structures and scaffolding are in place, to a certain extent, are not likely to change dramatically in the future.
>
> The linearity of these events is where the *structures* of structured and structuring structures come into the discussion. These events are a structure for the future. They are a guide, they are almost a railway track that determines how and why someone is the way they are today, and what they will become in the future. Yes, slight variations will occur and there will be exceptions to the rule, but Bourdieu's point is that, overall, what occurs in someone's life does not happen by chance. These occurrences are instead the variations that happen within a very set trajectory defined by the systems at play. In this example, those systems are around wealth and privilege.

In the description above, what habitus looks like and how it influences someone's history and future is very clear because the example intentionally provides stark life events that make cultural trajectory and habituses impact clear and predictable. Part of this clarity comes from the circumstance that the aristocratic child who attended Eton and Oxford before beginning a successful career in medicine is rewarded by habitus. They started life with a certain type of habitus due to their family's capital, then as they grew up, their habitus further evolved and enabled opportunities for elite education, and then for entering a desirable profession (Bourdieu 1996).

Let us also remember that the above example is purposefully simple to demonstrate structured and structuring structures. An example of habitus via a wealthy white male operating through school, university, and professional fields that reward wealthy white men make for a clear example. Yet, we must remember how fractured this system is as soon as someone is missing any component that is typically rewarded in the fields within which they are attempting to operate. When thinking about habitus, capital, or field (or many other Bourdieusian concepts) it is important to think about how the concepts apply to different situations. What impact would being a woman have on the example of structured and structuring structures? What impact would being non-binary have, what role does sexual identity play? How would the example play out differently if the person had a disability, was not white, or came from a working or middle-class background? In the example of elite English educational institutions and the medical profession, the answer is likely that the repercussions would be substantial and completely alter how, and even if, the person would attend Oxford or begin a medical career. Every deviation also complicates the analysis further, for example, the progression would be far more difficult for a woman, and more difficult again for a woman with a disability. The combinations and possible repercussions to this example are virtually endless, which makes them difficult to assess in a book dedicated to issues of higher education being explored through Bourdieu's concepts in an introductory fashion. However, it is crucially important that these factors are present and play a role in real life examples even if they are not present in the purposely simple examples selected in this text to demonstrate Bourdieu's concepts as plainly as possible.

It is vital to keep how issues around class, gender, and race can impact on social settings and someone's success in manoeuvring through one field and then another at the forefront of considerations because it is not just about situations becoming more difficult. Habitus becomes much more complex to think about when it can also *shut* gates and keep someone without the attributes rewarded in a field, such as a child born into poverty, from having a stronger likelihood of breaking out of the poverty cycle.

This cannot be examined through an example tied to higher education, for the sole reason that a child born into poverty, regardless of location, is less likely to attend university. Researchers and most governments may be dedicated to seeing people break out of the poverty cycle, or provide children from working-class families with the same opportunities as their middle-class counterparts. Yet, these measures are really about altering habitus (and capital) and is why these issues are a focus of many studies examining children and poverty, and children in the working-class.

However, to provide an oversimplified example that demonstrates the point of structured and structuring structures negatively impacting on the likelihood of a child from the working-class attending university, this circumstance is:

> *Structured* because they are born to parents who potentially did not have a good experience with education themselves, so their parents may not have a positive or encouraging view of attending school or pursuing post-compulsory education. Bad experiences with education can leave parents alienated by the system. These beliefs, regardless of how they form, can result in the child reaching school age with question marks over the value of education, and parents potentially unlikely to be encouraging or able to provide support. Being raised in this environment also means the child is less likely to be educated at home in the skills that transfer to classroom assessment such as reading and maths. Habitus can also be negative to schooling for the child from a working-class home or home below the poverty-line because teaching is inherently a middle-class occupation. This means habitus is structuring because even when parents see education as their child's 'way out', both they and their child need to first face the hurdle of potentially not having the habitus or capital that is valued in the middle-class school system. The family and child may not have the same interests, language, pastimes, holidays, social engagements, life experiences or hopes for the future as their middle-class

teacher, or the middle-class students. The result here is that the child does not have the *structured* habitus to engage with schooling in the same ways.

Thus, this example of habitus will be *structuring* because the child born into a house that has not been supported by education's middle-class focus will potentially be alienated by education. Achieving the grades to reach university, or the desire to seek out a career that requires a university education, is difficult to aspire to when it means fighting your way through a centuries-old system that is designed to benefit the middle-classes and few other groups. This is all about choice, however, the problem with *structuring* habitus is that it also works in the negative and removes choices. If the family or the child from a working-class family or family living in poverty wants the child to do well at school and go on to university, for the reasons listed in the above sections, they are less likely to succeed in the middle-class pursuit of university. There are also likely to be more life-obstacles in the way of a child from a poor or working-class background: they are unlikely to have the same resources at home as their middle-class counterparts that aid in their work (such as computers, stable internet connections, and assistance in gaining the required information). The culmination of these issues is the negative structuring of habitus. The cultural trajectory of the poor or working-class child is to replicate their parents because whether they want to or not, it is extremely difficult to shift out of one class and into another.

As with the example of the Eton and Oxford educated surgeon, for the working-class child, habitus is also a *structure*. However, as the Oxford graduate had a structure that allowed them to easily select a career that provided financial stability and have a life of secure housing and food, the structure for the poor or working-class child is that their own options will be only ones that move them amongst their social groups because the cycle of intergenerational poverty is extremely difficult to break.

It needs to be reiterated that both above examples are purposely simple and in direct contrast to each other to demonstrate that habitus can both open and close doors. It should also be noted that governments in many Westernised nations do make some attempts to enable or encourage people from non-traditional groups to attend universities and due to 'first in family' to attend university awareness, some support is provided once they get there, but this is still the exception to the rule of being unable to transition between classes (Hurd and Plaut 2018; Tamtik and Guenter 2020). The final point to note about these examples is that the class system is tied to ideas of money. Going back centuries, a working-class career provided less income than a professional career and that limiting of finances has restricted working-class people and their families in their education and life options (Laurison and Friedman 2016). In some traditionally working-class careers in recent decades, however, the income is exceptionally high, certainly higher than some professional careers, and this has provided situations where finances provide economic capital that can help bridge the gap from working-class to middle-class and allow these children options not routinely open to those bound by working-class structures (Manstead 2018). Though it should be noted, that success in breaking cultural trajectories is more about just economic capital. Economic capital might enable a child to attend a 'good' school, have resources, and have a steady home life that enables study, but aspects of habitus and social capital, such as language, interests, and experiences that pair with their teacher, may still elude them (aspects which will be discussed in future chapters).

Habitus on a Personal Level

The above examples demonstrate what habitus is in action as we see an internalised system shape what people believe and value, what is of interest to them, and subsequently what they think about the world around them and how they act. Bourdieu said of his own habitus:

> I either see or don't see certain things in a given situation. And depending on whether I see these things or not, I shall be incited by my habitus to do or not do certain things (Bourdieu and Chartier 2015, p. 58).

Habitus on a personal level is thus quite straightforward. The way an individual thinks, what they value, what they do as a pastime, what they aspire to achieve (among many other characteristics) rarely occur by chance but are often subconscious variations of what fits within their cultural trajectory. This situation becomes more complex, but far more interesting to researchers and anyone who wants to think about how and why society works the way it does, when different habituses cross paths.

Bourdieu refers to people and individuals as *agents*, and groups of agents operate in a *field*. Bourdieu sees habitus as being the defining factor as to whether someone *fits* within a group, or how well they fit within a group. To use his famous example, if someone's habitus fits within a field, it is akin to asking if they do, or do not, feel like a fish in water (Bourdieu 1990a). That is to say, for example, a historian of ancient Greece will have the correct habitus to 'fit in' at a conference about ancient Greece. They will thus have the knowledge, the life experiences, and the cultural trajectory that provided them with that knowledge, to enter the conference and feel like a fish in water; they likely also have existing relationships with people that have developed as their habitus to fit within the conference has grown. Habitus also ensures that the connections the historian has and can make within the field of the conference is not only about work, but they will also inevitably share interests around the books they read, films they watch, music they listen to, hobbies they might have, and holidays they might have taken. That is not to suggest that they will be identical, but it is to suggest that some connections will always be able to be made because inevitably the habitus of someone attending a conference about ancient Greece will not stray far from other attendees.

There are also sliding scales of an agent's habitus and how well they fit within a field. If we take the historian of ancient Greece and place them in the field of a physics conference, then their habitus will not fit quite so well. They will not be able to have detailed conversations about physics, they likely do not know people in the field, they likely have not read the most recent research, and they will not be able to contribute to detailed discussions about the field. However, the historian will not be a total 'fish out of water'. They will still be able to make connections because they and the physicists work at universities, they will have all climbed the ladder of academia, they can share stories of teaching undergraduate students and the promotion processes, the historian also possibly has some knowledge of the Greek ideas surrounding physics which could provide some avenues of conversation. As these groups are all academics, even in different areas, it is still possible that they share some of the same pastimes, hobbies, and other experiences. Thus, the connections may not be as direct as when the historian was at the ancient Greece conference, but the connections are likely still present at the physics conference even if the connections must be sought out.

The connections could be made because even if many of things about their lives are different, they are still of the same social group and will have had structurally similar lives and experiences which essentially guarantees that connections will be present. Bourdieu took this idea one step further and suggested that people are rarely able to ever wholly breakaway from the social forces that shaped their habitus; even if this is their aspiration. He argued that even when someone attempted to adopt a style, career, or way of life not necessarily aligned with their social class, that style, career, or way of life was destined to occur within the realms of what still 'fit' within their social class (Bourdieu and Passeron 1977).

Habitus is subsequently the dispositions and characteristics a group or person will hold, and whether someone is examining the habitus of an individual, or a group, it is not about groups being identical, that will rarely be the case. How well one person's habitus fits with another person, or how well one person fits within a given field, is about the pattens and similarities of one to the other.

It is also necessary to consider that though this discussion has been about habitus in individuals, and groups, and how, as Bourdieu would put it, the habitus of an *agent* impacts on how well they can operate within a *field*, habitus can also work on significantly larger scales and define cultural traits or beliefs. Webb et al. (2002) use the example of meat consumption in the Westernised world to demonstrate this point. They argue that habitus plays a large role in it being acceptable for cows, chickens, sheep, or pigs to be bred, slaughtered, and consumed as a standard part of the Western diet. People rarely consider why this is deemed acceptable because for generations people have had this acceptability structured into their upbringing. Webb et al. (2002) establish their point further by suggesting that it is cultural habitus that prevents cats, dogs, or rats being regularly consumed in the Western world, and is the source of the Western disbelief that it occurs readily in other areas. However, in those 'other areas', this diet is entirely acceptable because it is part of their habitus.

Bourdieu describes these variations as being part of the transcending dichotomy of habitus. Habitus can be used to examine the past, present, and future of an individual or group and determine with relative precision why someone is who they are today, and who they will likely become in the future. However, the transcending dichotomy is also that everything they are not, or that has not, contributed to their habitus is relevant because every person, group, and culture they interact with has their own habitus and some similarities can transcend some differences. For example, regardless of social structure or many subjective forms of habitus guided by upbringing, these can potentially be overcome when connections can be made via ethnicity, gender, sexuality, or nationality.

Habitus and Its Relationship with Field and Capital

The previous section outlines what habitus is, and the following sections examine some aspects of habitus in more detail to provide more ways, or tools, to identify habitus and think about how it impacts on individuals and groups in different social situations. However, before moving forward with this discussion, there also needs to be a brief examination of how habitus relates to capital and field; terms already used several times in this book, which are explored in the following chapters, but need further exploring before habitus can be examined in more detail.

Outlining the relationship between habitus, capital, and field is not a necessary step only for habitus, it just so happens that habitus was the Bourdieusian concept discussed first. Habitus, capital, and field are all individual concepts that themselves can be defined rather simply, but the exploration of how habitus and capital influence an individual's or group's (an agent's or group of agents') standing in a field is primarily about how these three concepts influence each other.

One of the most significant factors to consider is that neither habitus, nor capital or field, act alone; and the result of how habitus, capital, and field define a situation is what Bourdieu called *practice*. As with most aspects of Bourdieu's concepts relating to people and society, his emphasis was on highlighting that things rarely occur by chance and were instead the result of 'an unconscious relationship' (Bourdieu and Wacquant 1992, p. 126). Habitus, capital, and field are the components of a given relationship, but the result of how well someone's habitus and capital are received in a field is referred to as their practice; it is about how attuned or comfortable or familiar someone is with the practices that occur within a field. Bourdieu (1986) formed an equation to explain this process:

$$[(\text{Habitus})(\text{Capital})] + \text{Field} = \text{Practice}$$

To dissect this equation, we can begin with habitus, which as we know is the structures that have shaped someone to who they are today (and may be in the future). Thus, in the equation we can think of habitus as a value that does not change; someone's habitus at a given point is their habitus regardless of what other factors are at play. Someone's capital, however, is related to the field in which the equation is being applied and so will vary depending on the field being assessed.

To return to the earlier example of the history professor entering a history or a physics conference, the professor's habitus does not change in either equation. They have had a life of experiences, opportunities, and interests that were shaped by their family and upbringing, and has led them to become a professor of history. Thus, their history (their habitus) remains the same whether they walk into the field of a history conference, or the field of a physics conference. It is the field that changes and subsequently it is the field that plays a major role in how much capital someone's habitus holds in that field.

In this example, the field is either the history conference or the physics conference, and it is the field that dictates the history professor's capital, and subsequently, their practice (or result of their place in the field). Remembering that habitus remains the same at a given point, the equation thus leads to:

> A history professor in the field of a history conference will have significant capital because they 'feel like a fish in water' and so their practice will be a positive experience as they fit within that environment.

Alternatively:

> A history professor in the field of a physics conference will not have as much capital because they do not know the topic, research, or people involved in the field, thus, they may feel like a 'fish out of water', and so their practice will be stifled as they do not fit as well into that environment.

If we think about these examples as we return to *[(Habitus)(Capital)] + Field = Practice*, it becomes clear that if habitus is set at any given time, the capital someone can offer is connected to their habitus. However, what capital is valued, and to what extent, is defined by the field. Thus, habitus and capital define the success (the practice) someone has in a field.

While field and capital as individual concepts still have their own history, components, and intricacies that needs to be explored, it is the fact that habitus, capital, and field are always dependent on aspects of one and other that make being familiar with aspects of each necessary before they can be explored in detail. It is this relationship that led Bourdieu to conclude that when social situations are being assessed, the first step is to examine the subject's habitus, and the next is to determine how well that habitus fits within the given field (Wacquant 1989).

That practice is the result of how an agent's habitus fits within a field, and to what degree their capital will be valued within the field, also means that any assessment is only an assessment 'at a given point in time'. This is because habituses and fields have their own structured and structuring structures which means they are both constantly evolving and following their own trajectory. Thus, two examinations of how someone's habitus fits within a field at two different times will likely return slightly different results; or perhaps significantly different results if the habitus and field are on significantly different trajectories.

As this chapter has discussed in detail, habitus is the result of cultural trajectory and it is not about habits or choices that can be easily changed. It is the result of a life of being raised a certain way, by certain people, in certain communities. This setting provides a structure of who someone is and means who they become in the future is about their choice, however, their choices will often fall within very clear paths (Wacquant 2016). At the same time, though for slightly different reasons that will be discussed in forthcoming chapters, fields are also guided by their own structure that is shaped by the people within them, but also by the communities in which they exist. With habitus and field essentially operating independently of each other in most cases, someone's capital (or how they fit within the field) is not set because both are constantly changing. An agent's place within a field can grow due to the field morphing to value their capital more, or their place can diminish due to the field altering to value a capital the agent does not possess. This also means someone's habitus may fit within a field at one point, but it may not fit at another point; or vice versa (see Figs. 3.1 and 3.2).

The above figures depict how habitus and field can relate to each other in terms of structures and trajectories, but much of Bourdieu's work also explored what happens with different habituses within a field. As becomes clear in the chapter relating to field, fields are evolving, but everyone within the field is also ranked by what the field values, and what capital each agent's habitus represents within the field. Examining

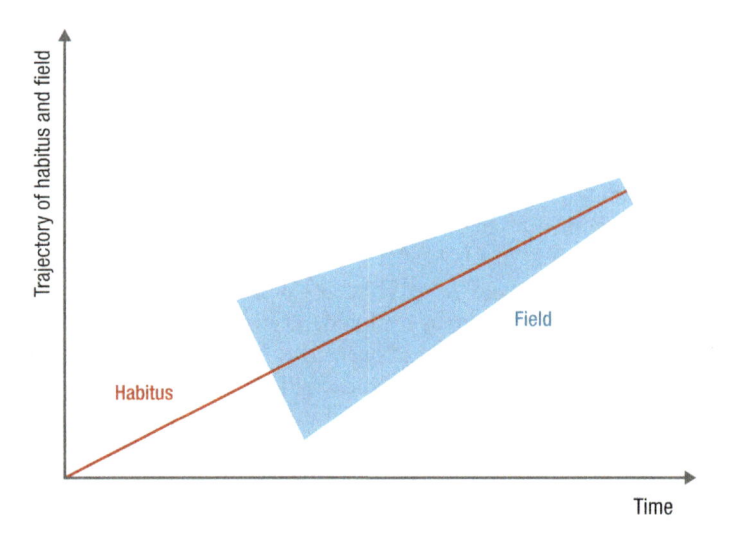

Fig. 3.1 Example of habitus and field evolving in sync

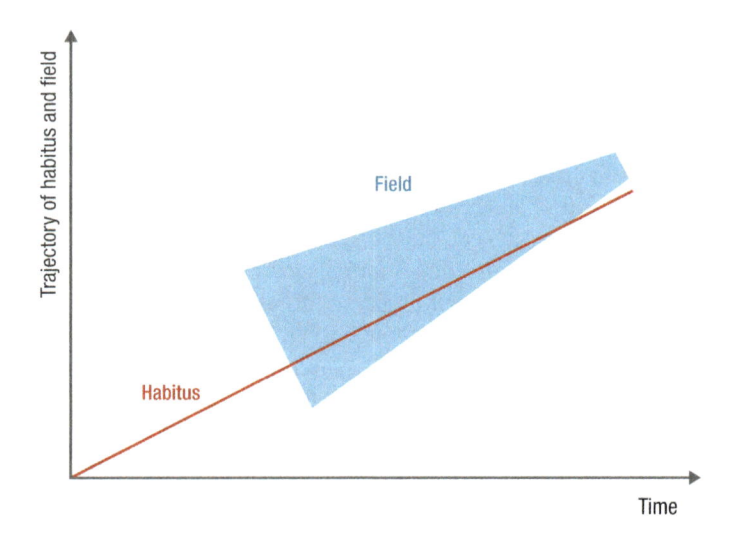

Fig. 3.2 Example of habitus and field evolving out of sync

these areas is not just a case of determining a hierarchical order of those within the field, it is about ascertaining that everyone within the field will have different levels of power, influence, and abilities to interact with others in the field. Thus, having a habitus that allows an agent to enter a field is one step, but once an agent enters the field a new set of parameters comes into play.

Well-Informed Habitus

An example of what happens within a field can be seen by those who have what Bourdieu (1977) called well-informed habitus. It is the agents with well-informed habitus, (for clarity, well-informed habitus is essentially an agent possessing the capital that the field values highly) that aids in ranking those within the field. Bourdieu suggests that well-informed habitus usually relates to *symbolic capital*. Hard capital is those forms of capital which are quantifiable. Economic capital is the easiest example of this; the more money someone has, the more economic capital they possess. If a field only values economic capital, then the wealthiest people are at the top, and the non-wealthy are at the bottom. In academia, hard capital could be the number of degrees someone holds, their academic level (lecturer, reader, professor etc.), the prestige of their affiliate institution, the number of publications they have, citations they have gained, or to add an economic component, the value of the grants they have received.

Symbolic capital is more about capital that influences perceptions within the field. If two early career researchers are attending a conference and have similar hard capital (quantifiable capital) such as number of publications, are affiliated with similarly ranked institutions, and neither have yet acquired any grants, then they will be ordered within the field via symbolic capital. At a conference, perhaps the easiest gauge of symbolic capital is who the early career researchers know, and the circles within which they socialise. If one of those researchers is known to be associated with a highly regarded professor in the field and they are presenting a paper together, or they can often be seen socialising with the professor's other equally-distinguished colleagues, then that researcher gains significant symbolic capital and will thus be ranked above the other early career researcher in the field. Symbolic capital in this instance was attributed to the distinguished professor bringing the early career researcher into their company. However, in academic fields, the capital stems from the potential inference that the professor's decision to work with the early career researcher is evidence that they deem the quality and potential of the researcher's work to be great enough to warrant the professor's time and support.

Another way to think about well-informed habitus is to take the concept one step further to what Bourdieu termed *distinction* (Bourdieu 1984). Well informed-habitus and distinction are both about knowing the rules of the game, but whereas well-informed habitus can place one agent in front of another at the lower end of a field's hierarchy, distinction is reserved for those at the top of a given field (such as a conference) or a field within a field (such as early career researchers at a conference).

Distinction

Distinction is subsequently another way an agent can set themselves apart in a field, but whereas habitus is about possessing the structures to fit within a field, distinction often also relies on knowledge and experience. To continue the examples of academics at conferences, let us think about academics at a sociology conference. Habitus and the resulting capital will be a component that enables people to know the conference is being held, have a reason to attend, and have the ability to travel to the conference. Being a sociology conference, the structures of habitus have likely led the person to be an academic (which is why they have a strong interest in sociology) and possibly work at a university (which is why they knew the conference was being held) and at their institution they work in the sociology field (which is why their university allowed them the time, and potentially some financial support, to attend).

As all our work on habitus indicates, an academic working in or around the field of sociology would be able to fit within the conference relatively well. If we think about an early career researcher, maybe someone currently completing their doctorate, they will be able to discuss the relevant topics, may know some people by name, and may even know some people personally from their academic networks (Heffernan 2020). However, what happens if we think about someone who gained their doctorate five years ago? They attend this conference every year and this is the seventh time they have attended because they first attended as a doctoral student. They know many other attendees personally, they know several of the publishing vendors by name, they know the system and patterns of this conference extremely well, and being that they have now been studying sociology for almost a decade, their knowledge on the topic is significantly greater than the doctoral student's knowledge. The result is that the academic who has attended the conference multiple times and has a significant knowledge of sociological topics can enter the field of the conference with distinction because they know, and have practical experience, of the detailed rules of the game.

That is not to suggest that experience must relate only to the field in question or that an agent must know people to enter a field with distinction; but these are methods by which distinction is regularly accrued. Distinction could also be attributed via notoriety. A globally recognised figure in sociology could attend the same conference (having never attended before) and know no one personally at the conference having elected on this occasion to attend as an invited keynote speaker. However, that person will still enter the conference with distinction because their place as a globally recognised researcher in the field (put simply, they are famous in the field of sociology) ensures they are instantly at the pinnacle of the field of the conference. They do not need to know anyone if everyone else knows who they are, people will approach them with enthusiasm and seek their knowledge on sociological topics, but they will also be keen to discuss topics that may result in forming closer bonds. This example is also interesting because it provides an insight into what we will be discussing in the future chapters in that fields are also moving and changing. That is because the globally recognised researcher has not just entered the field with distinction, they have entered the field of the conference with such distinction that the field has altered to accommodate the new and famous agent. Potentially, before their arrival, the pinnacle of the conference was nationally recognised researchers. However, that the field easily changed to fit the globally recognised researcher is why fields are always moving, and why the internationally recognised scholar could enter without knowing anyone but still gain the instant attention of many of the attendees.

Practice in a field is thus the results of structuring habituses, capital, cultural capital, symbolic capital, well-informed habitus, less well-informed habitus, and distinction (though the list exceeds these examples). Grenfell (2014, p. 111) summarised the long list of variables by stating that habitus, and subsequently capital, in fields would be determined by the 'accomplishment and transposability' of those habituses in the field. This is a succinct way of concluding that a field will value a selection of different forms of capital. The habitus (and subsequent capital) an agent has to offer will result in the relevant forms of capital being assigned a value, and the total combined value of an agent's habitus will determine their position in the field's hierarchy. This is a valuable observation because it highlights that (most) fields do not value a single form of capital, but instead value several forms and it is the combined value of the capital sought by the field that ranks an agent. Thus, having a significant amount of capital in a single area may bolster an agent's place in the field, but in most cases, their level of capital in other areas will also be relevant to determining their place.

Hexis

Bourdieu (1977) also spoke of the *hexis* of habitus, or unconsciously learning the values and disposition of the field. Bourdieu argued that this resulted in an 'installed generative principle of regulated improvisations' (Bourdieu, 1977, p. 78). The notion of improvisation is relevant because fields are always changing. For agents in a field with larger amounts of habitus, they are more attune to the field and its changes. As they have the habitus and capital to understand the field, they are most likely to be able to shift with the field as it changes and subsequently maintain, or even increase, their place in the field's hierarchy. As fields are always changing, this places some importance on being continually, or regularly, amongst the field so an agent can be aware of the changes and what the field is now valuing more, and valuing less.

Webb et al. (2002) use this point to examine Bourdieu's own life. Coming from a rural area, Bourdieu routinely discussed not initially fitting into the elite academic circles because he did not have the correct habitus. However, he soon learnt the rules of the game and became not only an agent in the field of elite academia, but one at the utmost pinnacle who was globally recognised and spawned an entire field of study dedicated to his theoretical concepts. This change in Bourdieu's habitus nonetheless came with consequences. At one point in his life, Bourdieu had the habitus to fit within that of a poor, rural farming community. Having left for Paris and become a world-renowned sociologist, he could not then return to his childhood community and fit back into that poor and working-class field as he did when he left. His habitus had changed; in being shaped by new structures to fit within Parisian academic circles, his habitus was altered in a way that meant he did not fit within the farming community as he once did. Additionally, in leaving for Paris (and later the world), this took him away from his childhood community so as the habituses that were most valued in those circles inevitably changed, Bourdieu was not there to witness these changes, and adapt to the new values (Bourdieu, 2000). This of course further distanced him from the fields where he once naturally fit. Bourdieu (1977) called this 'bodily hexis' because a person inevitably takes on traits from the fields within which they operate. He also took this one step further and pointed out that people are products of their habitus and the fields within which they move. Even when people feel as though they are making their own decisions and being independent, they are inevitably often making decisions that still fit within the expectations of their cultural trajectory, their habitus, and the capital they possess.

Bourdieu focused so intently on habitus, how it was created, and what its impact would be because habitus, in his and the view of many others since, provided the building blocks of who someone was, who someone is, and who they will become. The point is that statements such as 'all people are born equally' or 'hard work will be rewarded' may be true in exceptional circumstances, but for the most part, they are only true within the bounds of someone's habitus. Bourdieu (1977) thus spoke of habitus embedding itself into cultures, and it was the habitus of a community or social group that largely determined what options an individual possessed. As an extreme example, someone born into a working-class farming family in rural America is unlikely to gain an interest in fine art, study the subject in New York or Paris, and go on to become an artist or critic that circulates across upper-class social circles due to their prominence in the field. As Bourdieu has suggested, that is highly unlikely to occur (even if something similar did happen to him). However, habitus in culture goes one step further because Bourdieu (1977) also suggests a person born into a working-class farming family in rural America would not want to pursue this career path or associate with the upper-classes. Bourdieu says this is because of the *conditioning* of an agent's habitus. A person is born into a family, which is located in a community, which has a culture, and these groups all have their own priorities and interests that influence, or *condition*, someone's habitus. We have previously spoken about cultural trajectory. That trajectory is based on the culture someone is raised in and thus their habitus is not random. Habitus is conditioned by the community an individual is raised in, which is the culture many people are raised in, and is why the community conditions them into relatively the same structured and structuring structures.

Conditioning

A key point relating to habitus and conditioning is that someone's habitus, for example, explains why someone from a rural working-class family is unlikely to attend university. No one in their family has attended university, no one they know has attended university, there are no universities located near them, and the common sequence of growing up in that community is that someone finishes their schooling and begins a working-class career. The cultural trajectory is to remain in the community and seek out what jobs are available. Conditioning tells us that it is entirely possible that people in the community with the academic ability to attend university and leave the community perhaps do not want to make that choice; the notion of leaving the community to attend university may not have even registered as a possibility to them.

Bourdieu (1990b, p. 54) says this is because at an extreme, cultural habitus makes a 'virtue out of necessity', but if this notion is somewhat diluted, it also means that the most common cultural trajectory someone is surrounded by becomes their aspiration. That is to say, there is little connection between access (to an opportunity) and aspiration (to take up that opportunity). This is because decisions are not made freely, they are made with habitus as part of the equation. An individual will not take the 'greatest' opportunity presented to them if that opportunity does not fit within their habitus. Bourdieu (1990b) says that sometimes this choice is subconscious. The opportunity is sometimes so far out of the person's habitus that they fail to even consider the opportunity; it is an unfathomable trajectory, so it is dismissed, sometimes without thought. In other instances, the individual is aware of what is on offer, but because the opportunity is so far removed from their habitus, they choose not to take up the offer because it is not what they are familiar with, and they feel they will not fit in when they arrive. In higher education, an example of this relates to the line of study regarding students from working-class, refugee, first-in-family etc. backgrounds being accepted into elite institutions such as within the Ivy League, or Oxford or Cambridge, yet they electing to attend less prestigious universities (Hurst, 2010). Bourdieu would suggest this choice is made because they feel they do not have the habitus to fit into these spaces, and it is this lack of capital in the field, and knowing they will likely feel like 'fish out of water' that will only add pressure to an already high-pressure environment. Subsequently, attending less prestigious universities is slightly closer to the bounds of their cultural trajectory.

Bourdieu (1977) calls this *operating in habitus* and suggests that people are naturally strategic and aspirational, and this guides their decisions, actions, and negotiations within a field. Bourdieu also suggests that a great majority of people, no matter how aspirational or strategic they are, will only operate in the bounds of their habitus; but this is also how they have the greatest success. For example, when climbing the hierarchy of any field involves knowing 'the rules of the game', strategy and planning can only be carried out if someone knows the rules of the game. Thus, consciously or unconsciously, these issues can motivate people to remain within fields with which they are familiar. This has often been likened to Marsh and Parker's (1984) 'big-fish-little-pond effect' in that individual's make internal calculations (sometimes they are conscious of them, sometimes they are not) about what they can achieve. As knowing the rules of the game is imperative, this inevitably results in people choosing to be more successful in the fields they are familiar with than taking a lower position in the hierarchy of a field in which they are less familiar. These notions have strong ties with the occurrence of people from certain demographics being admitted to prestigious universities, but electing to attend less prestigious institutions as discussed above. This can be a very conscious decision and it can be guided by their own knowledge that they are less likely to have the habitus to successfully operate in the highly stratified world of elite universities (Hurst 2010). As a result, they chose an institution where their habitus fits, and they will thus likely be more successful.

It may seem extreme that some people are choosing not to attend the world's most famous universities in favour of less prestigious options, but it is crucial to point out that this decision is rarely about intellectual capability. These decisions are based on the social aspect of university; universities create and disseminate knowledge, but this is almost always done through social means. Bourdieu (1984, 1988) knew this social process was an advantage to some, but a disadvantage to others. He advocated for the notion of universities being a place that offered students the opportunity to share ideas and form bonds with particular types of people that shared their ideals (it could be argued that this also leads to networking opportunities in later life). These connections are all about shared habituses and cultural capital experiences, but it is the opportunities of these connections that are also negatives if someone does not have the shared experiences of the group.

It is also necessary to consider that the above discussion around 'fitting in' to higher education, and 'knowing the rules of the game' in terms of elite institutions are general terms that Bourdieu used, but in part cover (or disguise) the consequences of gender, race, disability, sexual identity, and other marginalising factors in higher education (Bhopal et al. 2016; Meekosha et al. 1991; Mirza 2018). At other times, people are acutely aware of the rules of the game and how to fit in, and it is knowing these rules which is why they choose not to fit in—because they know they will not be allowed to play 'fairly'. This can be the result of gender or disability or any other marginalising characteristic when the field someone is attempting to enter has clear parameters. Sometimes it is not about whether an agent can fit within a field, it is about whether the field will allow them to, or if they do, if they allow them an equal opportunity.

For Bourdieu, these are all issues relating to education and cultural capital. As we have already looked at, Bourdieu knew education was a significant component of structured and structuring structures, and the success of someone's formal education or training was highly influential in the trajectory of how the rest of their life formed. However, education, and subsequently both the academic and social aspects of education, that begin from the earliest years, was in Bourdieu's view strongly tied to the structure of the family home. Bourdieu (1977, 1988) said that success in schooling can be influenced by someone's social class, the financial situation of their family, where they grew up, or their religious affiliation (among many other factors). In his studies of students' academic and social relationships to their peers and educators, he found strong ties between parents' employment types and their children's success in the school system. Bourdieu's focus on employment type originates from the fact that social class is not always binary to income, particularly once the discussion surrounds people who are employed. Earlier in this book, we discussed the example of working-class occupations and trades (such as in the mining or oil industry) providing incomes higher than some middle-class occupations. It is from this starting point that Bourdieu knew success in school was more about parents' incomes, and that other factors were influencing the habitus they instil on their children.

Knowledge and Labouring Classes

Bourdieu divided these groups into the knowledge-class, or the labouring-class. A child whose parents were from the knowledge-class (so had attended university or were connected to knowledge if they worked at, for example, a school, library, office, or in administration) would do better in school both academically and socially then a child from a labouring-class family (even if that family had a higher income). This is because the habitus created by structures in the knowledge-class fits better within schools which themselves are creators of the knowledge-class. Children of the knowledge-class are more likely to have skills and interests aligned with what schools teach, assess, and value. The knowledge-class children are more likely to read as a pastime, receive instruction at home in reading, maths, science, and they are also more likely to have the language, interests, and thus ability, to communicate more effectively with their teacher (Nash 1990).

In many ways what Bourdieu is referring to is the knowledge-class being more likely, but also having clearer, paths to academic success because of their social cohesion in knowledge-class circles. This is, as with much of what he writes, reflective of his own experience of leaving a poor farming background for elite education. Attending elite universities may not be the usual cultural trajectory for most, though even if they do pursue this option, they can still face difficulties with fitting into new cultural environments.

This social lack of cohesion can also present itself in the university classroom. For example, in an ancient history doctoral programme reading group at one of the most prestigious universities in the world, it is entirely likely that a significant majority of the group have studied or holidayed in the locations they are discussing such as Rome or Athens. This is because the habitus of most people in an institution such as this is connected to wealth and privilege, and overseas holidays fall within the common pastimes of this group. For the working-class student admitted into the doctoral programme due to their academic ability, however, they are at a disadvantage. They might be as academically capable as everyone else in the room and have read the same books, but inevitably some of the class discussion around their work, and much of the social discussion not relating to their work, will be about these locations and what it is like to be there, walk there, and go on tours etc. For these discussions, the working-class student will find it hard to be involved, and so will find it more difficult to make meaningful personal connections (Lampert et al. 2016).

The concept amplifies outside of the classroom; because at least in the classroom there was the shared habitus of a passion for history and the process of completing a doctoral degree. Outside of the classroom, social connections will not be non-existent, but they will be fewer for the working-class student. Elite private schools are the feeder-schools for elite universities, so in some cases students would likely have attended the same schools, and even if they did not attend the same school, they would still have connections over the trials and tribulations of life in an elite school. The same concept continues into hobbies, holidays, houses, where people live, the cars they have, the forms of entertainment they enjoy. In both above examples, these are commonalities that will immediately draw some students together to form instantaneous social circles. An institute comprising mostly of upper-middle class students will be a difficult place for a working-class student to enter and create the same relationships as quickly or as easily as they might if they were from a different social class. These difficulties are not about hostility or aggression between classes (though that could exist). These difficulties are about the working-class student starting from a deficit position in creating social ties. This means they must work harder, and sometimes instant connections maybe lost which will take time to re-establish, or perhaps the opportunities in some situations will be lost entirely because the middle-class students have already formed tight bonds.

As this book is about universities and academics, it is crucial to note that these discrepancies in habitus do not end once someone comes to realise their habitus does not fit in certain fields. At this point, they begin altering their outward disposition to better fit within the field, or they remain true to their origin and risk a lower place within the field; it is rarely the latter option when education, work, or career success are at risk (Bourdieu 1977). Instead, university students will try to fit in, for the purpose of success and perhaps also social inclusion, but the issues associated with unaligned habituses continues throughout their studies and career opportunities.

Bourdieu wrote about these issues in detail in *Homo Academicus* (1988). Though questions could be raised about the relevance of issues that originated in a text from last century that summarised findings up until the late-1980s in the French university system, many of the elements Bourdieu discussed remain relevant today. As Bourdieu advances the discussion of habitus and field beyond the scenarios of initial undergraduate study, he moves onto circumstances as students begin their postgraduate study or doctoral study. I think most people would agree this is the time when a successful academic career can begin to take shape. Favoured students can find themselves invited onto their supervisor's (and their supervisor's colleagues) research projects, quickly be attached to funded projects, and soon have their name begin appearing in publications alongside established figures in the field. This is not the only way to start an academic career, and it does not guarantee a successful academic career, but it is one way that affords the selected students opportunities not available to all students. Bourdieu (1988) discusses how these students are selected, and the roles these students filled are often casual or short-term contracts, and as such, there's rarely any formal hiring process or checks; the student is selected because that is the senior academic's choice. The student must be potentially capable of performing the required tasks because this selection is not about blind favouritism. However, Bourdieu's point is that in a group of graduate students, or amongst a senior academics' likely large number of doctoral students, matching habituses and social connections is inevitably going to play a role in which students are selected to receive the senior academic's patronage.

This system has clear implications to working-class students and students from the labouring-classes. Students' with habituses that match the university environment and the senior academic are at an advantage when the selections are made. Ultimately, the senior academic wants tasks fulfilled (for example, literature reviews completed, interviews conducted, transcripts analysed etc.), and when presented with multiple candidates capable of completing that task, the selection will be made on personal preference which will likely be at odds with the labouring-class student, working-class student, or student from a marginalised background who has broken away from the more likely path of their cultural trajectory to attend university and pursue an academic career.

Bourdieu identified and explored this circumstance, but the rapid expansion of the university to a mass-market higher education system throughout the latter half of the twentieth century has led to many other researchers examining the issues in their own contexts (Ingram and Abrahams 2016; Reay 2001; Thomson 2017). These investigations further dissect the links between childhood habituses and how agents operate in universities, but they also explore a point not readily discussed in Bourdieu's work. Bourdieu examined these issues from a theoretical, almost mechanical standpoint where occurrences in childhood would have predictable results in adulthood; which is largely correct. However, the work of the above listed researchers involves multiple studies using qualitative methods and highlights an additional point. These opportunities (or lack of opportunities depending on habitus) that occur in universities are not happening in the background or hidden from view. They are open, and the people involved know why, or why not, they may be having more or less success as they enter the field of higher education. This scenario may be of little consequence to those who benefit from the process. However, to those unable to break into the inner-circle, they know they are not in the inner-circle. This knowledge predictably has an emotional toll that plays a role in motivation, career aspirations, and if they will remain in the academy at all. Scenarios with a negative personal impact, but also lower the representation of diversity in universities.

Summary

This chapter has been a brief exploration into habitus, with some introductory points on capital and field that will be explored further in the coming chapters. Habitus is the summary of an individual's or a group's structured and structuring structures and helps explain why cultural trajectory can be formed before birth, and why someone's thoughts and actions are rarely unpredictable, and are often only variations of what will remain within their habitus. As crucial as it is to understand habitus and appreciate how an agent's habitus is formed and will shape their opportunities in the future, this chapter has also explored the consequences of habitus in communities and society. Habitus is one part of the equation of how an individual fits into different social contexts because it is the culmination of an agent's personal structure, and how well it fits depends on what components (or capital) the field values.

This chapter's examples have intentionally provided stark contrasts to demonstrate why habitus and fields pairing well is so important to potential career pathways; but this has been done so readers can apply the theories behind the examples to their own contexts or interests. Children from working-class/labouring-class backgrounds will fit better in working-class environments that fit their cultural trajectory. Alternatively, children from lower-income knowledge-class families will likely still do better in school than their wealthier labouring-class counterparts because children from the knowledge-class likely know the rules of the game in a knowledge-based setting; such as a school. This chapter has also shown that while basic examples demonstrate the wider point, exploring the relationship between habitus, capital, and field can also be incredibly complex. Behind every conclusion relating to each of these three concepts there will always be another layer of analysis that can be exposed, and every layer has repercussions to the other concepts and so the analysis could be virtually never-ending.

However, this is a work about universities. We are less concerned with how habitus fits with different fields in society, and more concerned with how habitus fits in the field of a university setting. Every university will be different and value their own set of capitals, and this will again be different from faculty to faculty, and subject area to subject area. Understanding the frameworks of capital and field is thus the next necessary step before we can explore what these concepts look like in the rapidly changing global higher education sector.

References

Bhopal K, Brown H, Jackson J (2016) BAME academic flight from UK to overseas higher education: aspects of marginalisation and exclusion. Br Edu Res J 42(2):240–257. https://doi.org/10.1002/berj.3204

Bourdieu P (1990) In other words: essays towards a reflexive sociology. Stanford University Press, Stanford

Bourdieu P, Wacquant L (1992) An invitation to reflexive sociology. Polity Press, Cambridge

Bourdieu P, Chartier R (2015) The sociologist & the historian (trans: Fernbach D). Polity, London

Bourdieu P, Passeron JC (1977) Reproduction in society, education and culture (trans: Nice R). Sage

Bourdieu P (1977) Outline of a theory of practice (trans: Nice R). Cambridge University Press, Cambridge

Bourdieu P (1984) Distinction: a social critique of the judgment of taste (trans: Nice R). Harvard University Press, Boston

Bourdieu P (1986) The production of belief: contribution to an economy of symbolic goods. In: Collins R, Curran J, Garnham N, Scannell P (eds) Media, culture and society: a critical reader. Sage, London

Bourdieu, P. (1988). *Homo Academicus* (P. Collier, Trans.). Polity.

Bourdieu P (1990b) The logic of practice (trans: Nice R). Stanford University Press, Stanford

Bourdieu P (1993) Sociology in question (trans: Nice R). Sage, London

Bourdieu P (1994) In other words: essays towards a reflexive sociology (trans: Adamson M). Polity, Cambridge

References

Bourdieu P (1996) The state nobility. Elite schools in the field of power (trans: Clough LC). Polity, Cambridge

Bourdieu P (2000) Making the economic habitus. In: Algerian workers revisited (trans: Nice R, Wacquant L). Ethnography 1(1):17–41. https://doi.org/10.1177/14661380022230624

Grenfell M (2014) Pierre Bourdieu: key concepts. Routledge, Abingdon

Heffernan T (2020) There's no career in academia without networks': academic networks and career trajectory. High Educ Res Dev. https://doi.org/10.1080/07294360.2020.1799948

Hurd K, Plaut V (2018) Diversity entitlement: does diversity-benefits ideology undermine inclusion? Northwestern Univ Law Rev 112(6):1605–1636. https://scholarlycommons.law.northwestern.edu/nulr/vol112/iss6/12

Hurst A (2010) The burden of academic success: managing working-class identities in college. Lexington Books

Ingram N, Abrahams J (2016) Stepping outside oneself: how a cleft habitus can lead to greater reflexivity through occupying "third space." In: Thatcher J, Ingram N, Burke C, Abrahams J (eds) Bourdieu: the next generation: the development of Bourdieu's intellectual heritage in contemporary UK sociology. Routledge, London, pp 140–156

Lampert J, Burnett B, Lebhers S (2016) More like the kids than the other teachers': One working-class pre-service teacher's experiences in a middle-class profession. Teach Teach Educ 58:35–42. https://doi.org/10.1016/j.tate.2016.04.006

Laurison D, Friedman S (2016) The class pay gap in higher professional and managerial occupations. Am Sociol Rev 81(4):668–695. https://doi.org/10.1177/0003122416653602

Manstead A (2018) The psychology of social class: How socioeconomic status impacts thought, feelings, and behaviour. Br J Soc Psychol 57(2):267–291. https://doi.org/10.1111/bjso.12251

Marsh H, Parker J (1984) Determinants of student self-concept: Is it better to be a relatively large fish in a small pond even if you don't learn to swim as well? J Pers Soc Psychol 47(1):213–231. https://doi.org/10.1037/0022-3514.47.1.213

Meekosha H, Jakubowicz A, Rice E (1991) "As Long As You Are Willing To Wait": access and equity in universities for students with disabilities. High Educ Res Dev 10(1):19–39. https://doi.org/10.1080/0729436910100103

Mirza HS (2018) Racism in higher education: what then, can be done? In: Arday J, Mirza HS (eds) Dismantling race in higher education: Racism, whiteness and decolonising the academy. Palgrave Macmillan, pp 1–7

Nash R (1990) Bourdieu on education and social and cultural reproduction. Br J Sociol Educ 11(4):431–447. https://doi.org/10.1080/0142569900110405

Reay D (2001) Finding or losing yourself? Working class relationships to education. J Educ Policy 16(4):333–346. https://doi.org/10.1080/02680930110054335

Tamtik M, Guenter M (2020) Policy analysis of equity, diversity and inclusion strategies in Canadian Universities—how far have we come? Can J High Educ 49(3):41–56. https://doi.org/10.7202/1066634ar

Thomson P (2017) Educational leadership and Pierre Bourdieu. Routledge, Abingdon

Wacquant L (1989) Towards a reflexive sociology: a workshop with Pierre Bourdieu. Sociol Theory 7(1):26–63. https://doi.org/10.2307/202061

Wacquant L (2016) A concise geneology and anatomy of habitus. Sociol Rev 64(1):64–72. https://doi.org/10.1111/1467-954x.12356

Webb J, Schirato T, Danaher G (2002) Understanding Bourdieu. Sage, London

Chapter 4
Field

Abstract The chapter examines Bourdieu's notions of fields, what they are, what influences them, and how someone's habitus does or does not allow them to fit easily within a field. The chapter explores what fields can look like in a higher education setting. They can be the field of the university, the field of a faculty, the field of early career academics, or the field of an undergraduate classroom just to name a few. Each of these fields has their own requirements for entry, rules on how to act, and values that make someone more or less important within the field. The chapter investigates what these fields mean for people trying to enter these fields, and also how these fields are changing as the higher education sector adapts to the pressures of the twenty-first century.

In the last chapter we examined habitus as the first of Bourdieu's primary theories to understand who people are, how their life has been shaped, and what this means for them in different areas of society. We began with habitus because habitus tells us what shapes the person, and this discussion made it clear that habitus is directly related to someone's capital, but we are now going to jump forward to field. This is because while habitus is related to capital, habitus results in a person having an almost untold number of various capitals associated with every aspect of their life. However, only a select few aspects of capital will be valued (and thus measured) in any given field.

A primary focus of this book is how fields within universities are changing as different habituses and capitals are being valued at new and varying levels, this makes examining fields the most prudent next step in looking at Bourdieu's theories. Put simply, habitus is the evolving structured and structuring structure of the person, and fields (as we will soon see) are also the result of a different type of ever-changing structure that is primarily influenced by the field's members. Capital, it could be said, is the link that ties (or alienates) a person's ability to have their habitus fit within a field and connect with its members. Therefore, understanding the structure and composition of habituses and fields is the necessary first step before examining the ties between the two that capital provides.

Defining Field

We have already touched on several examples of field; the field of the classroom, the field of the university, the field of an academic conference. These examples tell us what a field can be, but they do not tell us what is going on inside. Bourdieu always being one for metaphors, regularly referred to any field as being like a sports field (1990), for example, during a soccer game. The players, the referee, and officials will all walk onto the field, and though they have different roles to one another, they all know the rules of the game, they belong on the field, and they will be accepted onto the field. That different groups can have valued roles and fit within a field is important to note as even the players have different roles beyond 'playing the game' as they take up different positions in the field; some may be attackers, some may be defenders. The field also usually contains a general hierarchy that, from a spectator's point of view, likely begins with a team's star players, followed by the other players, then the referee, then the officials. In a majority of games, the star players will lead the field in terms of hierarchy, but fields are not set. If one player makes a questionable attack on another, for a small moment the most important person in the field will become the referee as the players, officials, and spectators all wait to see if the referee saw the tackle, and if they will punish it with a yellow or red card. However, a game of soccer only lasts 90 min, as Bourdieu (1990) and a great number of researchers have argued since, social fields do not stop, the game never ends, and they are always morphing and changing shape. Even an academic conference that lasts for four days each year does not stop for the 361 days between one conference and the next. The field may slow down in how it changes. However, behind the scenes, all involved know the twelve-month period in-between is one where the papers published and the grants won (and the papers rejected and grants lost), will reshape the field when the academics next enter the conference.

The clear suggestion in the above statement is that fields are competitive and that is an argument Bourdieu (1990) and many researchers since have made (Grenfell 2014; Grenfell and James 1998; Schirato and Roberts 2018; Webb et al. 2002). The point here is that all fields are competitive if there is an option for the field to be competitive. In fields surrounding and involving academia, that it is generally believed that all fields are competitive will surprise no one who is part of the field. However, in the field of a university, the field will be led by the vice-chancellor or president, followed by their deputy vice-chancellors and vice-presidents, then by faculty deans, and finally the academic and professional staff. In a hierarchy of an institute that often includes thousands of employees, the field may be set if someone looks at these main groups. However, if we explore the hierarchy within a single group, of say, academics within a single faculty, then the instant and constant competitiveness of fields becomes clear.

In any field, people may be competitive, but this can vary from a very mild competition, to a very aggressive one. Bourdieu (1998b) makes it clear that fields are competitive because at their core, advantage can be gained by one person or party being ranked above another in the field's hierarchy. Theoretically this may be true, but the competition is thus linked to what is at stake. In academia, in a field of a faculty, what is at stake is quite clear. Internal funding, extra research time, time to attend conferences, opportunities to select classes and timetables, input into the faculty's direction, let alone likelihood of promotion, can all increase in likelihood by being higher in the field's hierarchy. These are not small opportunities; these are matters that will potentially enhance someone's work experience and thus they will be fought for with vigour; even if politeness of the workplace is maintained; though that is not always the case (Heffernan and Bosetti 2020a, b, 2021).

The clearest form of faculty hierarchy is likely academic rank. Without knowing anything about the faculty, one could assume with a great deal of certainty that someone who is a full professor has higher capital than someone else who is associate lecturer or adjunct. Capital will, however, also be attributed to volume and prestige of publications, grants received, invitations to deliver keynote addresses, research awards, teaching awards, and teaching evaluations—to name just a few things. Yet, different faculties will also attribute their own amounts of capital to various achievements. Some faculties, for example, may highly prioritise the importance of research outputs over outstanding teaching evaluations, while others may see teaching results as being more important to someone's value in the faculty. Another aspect to consider is that many fields will exist in a faculty, and each of those fields will have their own criteria or rank.

One field might be most concerned with leadership skills, the other may be research focused. Formal leadership is generally a straightforward hierarchy and a sample faculty hierarchy might begin with the dean of the faculty at the top, followed by deputy-deans, heads of research, degree coordinator's, course coordinators, and finally academics who teach into these courses. Other forms of capital might separate people of similar roles, but at faculty meetings when discussing leadership issues, the hierarchy is clear and set. However, at that same meeting when discussing research issues, the hierarchy may change to favour those with the most outputs and largest grants. These issues are separate issues in a meeting, and away from the meeting and in normal day-to-day faculty life, there will be a general hierarchy in place, and that hierarchy is defined by a multitude of ever-changing parameters. In this field, hierarchical position is linked to advantage, and just as Bourdieu suggested, people will use their own strategies and exploit the capital advantages they have to enhance their position.

The idea that different people will use their own strategies to get ahead is based on a clear premise that fields are not equitable places. This is because agents do not enter fields from the same starting position, and as Thomson (2017) argued, there is no such thing as a level playing field when it comes to Bourdieu. The exploration of habitus in the previous chapter makes it clear why people do not enter a field from the same starting point. The undergraduate classroom could include students who know each other, whose middle-class schools prepared them for university study (as was the cultural trajectory of the school's students) and the type of work expected in university level courses. Those students are at a better starting point to working-class, labouring-class, or first-in-family students who do not know anyone in the class and whose schools had not been focused on preparing their graduates for university study. This is also where factors such as gender, sexual identity and disability can play a role. These factors can set people apart from a majority of the class who 'fit' into the classroom, but it is also necessary to point out that the classroom is not set into people that 'fit' the mould and those who do not. Not fitting within the mould does not put someone in a social category of others who do not fit. In practice, it means they are more likely set aside and face their own challenge to fit within the classroom. To reiterate, little of this scenario has to do directly with academic ability or potential, but some students will enter the field in a more comfortable social state which immediately places them higher in the field's hierarchy. Starting higher, thus means they are likely in a better position as the class begins. This may be nothing more than a positional advantage (the closer you are to the front the better positioned you are in to succeed), but it is an advantage nonetheless.

At a faculty level, the same scenarios relating to starting points in the field are also true and can be based on an innumerable number of reasons. A new employee entering their first faculty meeting will need to be positioned into their faculty's hierarchy somewhere, but what will determine that position? If they are an esteemed and internationally recognised professor, they likely fit at the very pinnacle of the hierarchy—depending on their status, they may even rank above the faculty dean in terms of power and control and be second in title only. For most employees, however, they will enter the field and be ranked on predictable factors such as their rank (lecturer, senior lecturer, professor etc.), their research profile, and what they have been employed to do (research-only, research and teaching, teaching-only) which itself will be attributed an amount of capital depending on what aspects the faculty values most. They will also be ranked on unpredictable factors such as with whom they have existing relationships. A newly conferred (gained their doctoral degree) lecturer who only knows other lecturers will be limited in their hierarchical position amongst the field. However, if that newly conferred lecturer knows one or several professors, or the dean or associate dean in a visibly social/friendly context, then their position immediately rises. The differences occur because everyone in a field will be ranked (Bourdieu, 1998b) and that ranking will occur on the available information regardless of how much or how little information is accessible. It is also important to reiterate that every field will have its differences. The capital of the newly conferred lecturer walking into a faculty meeting at one university will be different to if they walked into another because each faculty will have their own set of values. When the lecturer's publications, research profile, and network are set at the time of entering the field, how they will be received will be determined by those filling the field and what the field values. The lecturer's publications may put them in a good position at a teaching-focused university, but may be average at a research-focused institution.

When discussing a new academic entering the field of their first faculty meeting it is also imperative to consider the other factors, away from publications and profile, that will have instant consequences to how they are assessed and viewed. For example, gender will play a role. This impact may be determined by the gender composition of a faculty. That is to say, a man will likely face fewer consequences regardless of their disciplinary area, but a woman entering a traditionally male field (such as maths or science) will potentially face a different outlook than if she entered a disciplinary area (or faculty) with an equal or predominantly female staff. However, the situation becomes significantly more complex when the new hire has very little chance of not being part of a small minority, if not the only person, in their faculty from a marginalised group. Non-binary genders, sexual identity that is not heterosexual, race, disability are all factors that may lead to a new academic entering their first faculty meeting and immediately being presented with a 'bridge' that needs to be crossed before they even have the opportunity of being on equal footing with their new colleagues.

The above scenarios highlight what happens as an agent enters a field, and this situation is easier to examine because the focus is on a single point in time—that of the agent entering the field. This single point means a sociological researcher can look at what capital the field values, and what capital the agent possesses at a static point in time, to determine how well and where the agent may fit in the field. This situation becomes far more complicated, and significantly more difficult to predict, once the variables of the ever-changing capital of agents, and the field's changing priorities, are taken into consideration.

That fields change in their shape and structure, and what they value, can be summarised by the fact that fields are made, not set. This notion was explored regularly by Bourdieu and scholars since (Albright et al. 2017), however, it is the different implications of this scenario that highlights why fields can be (and usually are) an extremely difficult area to examine (Grenfell and James 1998). The notion of a field being made and not set lends itself to thinking of a field from its inception because knowing how and why the field was created helps understand what capital it is likely to value. If this information is available, that may be a very logical starting point for anyone examining the field and subsequently how agents operate within it and vie for position. However, in most cases, particularly when focusing on fields within established institutions like universities, it is unlikely that the origin and original composition of a faculty, school, or department is going to be known in terms of what capital it valued. This is because fields are made (and maintained) by those within them. The creation of a new faculty or department within a faculty will thus be a newly created field and its values will be dictated by those people within them. A new department comprised of highly-research active academics will value capital associated with research activities (publications, grants, or prizes) more than teaching experience or teaching evaluation scores. The hierarchy of the department in this instance is much more likely to value researchers at the higher levels, with those more dedicated to teaching and administration positioned below them. The opposite is true of a new department comprising mostly those focused on teaching as experience and teaching prizes then becomes the most influential capital.

Field Trajectory

How a field starts is then linked to how it develops. The composition of those within a field at its inception essentially provide the framework for what the field is and what its trajectory is likely to be into the future. In this instance, it is possible to think of a field as having a habitus, and subsequently the notion of structured and structuring structures applies. The beginning of the field inevitably sets a tone that provides a trajectory, and it will not be altered without significant effort.

With the field's structure in place, it becomes clear how fields change and move in ways that are in some instances highly predictable, but in other instances, are not. Fields move in predictable ways because the habitus of those inside them give the field a habitus of its own and a cultural trajectory. Take the above example of the newly formed faculty or department. The habitus and trajectory of the field was set by the original members as their habitus, and their interests and skills (their capital) defined what the field was about, and what types of capital the field valued. This means the field changes in predictable ways. The new agents bought into the field will not be random, they will be invited into the field because they have capital that matches or complements that of the other members. A new department comprising of highly research-active academics will invite new members who are also highly research-active, and a department focused on teaching will be more interested in academics with teaching achievements.

These methods are a version of what Bourdieu called *reproduction* where, put simply, members of a field value their own capital so look for others with similar capital and so *reproduce* people like themselves (Bourdieu 2000). Reproduction subsequently can limit a field in who can enter. The research-active department will not easily make space for a researcher with a less-impressive profile and the department focused on teaching will seek those with innovative pedagogies and positive teaching records. It also cannot be ignored that a field's structure will prevent some from attempting to gain access to the field because they are not focused on what capital the field values and potentially provides its participants.

Fields can also be moved not by the accumulative habitus of all participants, but instead due to the influence of the most influential. A university faculty is a good example of this because faculty deans do influence a faculty's direction. If a faculty is led by a dean focused on teaching excellence, but their successor is driven by research prestige, even if no one else in the field of the faculty changes, the parameters of the field will alter as a powerful agent has made this decision. The dean's decisions can be guided by directing funding to research activities, providing staff with time to disseminate their research at conferences, highly active researchers may be encouraged to apply for promotion. However, depending on the dean's habitus and capital (their influence), the very fact that it is known that they highly value research-excellence will be enough to make many in the field self-regulate and increase their focus on research activities.

The above examples are all instances of fields changing predictably. Who is in the field will directly influence the field's trajectory, its changes, and what forms of capital it is likely to value more and value less. Fields can also change unpredictably, and these unpredictable changes often have the potential to lead to trajectory changes and a shift in what capital is valued. Unpredictable changes to a faculty could include the addition or subtraction of major and influential researchers. If a faculty has gained recognition nationally or globally because it was home to a pivotal researcher in the field, losing that researcher will have ramifications to the faculty's status. Similarly, a faculty with an influential researcher on its staff may gain significant kudos from employing such a person. Though, it cannot be ignored that the most likely faculty for such a researcher of such status is one at a globally recognised university that likely houses other major researchers.

Unpredictable shifts to the field can also come from politically driven policy changes, or factors impacting on funding. Clear examples of unpredictable field changes can be seen due to the unfortunate circumstance that this book is being written and edited during 2020 and 2021. COVID-19 has become a global pandemic and even within a single university, expectations have changed. Courses in education and health have sometimes been stable or grown in enrolment numbers due to the emphasis of these as critical areas and offer fields of stable employment as many other sectors are temporarily in decline. These changes have caused significant alterations within most faculties. Even if the agents in these fields have not changed, the unpredictable occurrence of a global pandemic and subsequent impact on the world and higher education sector has reshaped the capital many faculties value.

The goal of all faculties (and indeed universities) is primarily to remain financially stable. However, across the globe many news services are reporting the sector routinely needing to downsize with individual institutions sometimes needing to downsize by hundreds of staff members depending on location (Doidge and Doyle 2020). The pressure on universities and faculties is such that money is not needed to grow, money is needed to minimise downsizing. In most faculties this has shifted the priority to teaching excellence; if student numbers are decreasing across the board, providing good learning environments is the goal to keep current students and perhaps encourage enrolments in those areas with growing student numbers such as health and education. Even for faculties that are research focused, this will have an impact. Teaching and research both may be potential avenues of income, but in times of crisis, attention must be paid to the most likely methods that will help solve the problem at hand. An emphasis on positive teaching practices is one method, but for researchers, their capital within the field has likely now altered according to how quickly or likely they are to bring in research funding in the immediate future because, put frankly, creating long-term research narratives in the hope of securing funding a number of years in the future is a difficult practice to continue with many universities needing to downsize staff, and it is likely these researchers may need to refocus to more teaching duties (Doidge and Doyle 2020). Many books and journal articles are no doubt currently being written, edited, and published regarding the impact of COVID-19 on higher education. Nonetheless, COVID-19 stands out as one of the clearest examples in recent memory of how unpredictable circumstances can completely reshape and field and the hierarchical positions of those within them.

That fields change and are subject to internal and outside pressures also means that those within them, or hoping to enter them, have an opportunity to learn the field to maintain or perhaps improve their position. Learning the field can take on many attributes (Bourdieu 1984) including learning skills and knowledge, or adopting interests, language, or dress. However, Grenfell and James (1998, p. 116) argue that learning the field is a case of getting 'a sense of the game'. This then allows agents to make sure their habitus and capital match what is valued by the field so they can 'operate strategically' to improve their position.

Learning the field to gain entrance to it, or to maintain your position, or to gain a higher standing may sound straight forward theoretically, but it can be much more difficult to practically apply this technique. The first issue is that it can be difficult to gain access to a field if it is secured by gatekeepers. The clearest example of this in higher education is a student applying to a course to study, or an academic applying to a faculty for an employment opportunity. The student can make their argument via their academic record, and the academic can present their list of publications and grant successes, and make an argument for how they would fit within the faculty via completing the selection criteria. However, neither has a direct ability to enter the field. Their success at entering the field will be dictated by the selection process, which will in turn be influenced by the academic success of other students applying for the course, or the research success of other academics applying for the same role.

Some fields are less strongly defended. Larger academic conferences are often open to relatively anyone who wishes to pay the conference fee and/or are part of the association holding the conference. In this sense conferences are not open to everyone, but it is likely that anyone who wished to attend would by the very fact that only a certain set of parameters would lead someone to want to attend an academic conference (such as being a student or researcher in that disciplinary area), meet the criteria.

Once in a field, an agent's ability to find an influential position, or maintain their position during times of change, is about their level of capital or 'distinction' (Bourdieu 1984). As discussed earlier, this is about how much capital someone possesses and how much that capital is valued within a field. However, an element of capital is that the more someone has, the more avenues, networks, or connections someone has available to them. In most situations this leaves those with the most capital to be the most likely to be able to accommodate the changes within the field to stay on top. This is particularly the case with predictable changes because both the field and the agents have structures which make their general trajectory clear even if the specifics are not. For example, a research-intensive faculty is most likely to change by becoming even more research-intensive, or they might increase the attention they pay teaching practices, but not at the cost of their research priorities. For the highly research-active academic in the faculty, this change will make very little difference to them as the faculty's core priority remains on research. They may need to increase their publication number a little if the faculty has decided to increase its research focus, however, they may also find themselves with more research time to do this as they already held so much capital in this field. Unpredictable changes within a field are, of course, unpredictable and may significantly alter a field's priorities. It nonetheless remains the case that those with the most capital to begin with, are most likely to fare best with the changes within the field.

Bourdieu (1984) also connected changing values with a field, with the changing borders of a field. In most scenarios, Bourdieu argued that fields never have set borders, but floating borders that are not only prone to change, they open up the possibility of agents having the ability to operate within adjacent fields (Bourdieu

1998a). Bourdieu argued that people naturally enter fields that share interests and values to their own primary field, and take with them ideas and technology, and thus return to their own field with similar new ideas. These movements within adjacent fields subsequently alter both fields, and as each field will itself be adjacent to another field, this is a constant source of change to all fields. The idea of floating borders is particularly clear within a university setting. Take for example an education faculty. A professor of science education is likely able to enter the field of the science faculty with some success and share ideas with professors from the science faculty regarding science, but also ideas about teaching students a scientific discipline. These meetings provide the professor of science education with the ability to return to their own faculty with ideas relating to the most recent research in their scientific field, and they have new insights into pedagogical practices in the science faculty. Similarly, the science faculty members have teaching insights from someone's whose research is primarily around the pedagogy of science education. Thus, the floating borders has allowed one person to visit another field, but both fields have shifted (to varying degrees) because of the relationship. Members of the science faculty will also take their newly formed ideas around pedagogy, that have been influenced by the education academic, to other fields. This action may take the education academic's ideas around pedagogy to faculties where an education academic (regardless of their specific disciplinary area) may be less likely to enter but an academic within the science faculty might; such as the engineering or medicine faculties. Multiply this same scenario by everyone in a faculty having different interest areas and exchanging knowledge with different faculties, and the value and impact of floating borders becomes clear.

Entering a field and crossing borders into another field is about habitus and capital, but as we touched on in the last chapter, there is a difference between being able to access a field, and feeling like you belong there. Bourdieu emphasises the sense of belonging to a field as a predictor of whether someone wants to enter the field and specifically uses the example of working-class students electing to not pursue opportunities to attend prestigious universities. Bourdieu (1984) points out that these decisions rarely occur subconsciously, and he reiterates that everyone from every social field is often acutely aware of where they fit in society and where they are most likely to succeed. Bourdieu (1977) make the point that these decisions to some might be about self-limitation, and a desire for the agent to stay within their social-class, however, dissecting this statement makes it clear several other factors are at play.

The first is a belief that social climbing is the goal of all people in all classes; that is, working-class aspire to be middle class, middle class aspire to be upper-middle class etc. Social mobility is nonetheless primarily a pursuit of the middle-classes because they know they already possess the social capital to step into higher social-class environments. A middle-class person who gains the economic capital to move to an expensive part of an expensive city, which may not be in the state or country they currently live in, can because they also have the social capital to do so. This change of address is not about money, just as the working-class student electing not to accept enrolment at a prestigious university is not about the opportunity; these decisions are about being able to fit into the new social fields. The middle-class person moving to the expensive part of the city knows they will fit. Even if their experiences are not identical, their social climbing can happen because their history is similar enough to that of their neighbours. They will have a professional career or run a successful business, they will share similar interests, so they will be able to adapt and fit within their new social fields. As was discussed regarding changing fields and floating borders, the more capital someone possesses, the more likely they are to succeed during changing circumstances.

In the twenty-first century, universities are going to great lengths to increase their accessibility and diversity. In part, this is financial: up to 40% of school leavers now attend universities so there is a large market share to attract. However, it cannot be ignored that a large part of this increase is because the middle-classes have expanded so much in recent decades (Forsyth 2014). Nonetheless, universities are working hard to include people from groups who for decades, or centuries in many countries, were excluded. The result may be that many people from many groups that traditionally may not have attended universities are now doing so, but many groups are still excluded. The institutions being attended by these groups are also often not the elite and prestigious universities; these institutions have a much more difficult time overcoming their elitist roots even if they are taking steps to aid in the process.

Bourdieu suggests that fields in education do not have as many of these inclusionary and exclusionary practices but only because of their structure and the habitus of the people they attract, this is in part due to all field's *heteronomous* and *autonomous* poles. Bourdieu argues that fields will contain aspects that are isolated and removed from society (the autonomous aspects of the field where one must be part of the field to understand). While there will also be those heteronomous aspects which are closely related to factors outside of the field and wider society (Webb et al. 2002). In higher education the distinction is clear. The autonomous aspects of the field are those connected to lectures, tutorials, grading, research, graduations etc., in many ways the aspects people associate with the field. The heteronomous aspects are those like government funding, grant applications, industry partnerships, accreditation, community engagement; aspects that shape the field, but that occur outside of the field or not wholly inside of the field.

Webb et al. (2002) highlight Bourdieu's argument that mapping the heteronomous and autonomous poles of a field provides insights into how it is structured and to which outside pressures it might be subjected. However, in higher education, tracking these poles also results in a clear portrayal of how outside influences have changed rather than grown. A century ago, most universities relied on significant government funding to exist; even if at that time universities then ran themselves fairly autonomously. In recent decades, however, government funding has decreased, governments have become more involved, and universities now seek funding through grants, businesses, and partnerships. Thus, the heteronomous aspects of higher education were always there because globally most university systems relied on government funding (or funding from somewhere such as a Church system), universities were never self-sufficient. In the twenty-first century, the heteronomous pole of higher education is divided between many more stakeholders than it was in past decades (Forsyth 2014).

Identifying the autonomous and heteronomous poles of a field can help in understanding what a field's purpose may be and what pressures it faces in carrying out their work. Nonetheless, Bourdieu (1998b) knew those poles and who interacted with then and influenced those decision came down to the *field of power*. That is to say, every agent in a field will be impacted on and part of what happens in a field, and what outside pressures force changes in a field; but only a select group within a field will be directly involved with shaping these practices. The field of power is thus a subset within a field; Bourdieu would call the field of power a social space within a field (rather than a field within a field). The difference being that a field of power is members within the field, but who are at the top and thus have the most controlling influence. They are not wholly separated (Bourdieu 1998b).

In the field of a faculty, the field of power might be held by the committees that make the decisions and will likely be made up of more senior members. The professors who form these committees might nonetheless be subject to the same faculty pressures as teaching and research to every other academic in the faculty. However, they were higher in the field's hierarchy and this has put them in the social space of the field of power to now be part of the decision-making process that will impact on the rest of the field. So, while this group is pivotal in determining the autonomous and heteronomous aspects of the field, Bourdieu also reminds us that this all comes back to capital (1998b). Those with the most capital gain entry to the field of power, and those in the field of power make the decisions that determine what forms of capital will be more or less valued as the field evolves.

It is also crucial to note that in some areas, such as higher education, fields fit within a hierarchy and some fields may be dominated by another. For example, there may be a field of senior university governance, a field of faculty leadership, and a field of department leadership. Each of these fields will have a field of power and a ruling group of field members, but those at the department level will be influenced by the faculty level which will in turn be influenced by the senior management level. Any hierarchical field of governance will also set parameters for the fields below. In a university, this typically looks like the senior management setting the vision for the university and outlining the constraints in enacting this vision (primarily financial and policy constraints). A faculty will then apply their own vision within those bounds, and so too will the department make decisions that fall within the bounds of the faculty.

Unsurprisingly, how some fields could control others led Bourdieu to apply and explore his theories in relation to governance. From the outside, it could appear that these acts of one field governing another (such as in the example above) were about dictating what other fields could do; but Bourdieu argues it is more nuanced than dictatorships. Instead, he returns the discussion to habitus. To understand Bourdieu's point, let us begin with dictatorships. A dictatorship in the literal sense refers to the controlling fields dictating what the lower fields can and cannot do, and with those lower fields having no voice or options to change this course. In a democratic country, the controlling party may create laws, and make decisions that impact on the entire country. The party may be dictating laws in that sense, but it is not a dictatorship, and they can be voted out of office. The same is true of the university hierarchy. It may seem as though the senior executive control certain aspects, the faculty level controls others, and the department heads control more still, however, just like a democratic nation, people do have options to have their voice heard. The complication is that having a voice heard in either scenario is about habitus, and more likely, the collective habitus of the group airing their support or criticism of the decisions being made.

In a democratic nation that voice can be exercised through voting so the habitus is about the number of people who can legally vote choosing to vote for the desired outcome. In a consultation society, such as might be found in a university, certainly voices may be heard, and the more voices who speak up the more they may direct a decision, but status likely becomes far more important. In the scenario of a department decision, a professor's view is more influential than a lecturer or a casual employee's opinion. This can be because of the pure habitus and capital that comes with being a professor, or it can be because the professor more likely has a closer working (and potentially social [which brings them more capital]) relationship with the department leaders. It is also not impossible that the professor has the option of seeking admittance to the department leadership team and the habitus that enables this option is also the habitus that ensures their voice is heard. A lecturer or casual employee does not have these options and thus, for their views to be considered, the likelihood of them needing support from others at their own levels, or from those above them, is much greater.

Bourdieu is quick to point out that democracy and consultation, who gets to lead, and who gets to have a voice, are intentionally set up so that theoretically all participants have options. We all know, of course, that this is not the case. Limiting fields is a method by which the controlling parties maintain power, and ensure that even when options are presented, they are options and selections that work in the leaders' favour. For example, any country with a two-party political system is democratic and the people within those countries can vote for any of the many parties that are listed on the ballot, but only one of two parties will lead. Regardless of who wins the election, there's also the case that these two parties usually consist of a conservative party and liberal party. People vote for one and then the other so even the party who loses the election will gain control in the next election or at some time in the future because they are the only alternative. Thus, for the leaders of any two-party political country, even losing the election is not really losing, it is simply deferring success and political careers are still made without being in power. This is the power fields can hold, for those at the top, in the field of power, they can create systems that orchestrate their control over those below them. In the case of politics and consultation, this is also ratified by the votes of people which is touted as those in lower fields choosing on their own accord who they wish to be their governing authority.

Governance in universities looks different to that of politics, but fields being fields, many aspects remain the same and primarily they are based on protecting those at the top. The hierarchy of governance that controls most universities (for example, the fields of senior management, to faculties, to departments) limit their ability to control, but also enable it. For those leading a faculty, they are limited in how they instruct their departments because they are being told what to do by senior management, but this very act also provides some insulation for those in the faculty's field of power. When it comes to decisions (though most notably unpopular decisions) relating to cutting courses or working with smaller budgets, faculties can provide departments with options of how these issues might be handled. However, the faculty can do so without taking any responsibility themselves because faculty budgets are determined by the university's senior management, not the faculty. In this instance, the people (in the departments) are being forced to make a decision by the field above them (the faculty), but the faculty is somewhat protected from retaliation from the departments because the faculty is carrying out a university directive. The same principle applies to senior management when the university is making budget cuts or negative decisions (which are usually budget related). Staff can be asked to vote or provide input into even the most unpopular decisions, but budgets are tied to government policies and funding. Thus, management's objectives can sometimes still be met with minimal damage to them as the fault can be attributed to government and not their own choices.

Status in Academia

The debate about hierarchies in fields, fields dominating others, and who gains access was interesting to Bourdieu (1988) theoretically in terms of understanding social structures. However, he also dedicated a great deal of time to the practical application concerning education, and higher education in particular. In the above section, we examined the fields of universities in the form of the clear hierarchy of management. Bourdieu nonetheless also emphasised the importance of understanding what happens even at the theoretically similar field-levels. For example, all faculties within an institution are not equal, they are all within the *field of faculties* and thus, like agents in a field, will be ranked. Bourdieu (1988) suggested that prestige and rank might be attributed to those areas closest to the purest pursuit of knowledge or the fundamental role of the university, which would place philosophy or physics towards the top of the field. This is, of course, a judgement based in Bourdieu's time and perhaps a judgement of the French social system because Bourdieu's ties to knowledge and prestige remained prominent in much of his work until his death.

Several decades into the twenty-first century, an element of faculty rank is now connected to income; which likely sees the prestige of the knowledge of the arts fail to overcome its financial constraints. Faculties are thus today more likely gauged on their income, but even then, different incomes hold different levels of prestige. Institutions with undergraduate education or nursing courses often have extremely large portions of their income generated from the fees of those becoming teachers and nurses. These courses have high numbers of enrolments but do not require specialist training facilities because practical training is interwoven into their course placement in schools and hospitals. However, far more prestige is attributed to income that stems for research funding, and in this arena, multi-million dollar grants are more likely directed towards the medical sciences than social sciences. Thus, despite what financial benefits areas like education and nursing provide to universities, the capital they offer is rarely the most prized type.

One area of difference concerns outside elements, such as global research and prestige rankings. Whether it be *Times Higher Education, QS, or Academic Rankings of World Universities* (*ARWU*, or sometimes called *Shanghai Rankings*), these rankings matter and do make a difference to faculties internally and externally (Pusser and Marginson 2013). For a faculty, the critical aspect is that these ranking bodies all provide annual university lists, and subject lists which rank faculties. A faculty can set itself apart via this method. For example, if the university is ranked 100th in the world, but the faculty is ranked 20th in their subject area, prestige can be gained which can likely also turn into extra funding and support to maintain or enhance this position (though in times of financial downturn, it could also be the case that funding is reduced in the hope this prominent position can be maintained with a smaller financial outlay). The other method for a faculty to gain extra kudos within the institution is by containing faculty members of prominence. This might be through research profile, or research profile that edges into the media (impact outside of academia is now a valuable trait), however, a faculty with a celebrity academic/s will nonetheless gain extra value within the institution.

Faculties also are not only ranked within the institution, but also amongst each other across regions, countries, and internationally. The factors that rank them in the field of their discipline are largely dominated by the institutional capital of their home institution. Assessing capital, as is discussed in the next chapter, is about assessing the available information, thus, if the only known piece of information about a faculty is which university it is located within, that fact still provides ample information. The faculty is part of the university's habitus and structures, which makes their habitus relatively predictable. A faculty from a globally renowned university will be well funded and attract academics with sizeable research profiles; a faculty in a lesser-known university with less funding will likely, overall, attract academics with smaller research profiles. In recent decades, the research and reputation rankings have provided a new and closely followed measure by which faculties are assessed. To those outside the field looking in, they are likely primarily informed by the ranks of institutional capital, but for those within the field, these subject rankings are watched closely (Heffernan and Heffernan 2018). Another way by which similar faculties are ranked is tied to the prominence of those within them. Academic profile might be about the number of publications, producing a work that guides a field, making a research breakthrough, or (in the modern age) being known through the media. The field of faculties within a discipline is quite limited and the prominent figures are well known. Thus, a prominent figure whose habitus is potentially viewed as higher than that of their home institution will benefit the faculty and its rank within the field.

Field Theory

This chapter has been about what a field is, what shapes a field, why fields move, and how this movement corresponds with an agent's habitus. Bourdieu spent decades forming and refining these theories, and some of them were shaped in direct response to education and higher education occurrences. However, Bourdieu and researchers since, have spent years dissecting every aspect of education using his tools to better understand the mechanics and social implications of people in education fields, and all fields in society. Bourdieu believed offering sociologists a broad variety of tools to use to understand fields was not ideal. His belief is why he produced his 'field theory' in an effort to provide guidance (rather than instruction) on aspects that must be considered when examining a field (Bourdieu and Waquant 1992). Bourdieu's field theory provides three steps which could guide any examination of a field.

1. Analyse the positions within the field. This step includes identifying the field of power, gaining some understanding of how many hierarchies are within the field, and who will be positioned in each.

   In a faculty, this could involve identifying the faculty leadership team as filling the field of power, identifying the professoriate, the faculty's highest research publishers, highest grant achievers, the early career researchers, the research-focused academicsn, and the teaching-focused academics.

2. With the positions and hierarchies of the field identified, map out the structures within the field and how they relate to each other.

   If step one was about ordering the hierarchies in the field, step two is about examining how the hierarchies can, or cannot, influence each other. In the faculty example, this means examining how the hierarchies can influence each other. The professoriate, for example, likely has some influence over the field of power, and some members will be in the field of power. Early career researchers, however, likely have less influence over the field of power and the faculty's direction. Different issues within the faculty will also gain some groups more voice than others. On issues of research, the research-focused academics will likely have a strong input. On teaching issues, it will be the teaching-focused academics who may have the greatest influence in shaping how the faculty moves forward. More broadly speaking, it could also be examined whose voices are valued most. As the traditional purpose of the university is to create and disseminate knowledge, it could be argued that for centuries it was the researchers. Today, however, in an industry that must respond to its customer-base, this could mean that teaching-focused academics are most influential, but this will be highly dependent on the focus and achievements of each faculty.

3. Examine the habitus of each agent in the field (or type of agent if there are multiple) to understand their current influence but also the history of their trajectory within the field to determine their likely future.

This step is primarily about identifying those agents in each section of a field's hierarchy that have habitus different from those amongst them. This might be because their current trajectory is at a cross-point with those around them, but their trajectory is nonetheless heading towards a different endpoint. In a faculty, this might see the high achieving early career researcher be given extra research time and a larger than average voice in the faculty's research directions. It might also see the high achieving teaching academic asked to help shape professional development around class design. It could also involve analysing the collective power of several sub-groups within the field. The research-focused academics have some level of influence, and the teaching-focused group another, but if they combine (even from an early career researcher standpoint) then they will have a stronger voice with a greater influence on the faculty's direction.

Summary

Bourdieu's explanation of how he uses field theory also provides an excellent summary point for a chapter focused on fields. Field theory provides a roadmap for researchers to use that can be as general as needed, or they can use the full array of theories and considerations that Bourdieu created and researchers have continued to shape and refine. What is important about Bourdieu's work around fields, and indeed all his work, is that the research and ideas he prompted are vast. This chapter has been a summary of fields, but countless journal articles and books have been written about every individual aspect discussed in the chapter relating to education and virtually every aspect of social and professional life. For new and existing researchers working with Bourdieu, an almost endless collection of critiques and applications of Bourdieu's work exists, and all are dedicated to helping researchers better understand society's mechanics.

References

Albright J, Hartman D, Widin J (2017) Bourdieu's field theory and the social sciences. Springer Singapore, Singapore
Bourdieu P (2000) Pascalian meditations. Stanford University Press
Bourdieu P, Wacquant L (1992) An invitation to reflexive sociology. Polity Press, Cambridge
Bourdieu P (1977) Outline of a theory of practice (trans: Nice R). Cambridge University Press, Cambridge
Bourdieu P (1984) Distinction: a social critique of the judgment of taste (trans: Nice R). Harvard University Press, Boston
Bourdieu P (1988) Homo Academicus (trans: Collier P). Polity
Bourdieu P (1990) The logic of practice (trans: Nice R). Stanford University Press, Stanford
Bourdieu P (1998a) On television and journalism (trans: Parkhurst Ferguson P). Pluto Press, London
Bourdieu P (1998b) Practical reason (trans: Johnson R). Polity, Cambridge
Doidge S, Doyle J (2020) Australian universities in the age of Covid. Educ Phil Theor, pp 1–7. https://doi.org/10.1080/00131857.2020.1804343
Forsyth H (2014) A history of the modern Australian University. NewSouth Publishing, Sydney

References

Grenfell M (2014) Pierre Bourdieu: key concepts. Abingdon: Routledge
Grenfell M, James D (1998) Bourdieu and education: acts of practical theory. Routledge, Abingdon
Heffernan T, Bosetti L (2020) University bullying and incivility towards faculty deans. International Journal of Educational Leadership. https://doi.org/10.1080/13603124.2020.1850870
Heffernan T, Bosetti L (2020) The emotional labour and toll of managerial academia on higher education leaders. J Educ Adm Hist. https://doi.org/10.1080/00220620.2020.1725741
Heffernan T, Bosetti L (2021) Incivility: the new type of bulling in higher education. Camb J Educ. https://doi.org/10.1080/0305764X.2021.1897524
Heffernan T, Heffernan A (2018) Language games: university responses to ranking metrics. High Educ Q 72(1):29–39. https://doi.org/10.1111/hequ.12139
Pusser B, Marginson S (2013) University rankings in critical perspective. J Higher Educ 84:544–568. https://doi.org/10.1353/jhe.2013.0022
Schirato T, Roberts M (2018) Bourdieu: a critical introduction. Allen & Unwin
Thomson P (2017) Educational leadership and Pierre Bourdieu. Routledge, Abingdon
Webb J, Schirato T, Danaher G (2002) Understanding Bourdieu. Sage, London

Chapter 5
Capital

Abstract This chapter is the culmination of the previous chapter's focus on habitus and field. The chapter explores what capital looks like in a higher education setting such as the number of publications someone has, the value of their grants, their position in the academic hierarchy, and the collaborations and networks they hold. The chapter then investigates how capital means different things in different fields, and can even mean various things to different people in the same field because how much capital someone holds can change what they expect of others. The chapter finally acts as an end point for the theoretical discussions about Bourdieu's notions and what they can mean in higher education. The chapter demonstrates that in the many facets of the higher education sector, many different fields exist, and the fields are changing. However, in every instance, capital and habitus combine to form structures that allow some people potentially easier and greater success, while these same aspects can be detrimental to those who do not possess the traditional capital and habitus the sector tends to value.

After two chapters examining habitus and field, capital as a broad notion has been discussed frequently as it is difficult to discuss a single component of $[(Habitus)(Capital)] + Field = Practice$ without touching on each aspect. That Bourdieu would pair capital with habitus makes sense because the habitus someone possesses is linked to the capital they possess and have to offer. However, it is because a field, and its everchanging values and borders, dictates what forms of capital are valued, that the discussion surrounding capital should take place now and not following or in conjunction with habitus.

In an evaluation of a social space, we need habitus to tell us what forms of capital are potentially on offer, and field to tell us what forms of capital are desired. Only then can we examine how capital can be used or manipulated to fit the field. I intentionally use the word manipulate because, as we will see, capital involves quantifiable and unquantifiable components. In the coming discussion, we will see how capital can be used, but also how it can be leveraged if someone 'knows' how to use their capital because they know the rules of the game. As is a common theme when discussing

Bourdieu and society, it will also become clear that those with the most capital are most likely to succeed across the most fields, and know how to leverage their capital most effectively.

Bourdieu on Capital

Bourdieu was aware that the idea of capital ranged from a very basic premise that was easily assessable via basic investigation, to a highly complex component of intricate equations with blurred lines that could not easily be mapped. He knew in many circumstances that capital meant different things in different fields, and even meant different things to different people in the same field. Despite the complexity that surrounds capital, he was nonetheless aware that capital was pivotal to understanding how society and those within it were structured and the positions they would hold (Bourdieu 2006). Thus, even small insights into someone's capital could pay great dividends in dissecting their place within a field.

Economic Capital: A Starting Point

Using economic capital as a starting point to define and discuss capital more widely is both a blessing and a curse even from Bourdieu's (2005) viewpoint. It is a blessing because it outlines what capital is in its most basic and quantifiable form; and is why we used the example earlier. Capital, in economic terms, is how much money someone possesses. Thus, in a field where economic capital is the only capital the field values, setting the field hierarchy is only a matter of ordering agents from those with the most money in their bank account, to those with the least money. Bourdieu's concern (2005) was that this example was so straightforward that it then skewed perceptions of how complex and influential capital could be in understanding social settings. Bourdieu argued that it was impossible to dissect the structures and functioning of the social world without understanding capital and all its forms in a field, or in groups of neighbouring fields, what they valued, and how capital related to habitus and field.

The point remains, however, that if discussions surrounding economic capital oversimplifies the issue, these discussions can also be used to begin exploring capital's complexity. Take the above example of ordering the field by how much money people have in their bank accounts, but now consider that how much money someone has in their bank account is not overly relative to how much wealth they possess, or to how much money they can access. If two people both have the same amount of money in their bank accounts, but one person has good credit and gets a bank loan, does borrowed money still count as capital? What if someone else has less money in their bank account, but they own a house? What if someone has a lot of money but it is from a trust fund and they have never worked in paid employment?

Does their money count the same as someone who has worked for the entirety of their adult life?

For all these questions, and the myriad others like them, there is no clear answer because the field collectively decides on what does and does not count, and fields are always changing. If most of the richest people in the group are rich because of inherited money (and remembering that those with the most capital have the most influence), then inherited money will likely count. However, if several of those people were to leave the group, it may be the case that the field evolves to no longer put so much value in inherited wealth. Once again, how much something is valued will be determined by the group and its composition, and this will always be changing.

Economic, Cultural, and Social Capital

In addition to economic capital, Bourdieu suggests there is also cultural and social capital; and it is the mix of these different capitals that ultimately shape the capital someone has to offer within a field. However, it cannot be denied that economic capital enables many aspects of cultural or social capital to occur, or at the very least, increases the opportunity and likelihood of someone possessing them.

Bourdieu suggests that cultural capital is the product of education, and though he does not specifically mean this to refer to formal education in all aspects, formal education does nonetheless play a strong role. Bourdieu argues that cultural capital can be divided into three categories, the first of which is institutional capital, and does relate solely to the schools and other institutions to which someone has access. In most of society, institutional capital matters because that alone provides an indicator of a person that assists in them being placed in a field because institutional capital tells the field something about the person even if the field knows nothing else. If someone attended a globally known university this says something about their level of intelligence, though perhaps also their family's wealth and networks. The same is true of secondary schools but there are far fewer globally recognised secondary schools. However, even words like 'Grammar School' and 'College' carry some institutional capital as in many parts of the world this separates them from government funded education. Government funded schools can nonetheless hold significant cultural capital if they are located in desirable areas. Simply knowing someone attends or attended (with the inference being they lived nearby) a school in an expensive or exclusive area aids in developing their economic capital. As far as schools are concerned, names can also give an indication of religious affiliation and separate someone from state education; this may be valued not at all in a field, or it may make a great difference.

For all of what institutional capital looks like for the general public, it looks a little different for those in higher education because the educational institutions someone attended is then paired with where they are employed. That is not to suggest that where someone attended is superseded by where they work, where someone studied can remain somewhat relevant throughout their career. Where they studied will forever be a topic of conversation, and in resumes and biographies for conferences and books, where someone gained their doctorate remains a commonly cited piece of information. Thus, an agent informing the field of this information is particularly likely to do so when their alma mater contributes heavily to their capital.

It is the fact that where someone studied remains relevant throughout their life that can also have an impact in university careers. Within the faculty people will be jostling for position, and particularly at the start of someone's career when publication or grant success is not yet determined. At this time, where someone studied provides an indication of their academic skills and potential research ability. Educational capital in this sense exists because it tends to be an indication of ability. The most prestigious universities generally have the most research funding, and attract global applicants when positions become available, and they likely have the largest number and most capable student applicants so the potential quality at every stage is inevitably extremely high. Thus, it is fair to assume (and is usually correct to assume) that graduates from the most prestigious universities are quite capable. However, the scenario of institutional capital can take a negative turn if someone does not live up to their institutional expectation. A graduate of a globally known university employed at a small, non-prestigious, teaching-focused university might find their institutional capital work against them because working at the teaching-focused university is not the cultural trajectory of someone who attended a world-renowned institution. Conversely, someone who attended a teaching-focused university but now works in a prestigious university might be able to take advantage of their situation by highlighting the change in their cultural trajectory as evidence of their abilities. Of course, in both examples, changes in cultural trajectories can also be fraught with issues of 'not fitting in' and feeling like a 'fish out of water'.

Cultural capital can also accrue via the objects someone owns. Remembering that capital is relevant to the field someone wishes, or has, to enter, capital can be gained by the books they own, their furniture and possessions, and albeit an extension of their education, their qualifications. Cultural capital in objects largely originates from Bourdieu's belief that seeing even a small sample of someone's possessions can tell a sociologist a significant amount about the person (Grenfell 2014).

Qualifications are perhaps the simplest example. If you walk into a stranger's office or house and see a diploma it provides clear indications of the person. The disciplinary area shows their interests or trade (for example, accountancy, dentistry, teaching, medicine). A diploma in medicine or doctoral qualification suggests they are academically high achieving. The prestige of the university likely gives some indication of their family's habitus and cultural trajectory, or gives extra indication of the person's intelligence and capability as they may have attended via scholarships or bursaries. The location of the institution could also be telling, if it is located internationally, the person may be from that location, or, their family possessed the economic capital (or the individual gained scholarships) to study at an international institution.

Bourdieu suggested that books provided similar information, but in the twenty-first century, this must also include the types of music and podcasts people listen to and what they watch on streaming services. If someone has books and listens to podcasts about history, they might be educated at the university level or raised in a knowledge-class household. If someone's interest seems to be in equal rights activism, that gives an indication of their political views. Do they watch sport? Is that sport sailing or polo, or is it soccer or NFL; these even on their own can be indicative of someone's level of capital. The music someone listens to has the same impact. Music can give indications of age, where someone was born, and what their interests might be; at the extreme, a music collection of rock music likely aids in building a different picture than someone who enjoys classical music.

The furniture someone owns provides similar information. Is their furniture the epitome of Danish design, is it purchased from a chain store? Is it antique, and if so, is it purchased from an antique store or is it inherited? Is it handmade, and if it is, did the owner make it or purchase it? These are all questions and scenarios that give insights into people (Thomson 2017). It is partly about money, but the point remains, that we are rarely confronted with situations where we know nothing about the person we are approaching, so in this instance cultural capital is exhibited by exploring aspects behind someone's economic capital.

Social capital is the third type of capital and is about someone's network, who they know that has capital in a field, or with who the field values. Social capital has been discussed regularly in this book because in academia, though it is essentially the same in any business/work environment, social capital can aid in success. Even at social capital's most basic form, the networks one can exhibit are indicative of someone's potential skill and success. These scenarios are clear in academia. A doctoral student or early career researcher being mentored by a renowned senior academic provides the student or early career researcher with social capital; their relationship with the senior academic raises their position in the field. However, this change happens not because of a relationship, but because the relationship indicates that the senior academic believes their mentee's potential is such that they are worth the senior academic's time. Further social capital can be gained if the starting points of the doctoral student or early career researcher to the senior academic are further apart and not clear. If the student or early career researcher was the senior academic's masters or doctoral student, or was at the same university, or had some clear connection, this relationship would have ample social capital. Though, if the senior academic, for example, essentially 'selected' the student or early career researcher after reading one of their papers or seeing them present their work at a conference, this relationship which was based on no clear connection, would hold more social capital if this information was known. What the above example makes clear, is that perceptions matter. It is not just about who someone knows that builds social capital, but also why.

This may seem like a trivial difference, but in academia, mentorship, patronage, and networks are powerful forces. As will be discussed in the second section of this book, networks can directly result in hiring and job promotions. However, they can also indirectly contribute to these by enabling opportunities that are valued in job applications and promotion documents such as special invitations for books, journals, keynote addresses, and panel discussions (Heffernan 2020a, b). It is also the case that network research finds similar circumstances to be true in business, law, and most professions, so it should not be a surprise that social capital and networks are pivotal in academia. Bourdieu's issue in academia is that he argues that the *doxa* (the naturally linked belief) of education and higher education is that it is a meritocracy; thus, the most deserving applicant with the highest merit gets the job or wins the prize (Bourdieu 1977, 1988). Despite this widespread belief by many regarding education, Bourdieu argues that social capital and networks combine in academia to skew the concept of merit just as much as it does in many other professions. Potentially, however, this occurrence is more dangerous in academia because it appears, particularly from the outside, like this is not the case and that merit and hard work remain the primary factors in attaining success.

Capital Attracts Capital

An element of Bourdieu's social theories that have been evident throughout this book is that the more any element of habitus or capital someone or a group of people have, the more likely they are to gain even more. In the wider world this is really about Percy Shelley's notion of the rich get richer, and the poor get poorer. Generations of middle-class families have the disposable income available to one generation after another afford better schooling, live in more prestigious areas, attend more renowned universities, and essentially 'buy' their way into a better life. For generations of working-class families, however, there may not be enough money for the necessities let alone extra finances to improve social aspects. Not to mention the issues associated with altering cultural trajectory and a potential desire to not aim for altering their life course to the middle-class or upper-middle class expectations.

In academia, however, it is more a case of the rich get richer and the poor stay the same. Capital does attract capital and one form of capital is often convertible into another. Publications can result in being invited to contribute articles for special issues of journals or chapters in edited books, and thus, further publications. Publications can result in being invited to give keynote addresses, and a mix of the above can result in successful grant applications and likely successful promotion applications or job applications at more prestigious universities. It could be said that in academia there is somewhat of a snowball effect when it comes to success, but social capital and networks can play a role in getting the snowball started and/or increasing its momentum. For the academics who never get to stand out from the crowd, or never get the chance to, there is no real punishment. They will still rise through the academic ranks and can gain employment at more prestigious universities. That capital attracts capital, is ultimately what can result in two people from the same starting point to end on different trajectories. In academia, assuming satisfactory work is being completed, both people will build a research profile and career. Though, regardless of what happens, the party with more capital will likely have a faster and higher ascent as they build a more widely known research profile.

Bourdieu also notes that there is some reasoning, potentially even advantage, to only some people using capital to build even more. Bourdieu (1977) suggests that the more agents in a field that possess a certain capital, the less value that capital eventually holds. In education, this can be seen in the example of teachers and principals possessing master's degrees and doctorates. Even only two or three decades ago, this occurrence was quite rare, and these were qualifications that could be leveraged in job applications, or in some cases, they could not be leveraged because they were so rare that they held no capital. However, for the most part, the rarity of this capital thus made it more desirable to hold these degrees and inspired more teachers to acquire them. As a result, doctorates and master's degrees have become almost commonplace in schools. The increase in the amount of this form of capital means that in some fields (such as the independent school sector), a doctorate is increasingly becoming a standard qualification of those hoping to gain a leadership position. Thus, the capital of a doctoral degree (which is a significant personal and professional undertaking) in a school was once rare and valuable, but its value has led to this enormous amount of work now becoming almost commonplace in some school systems as others have attempted to gain the same capital, which eventually begins to devalue the capital's worth.

Reproduction

An aspect of social capital, and the idea that capital attracts capital, is the suggestion that those at the top of the field, may identify those lower in the field, and aid in them climbing the hierarchical ladder. Bourdieu (2000) discusses this notion as being part of *reproduction* and argues that the process does not begin the those at the top looking down the field's hierarchy for potential proteges, but with agents lower in the field setting themselves apart. Bourdieu's point is that though the combination of different types of capital may be difficult, or virtually impossible, to quantify, capital is nonetheless not invisible, it does not occur in secret, and agents are not unaware of its existence. Agents know if they have capital, and they know if they have more than those in a similar position, and they will leverage this attribute (Bourdieu 2000). In academia, this theory in action is clear. For example, early career researchers know if they have increased capital (in terms of academic ability and network connections). This will lead them to push harder for opportunities, gamble more on the likelihood of their success, and situate themselves in areas that match their potential ability rather than current achievements. What is important to note is that none of this situation has to do with 'luck' or 'having an easier path'. That is something that capital can assist with, but when it comes to reproduction, however, reproduction is about people knowing they will be, or will likely be, recognised for their efforts and so put in extra effort in the hope that their investment pays dividends.

Bourdieu (2000) and other higher education researchers (Atkinson 2012; Heffernan 2020a; Mills 2008) have found and argue that these actions are usually only carried out by people aware of their capital. Subsequently, their actions are noticed, encouraged, and aided by those academics higher in the field and thus the 'reproduction' occurs as higher members in the field help those they believe can climb the field's ladder. As with most aspects of capital in education, Bourdieu notes that reproduction is not about merit, but is about holders of significant capital assisting those who already possess some capital to gain even more (Webb et al. 2002). Capital can be acquired via merit-based activities, but it can also be sourced through networks and network activities. An important point to reiterate about capital, networks, and reproduction, however, is that it is not purely based on merit. It is possible that someone with fewer skills can market themselves better, and someone with ample skills may be able to gamble on themself in a way that overshadows similarly skilled rivals within the field. However, that is not to suggest that an agent with no skills or potential will reach the top of the field due to their social capital. The systems may not be entirely merit-based, but skills are still necessary.

There are of course noted downsides to social capital resulting in promotion and advancement within the field. Business and management literature make it clear that risks to the integrity of the business (or the field) can occur because of hires made this way. In academia, Hadani et al. (2012) suggest that merit-based hires are more likely to achieve a higher-quality and larger number of publications, are more likely to have grant success, and will more quickly rise through the ranks. This is a valid finding as social capital and networking is about increasing the group's capital even if different people in the group are positioned at varying levels of the field's hierarchy.

Bourdieu would suggest that the scenario of someone being elevated in the field due to their social capital not meeting expectations is possible, but argues it is unlikely for at least three reasons. The first is that reproduction begins because the chosen individual has a higher level of capital compared to their similarly positioned counterparts in terms of career stage. Thus, capital can accrue via various methods, but some baseline of skills and ability is a necessity because these are what the network values and will aid in developing (Bourdieu 2000). Secondly, the collective actions of the network are based on increasing the network's capital, therefore, aiding in the elevation of a network member occurs because this action is deemed beneficial to the group (Bourdieu 1989). Finally, just as the network used their influence to see the member increase their position in the field, the ascending agent will likely not fail because the network will not allow that to happen. The new member will still benefit from all the advantages academic networks can bring to its members and this will likely see their career progress at a rapid rate (Bourdieu 2005).

A key consideration of this discussion must also centre around who is likely to benefit most from reproduction. In the above examples, reproduction was framed as success building on success so a starting point of publications and profile is what leads the new academic to be promoted via the more senior member. Thus, this leads to the question of what factors lead to a beginning academics relative quick success that will be noticed by more senior members of the academy? Far and away, the likely answer to this question is that they entered the academy with the correct habitus and capital to succeed almost instantly. This, of course, means those most likely to benefit from reproduction are those who fit the mould of higher education. For women (depending on faculty), or those from other genders, racial backgrounds that are not the majority in their institutions, or who have a disability (among many other possible factors and combinations), they are less likely to benefit from phenomena such as reproduction. This is because, to return to the earlier idea of having to 'bridge the gap' presented by being part of a marginalised group, it is likely that by the time the bridge has been crossed (assuming it ever can be), those who fit the university's mould have already been noticed and brought under the senior academic's wing. Thus, this is the group to further benefit from the career advantages of reproduction while those from marginalised groups are largely left to continue career building on their own and without the assistance of senior members.

Bourdieu's point is that by and large, agents are conscious of the capital they hold within a field; that is to say, that most agents are conscious of their limitations, though some will always overestimate or underestimate their capital. In academia, the capital that counts in most fields includes publication record, grants received, keynote invitations, awards, social capital, and institutional capital. Bourdieu (2000) suggests these forms of capital are usually clear and place a relatively well-defined estimate of where agents will begin in a field, but also how their trajectory within the field may be shaped. As we discussed above, for those with high capital and networks, they are likely to gamble on themselves and this method is likely to pay off assuming their capital matches their expectations. Bourdieu also points out that those with the least amount of capital will be aware of this circumstance (whether it be quantifiable in terms of publications or grant money, or options of social networks), and adjust their expectations accordingly. The result of this situation is that those with the least amount of capital tend to be less likely to gamble on themselves, and essentially accept their situation. That is not to suggest they enjoy their situation, it is that they accept that without capital, their position within the field is limited in how it will change. More broadly, Bourdieu (2000) summarises this by suggesting that people are realistic, and that their expectation of success is based on the probability of achievement, that is, people are more accepting of unlikely occurrences not taking place. This suggestion, however, must be viewed in context.

Increasing Status in a Field

In academia, it means people with high teaching loads know they are unlikely to produce significant publications which may result in not gaining grants or attaining a position at a prestigious university. Thus, their situation may not match their dream when they began their career of becoming a globally recognised professor with a palatial office in a centuries old building at a famous university, but they still have a career in academia. In society, Bourdieu's notion of people accepting their position based on the capital they have available is linked to why dominated classes and oppressed communities historically fail to rise and combat their oppressors. Even when the dominated classes possess the numbers and the power to defeat the ruling minority, Bourdieu argues it is almost a fatalistic flaw that the oppressed often accept their position and this is a trait exploited by the powerful. It is necessary to highlight these differences because what capital looks like in different scenarios predictably has significant variations in how they impact on people's lives and occupations. This book is about universities, which means even when it is discussing the negative or difficult aspects of university life for staff and students, it is nonetheless assessing situations within a privileged field. It should thus be reiterated here that Bourdieu's theories of habitus, field, and capital can aid in dissecting any social field or community. These results can sometimes be about how those within privileged fields operate, and at other times, these theories can help explain centuries of oppression and degradation, and lasting impacts that are still felt today.

As much as the field is set, fields also overlap and have shifting borders, and capital in one field can influence someone's capital in another. This is evident in higher education by ways academics can add to their profile in other areas which may subsequently influence their position within the academic field. This can include media engagements, working with policymakers, and working with industry partners. In each case, the reason these activities can provide some capital in the academic field is that they represent elements of what the field values. Media engagements help build an academic's profile, working with policymakers provides an avenue to turn research into policy decisions, and thus allows research to be practical rather than theoretical in its findings and recommendations. Working with industry partners can have the same impact as policymakers as it helps enact research, though, industry partners can often also have the prospect of potential funding to conduct research to aid the industry in moving forward. The connection in these examples is that each instance contributes to the academic field, and depending on the situation, to an increasing degree. Media engagement is publicity, publicity is marketing and draws attention not only to the academic, but also their faculty and university. Working with policymakers and industry partners both have the advantage of turning research into impact, practice, and action with potential funding benefits.

That activities in neighbouring fields can benefit the primary field was not lost on Bourdieu, and these actions are what he had in mind when he was referring to fields changing to accommodate new forms of capitals. It could be argued quite easily that universities in the twenty-first century are more concerned with academic profile and partnership than ever before. Marketing now plays a strong role in institutional development and as universities vie for students, and with government funding appearing to be ever decreasing in most countries, the need to source external funding grows. Thus, despite the primary capitals the field of academia values (publications, grants, awards etc.), success in neighbouring fields can have the benefit of seeing someone's position elevate in the academic field. Furthermore, considering what we know about fields and capital, the fact that people are successfully moving positions in the academic field because of new forms of capital, changes the academic field as it begins to place more value on the new capitals being introduced.

Bourdieu, however, was always realistic about what this meant in practice. Capital formed from other fields can count, they can even change the shape of the field within which someone is trying to improve their position, but that field will still be bound by the habitus and capital that the field deems most important. Bourdieu (2000) examined this concept through migrant families, or families from some poorer countries, pooling resources together to see one child educated at a school that is intentionally above the usual cultural trajectory of the family. This is done in the hope that the child would gain entry to a higher social class so that they could essentially 'bring' other family members with them.

Bourdieu (2000) sees this as using the collective economic capital of multiple family members to gamble on turning that economic capital into cultural capital (education), and hopefully then into increased economic capital so the pattern can repeat. Bourdieu uses the term gambling because this process can come to fruition. People from migrant families or poorer communities have seen this happen successfully and is why it is a method employed to raise finances and social status. It is, nonetheless, a gamble because people are more likely to ignore when they have witnessed this process fail, they rely on the gamble in the hope that it will work for them. This situation of course places an enormous amount of pressure on the family member selected to receive this education, but using what we know about habitus, capital, and field, Bourdieu also highlights the unlikelihood of the scenario playing out as planned.

These situations fail because the economic capital to enter the field has been gained by methods not usually used; a collection of people rather than the student's immediate family. Thus, the student rarely has the habitus to fit the economic capital they possess which leads Bourdieu to argue that without the necessary habitus, most students will be quickly disqualified from success. They may complete their studies and gain their degree, but without the habitus to build the necessary relationships, the chances of turning educational capital into social capital is minimal. Bourdieu (2000) also argues that whenever it comes to habitus and a compatibility with fields, people know whether they fit in or not even if they do not think about it in terms of habitus and capital. We have regularly used the example of working-class students knowing they may have trouble fitting within elite universitas as they had not had the same experiences or upbringings as the other students which is a social gap only some could cross. Bourdieu says the same situation occurs when migrant families or communities from poorer countries pool their resources to send one child to receive a privileged education. The student know they will likely not fit in, and they know this even before their arrival. They will know that everything they do and say will be slightly different to everyone else, and thus contribute to them expecting and accepting failure.

One could also argue that this is an inherent problem today even as universities see their privilege and encourage diversity and inclusion through scholarships and attempting to make their institutions more inclusive and equitable. These programs 'open the gate' in terms of helping to ensure that people are not excluded because of wealth or being part of a marginalised group. However, these programs cannot account for outside factors such as some students doing well because they are naturally gifted, but money means other students receive high grades because of small class sizes in exclusive private schools, private tutoring, and other resources to ensure their academic progress. Perhaps most importantly though, scholarships and diversity programs allow people to walk into a field, but they do little to make sure people will be socially welcomed, fit in, and have the social capital to 'use' their degree afterwards in the same way as the traditionally privileged students many universities are accustomed to educating. The goal of this activity is to social climb, not just receive a degree, and in many professions, the degree might give someone permission to partake in the occupation, but it is social capital that invites you to 'win' and gains you a position at a (for example) desirable law firm, stockbrokerage, or within another industry.

I have intentionally used the word 'win' here to fit with Bourdieu's broader summary of events. Bourdieu tells us that people 'forget that social games [...] are not fair games' (Bourdieu 2000, p. 214). That is to say, if we refer to Bourdieu's frequent use of the sports field metaphor, someone can have the necessary equipment and knowledge of the rules, but field success is a competition, and someone is still going to lose. Often, it is social capital that bridges the gap between knowing the rules, and victory in the game.

This example demonstrates what is going on both in the scenario of multiple families pooling resources to see one child be educated, and academics using capital gained in fields bordering education to increase their capital in the academic field. The capital being gained can set them apart from others around them and they will have a better standing in their desired field than they did before. However, success in any field is primarily driven by success relating to the capitals the field values most, and if these criteria is not met, in most cases success will be limited. Thus, the academic's work in bordering fields will not have a huge impact on their academic standing, and the child being educated outside of their cultural trajectory will likely not have the same opportunity as their peers being educated in ways that match their natural habitus.

Vying for positions in a field, and more importantly, the fact that people will go to great lengths to increase their position in a field, also has the impact of what Bourdieu calls *illusio* (Bourdieu 1998). The concept is that people are fighting to get ahead in a field (and more so, that they will try to advance themselves in bordering fields for the purpose of getting ahead in the primary field) only builds the field's *illusion* of importance and legitimacy. This has the result of not only helping build the field's place in the wider hierarchy (in academia this might be the broader education community), it also sends the message that this is a field worth competing in, and that what is on offer is worth the effort of sourcing capital from other fields in an attempt to try and get ahead. Illusio, however, also scales up. That people are vying for success, and this demonstrates the field's importance and tells people that this is a field worth fighting within, only encourages more people to participate. This has the chain reaction of raising the amount of capital required to succeed in the field, which only makes the stakes higher, and subsequently encourages more people to seek more methods of gaining capital.

Education is Capital

The final section of this chapter is concerned with the idea that education is capital. Within this chapter we have spoken about what aspects of education build capital, what capital can do in education and in life, and why people might seek out ways to use education to grow their place in the social world and why these methods will have differing degrees of success. This section, however, looks at education *as capital* because education is a powerful tool, and Bourdieu emphasised the importance of what it can represent.

In this instance, Bourdieu is focused on formal schooling and less concerned with the technicality of educational capital; that being that education is only important if it is valued in the field being assessed. Bourdieu knew that learning and skills were passed from one to another for thousands of years and do not require the full school-experience of secondary school and university (such as learning a trade). The idea of education being capital is largely dedicated to formal schooling, and types of formal schooling, because formal education is part of society's institutional barriers and acts as a gatekeeper to other successes.

This is strongly connected to one of Bourdieu's primary arguments surrounding education, that being that meritocracy in education is a myth (Bourdieu 1977). We have already talked about this notion several times, but ultimately it is a pivotal concept to explore because success in education depends on societal capital, and societal capital depends on success in education. This is why children with certain sets of capital are predisposed to succeed at education, others are not, and it makes scholarships and inclusionary programs difficult to be executed successfully. These practices, and the myth of meritocracy, disguise the powers and prejudices that are really at play. As Thomson declared (2017, pp. 18–19), some children are 'positioned to be successful at the game of education right from the moment they walked through the nursery gates'.

These are vital issues to address because for all of education's apparent qualities, there is a very dark and shadowy undercurrent that guides who is allowed in, and with what advantages they will be allowed to leave. Bourdieu spoke of education as being a 'gift exchange' in that it is a system whereby social inequalities can be relabelled as not being very intelligent or failing to try hard enough at school (Bourdieu 1977, p. 95). Conversely, education can also be used as a system to launder (think money laundering) decades or even centuries of a family's generational wealth, privilege, and networks so all that is left is the signs of academic ability, effort, and achievement.

What is at stake is enough to make the efforts worth strategic positioning by people to use education for this very purpose. It lets some groups declare to have a nice house and car (signs of economic capital) due to their academic ability and efforts in their study which resulted in a high-salary occupation. Thus, the economic capital and cultural capital of generational wealth and privilege is refined into a product that appears to be economic capital because of the belief that education is a merit-based system. As might be expected and has already been made clear, the people most able to use different forms of capital for their own shuffling of positions at the higher end of the field, are those who began with the most capital. Bourdieu (1990) points out how important this is to people's capital because power (in society or management) that appears to have been gained because of hard work and intelligence tends to be much better received than power inherited or acquired via family connections. However, their actions also hide one of the worst aspects of education.

In the twenty-first century, it is still the case that most of society sees education as those putting in the most effort being the ones who succeed and are rewarded. The above example shows how those with the most capital exploit the system for their own gain (which in turn publicly reinforces these beliefs). For those in poverty or in labouring/working-class families who want to move to the knowledge/middle-classes, however, the illusion that education is merit-based only acts as a barrier preventing people from aspirations no matter how strong their dedication or ability. As has been made clear and reiterated in this book, education is not solely about effort, ability, or intelligence, it is also very much about having the habitus and cultural capital in place to succeed in the field of education. These characteristics are also not learnt, and cannot be acquired, for the most part they are already set in a child's cultural trajectory before they are even born.

Scenarios that tend to get attention also act to reinforce the belief that educational success is about effort. The notion of 'pulling up your own bootstraps' and the connections to self-reliance, along with many 'rags to riches' stories that often tend to gain a lot of media attention, but these are the lucky few. What makes the situation worse, is that people transcending the classes are less likely to see themselves as 'lucky', and more likely see their success as a result of their hard work. The crucial element here is that they most likely worked extremely hard, their success may have come at the end of decades of toil, but many people work extremely hard at something they are dedicated to and never succeed. Working hard alone is not enough to overcome the societal barriers in place blocking many people from achieving their goals. That Bourdieu was one of the 'lucky' ones who transcended rural farming to academia's elite circles was never lost on him, and was a primary motivator in what guided his research. He suspected, and his research and theories show, how and why a child from a poor agricultural labouring/working-class background who attended prestigious universities because of a system of scholarships overcame a series of hurdles that would prevent a significant majority of the population following a similar path, and yet he was successful, but he was the exception.

Where education and capital are concerned, the most important aspects are to remember that formal education is not just something you do or do not have, and it is about more than it being shrouded in an almost everlasting cloak of merit. Formal education can be entered and attained by ways not always based on merit, and those who succeed will usually enter with additional capital, and people make these efforts because formal education has practical consequences. Knowledge is capital because it greatly assists in buying prestige. Directly, it can aid in status through qualifications, cultural capital through networks, and institutional capital from the prestige of the university. However, it also often results in secure and higher paying employment; and this is the perhaps the capital that transcends most fields and assists in ordering many field hierarchies. We do live in a capitalist society driven by material objects, and most people do adhere to these aspirations.

Summary

The end of this chapter also brings us to the end of this section relating to Bourdieu's concepts of habitus, capital, and field. Bourdieu and other scholars have spent decades and hundreds (probably thousands) of journal articles and books further examining these concepts and applying them to different situations. Being that we know that fields are always changing what they value, having their borders shift, and habitus is part of a cultural trajectory that is always changing and altering the value of someone's capital; these studies have a virtually infinite timeline of relevance.

Bourdieu created a whole host of other theories too, many that we have already touched on, like doxa and illusio, and others that we will discuss in the following section. However, habitus, capital, and field are the primary tools for any discussion of social settings, and we will use Bourdieu's other theories to help explore what is happening inside the primary focuses. Habitus, capital, and field are so important to us moving forward because this book is about exploring Bourdieu's concepts as they relate to higher education, and then dissecting life in the modern university for which Bourdieu provides some of the best tools available. Ultimately, it all comes down to the *practice*, of *[(Habitus)(Capital)] + Field = Practice* because it is the practice that concerns us most.

The following section focuses on why universities operate in the way they do, how they got to this position, why they are practically so different to the theoretical or imagined perception so many people have, and what it really looks like for those operating inside them from vice-chancellors to casual employees.

References

Atkinson W (2012) Reproduction revisited: comprehending complex educational trajectories. Sociol Rev 60(4):735–753. https://doi.org/10.1111/j.1467-954x.2012.02131.x

Bourdieu P (1989) Social space and symbolic power. Sociol Theory 7(1):14–25. https://doi.org/10.2307/202060

Bourdieu P (1990) In other words: essays towards a reflexive sociology. Stanford University Press, Stanford

Bourdieu P (2000) Pascalian meditations. Stanford University Press

Bourdieu P (1977) Outline of a theory of practice (trans: Nice R). Cambridge University Press, Cambridge

Bourdieu P (1988) Homo Academicus (trans: Collier P). Polity

Bourdieu P (1998) Practical reason (trans: Johnson R). Polity, Cambridge

Bourdieu P (2005) The social structures of the economy (trans: Turner C). Polity, Cambridge

Bourdieu P (2006) The forms of capital. In: Lauder H, Brown P, Dillabough J, Halsey A (eds) Education, globalisation and social change. Oxford University Press, pp 105–118

Grenfell M (2014) Pierre Bourdieu: key concepts. Routledge, Abingdon

Hadani M, Coombes S, Das D, Jalajasi D (2012) Finding a good job: academic network centrality and early occupational outcomes in management academia. J Organ Behav 33:723–739. https://doi.org/10.1002/job.788

Heffernan T (2020) Understanding university leadership and the increase in workplace hostility through a Bourdieusian lens. High Educ Q. https://doi.org/10.1111/hequ.12272

Heffernan T (2020) There's no career in academia without networks': academic networks and career trajectory. High Educ Res Dev. https://doi.org/10.1080/07294360.2020.1799948

Mills C (2008) Reproduction and transformation of inequalities in schooling: the transformative potential of the theoretical constructs of Bourdieu. Br J Sociol Educ 29(1):79–89. https://doi.org/10.1080/01425690701737481

Thomson P (2017) Educational leadership and Pierre Bourdieu. Routledge, Abingdon

Webb J, Schirato T, Danaher G (2002) Understanding Bourdieu. Sage, London

Part II
Life in the Modern University

Chapter 6
The End of the Ivory Tower

Abstract This chapter offers a brief history of what universities were once like and how they might be perceived by the public today to assist in determining how strong the contrast is between memories and the fiction of the entertainment industry. This is not simply for the purpose of pointing out the differences, this is because of the damage these memories and perceptions have caused, and continue to cause, as the global higher education sector faces funding cuts and less-favourable changes to funding models. The chapter outlines how the reality of what happens in a university today rarely reflects people's perceptions, even if the buildings and titles remain the same. This discussion thus outlines why political and funding pressures have changed the characteristics of the sector as a precursor to the following chapters which discuss the institution from the field of senior executives, middle leaders, and academics.

This book is concerned with life in the university today and what it looks like as we approach the mid-twenty-first century. In the Western world, there have only been a few small changes to what has happened in and around universities since their inception, but these changes have completely altered how universities operate. These changes are important because they have predictably impacted on the objectives of those who lead them, work in them, and the students who attend them. However, to see these changes we must scratch below the surface because on the face of it, things may not appear to have changed that much. As the rest of this book investigates, universities are in the same buildings (sometimes centuries old) that they have always been in, but what goes on inside is very different.

There has long been a general understanding through popular culture and public discourse about what a vice-chancellor or university president does, what a faculty dean's role is, and what the tasks of an academic are, but today, those ideas are usually not quite right (or sometimes very wrong). The titles like dean and academic remain the same, but the roles are very different. Perhaps most confusing is that peoples' understanding of universities often comes from the media or popular culture (television, movies, and books). This is understandable being that while anywhere from 30 to 40% of children in school today will attend university in countries like Australia, Canada, New Zealand and England, only a few decades ago that figure was closer to 10% (Forsyth 2014). Thus, of older generations, only a fraction attended university. Furthermore, that 10% was not representative of a diverse community—it was primarily made up of white, middle/upper-middle class students of professionals replicating what the generation before them had done (Forsyth 2014). Thus, though university attendance increases on a sliding scale as the population gets younger, a majority of the older and retired populations did not attend university and did not have the option of attending university. Those who did, tend to be in closed-off social fields where many people in their social circles attended. Subsequently, those who did not attend university are left with very few opportunities to know what really goes on behind the sometimes-imposing gates.

This chapter offers a brief history of what universities were once like, and how they might be perceived by the public, to assist in determining just how strong the contrast is between glorified memories and the fiction of the entertainment industry. This is not simply for the purpose of pointing out the differences, this is because of the damage these memories and perceptions have caused, and continue to cause, as the global higher education sector continues to face funding cuts and less-favourable changes to funding models. The reality of what happens in a university today rarely reflects people's perceptions, even if the buildings and titles remain the same (Annansingh et al. 2018; Sin et al. 2019; Teichler et al. 2013).

The Doxa of the Ivory Tower

We have already spoken about doxa within this book, but the doxa of higher education and the concept of the 'ivory tower' is a topic that allows for a more detailed examination of the Bourdieusian concept. It also helps dissect why long-standing notions that rarely match reality can cause significant issues. The doxa of higher education is that universities are closed off arenas, isolated areas of learning and study separated from society and government, and only accessible by a select few. Add to this, for many people who have not attended or been employed by a university, their understanding of what a university does is driven by the media and popular culture, and in the twenty-first century, the media often mimics political stances (which tend to promote the obscurity of higher education to justify funding changes). At the same time, popular culture generally seems to go on reinforcing early-twentieth century stereotypes of academics strolling across the green grass of quadrangles in centuries old buildings, or highly intelligent people in science labs (Clark, 2008; Peacock et al., 2018). These portrayals matter because, to begin with, they are rarely true. These depictions may cause apprehension in students to attend university for fear their habitus does not fit the falsely advertised depiction, and also because these suggestions form a doxa of higher education that masks what universities are trying to achieve in the twenty-first century.

One of the key points about doxas, and particularly as they relate to higher education, is that the doxa has some basis in reality. Even brief examinations of the history of the university make it clear why the notion of the ivory tower exists. The primary reason is that historically universities were extremely closed off communities of scholars who for centuries were also governed by scholars, and all parties were dedicated to the creation, preservation, and dissemination of knowledge (Fitzgerald 2014; Forsyth 2014). The internally governed community of scholars was very much a purposeful design element. This system was intended to separate the university from external influences as much as possible, such as business and government, for fear that these could interfere with the creation and dissemination of knowledge. However, it was also this separation that aided in the doxa of the ivory tower. The community of scholars was seen as an impenetrable community who were free from the pressures to which most other members of society were subjected. On top of this, it has been noted that from the eighteenth to perhaps mid-to-late twentieth century (eighteenth century is of course limited more to Great Britain, Europe, and America), academics received remuneration that was on average three times higher than the national average (Morris 2002). Thus, academia allowed people to focus intently on their area of interest and they were well paid which allowed for the eccentricities of academia to grow. This is an element that was commonly noted in the literature, continues to be perpetuated today in much of popular culture, but only serves to further separate the university and academics from the rest of society (Morris 2002; Peacock et al. 2018).

The idea of universities being small, elite institutions full of well-paid eccentric academics also meant that this was a place only available to white, upper-middle class, and aristocratic students and academics. In some instances, women were admitted (in some cases) centuries ago, but their introduction in no way equated to equality, and was the exception rather than the rule. In most cases, regardless of university entrance and success being a question of gender, ethnicity, or wealth, students and academics were filtered out through habitus and capital alone. Thus, even if institutions were elite as a result of exclusionary practices made to look like merit-based decisions, they were nonetheless elite.

Even during the 1960s to the early-1990s as the reality of the elite university and eccentric academic was lost in all but the world's most prestigious universities, the idea of the ivory tower altered, but was not lost. The expansion of the mass-market education system meant the number of universities across the globe expanded quickly (Esson and Ertl 2016), as did the number and demographics of people attending, but this did not dilute the doxa. Instead, the idea of the eccentric academic was replaced by the idea of someone detached from the realities of the world around them; and particularly the realities workers in other industries face (Forsyth 2014).

The expansion of the mass-market higher education system had two impacts for those working in universities that reshaped the doxa but remains troublesome today. The mass-market higher education system started quickly. There was an expansion of the university system across the globe after the Second World War, but it was as the baby-boomer generation reached university-age that higher education expanded at an incredible pace. This period saw Australia grow from less than ten universities to more than thirty, the likes of Oxford, Cambridge, and the Red Brick universities in England were joined by the extensive network of more than one hundred universities they have today, and in the United States, the full system of state universities and community colleges took shape.

This increase of institutions at an incredibly fast pace meant academia as an occupation also grew in employment opportunities. Many universities were technically understaffed as the elite system of education meant there were not enough academics to fill the new offices and meet the increasing student demand. For those in academia, supply and demand meant very favourable circumstances. Doctorates were attained, academic positions were usually gained without trouble, and once in employment, promotion through the academic ranks was rapid. Being understaffed meant the expansion of higher education effectively instigated a conveyor-belt from the bottom to the top of the academic hierarchy because when there was not enough staff, the cycle of new staff entering universities and the faculties only pushed the existing academics higher up the hierarchy (Forsyth 2014).

This was also a period where most countries invested heavily in higher education to aid in economic growth, and essentially educate many countries out of recession. This scenario may seem foreign to many in the twenty-first century, but it was worth noting that in the 1960s to late-1980s, the Cold War was taking place which made scientific research a must for many countries. At the same time, medical advancements were leaping forward, and it was a period where many occupations became professionalised (such as teaching, engineering, accountancy). As this was also a period where working-class/labour-class jobs also attracted low salaries, universities were seen as a way of educating people into middle-class salaries and middle-class spending to fuel economic growth (Forsyth 2014).

Combined, these scenarios painted a picture of academia that was foreign to most. Academics were paid well, were promoted quickly due to a lack of academics (which would have been invisible to most outside of academia, but the financial repercussions of academia as a career and fast promotion would not). During times of economic trouble and recession, universities often enjoyed safe or increased funding to aid in economic growth which meant academics were safe from layoffs when most other occupations could and did fall victim to economic downturn.

The fact that the mass-market system of higher education that led to these benefits continues today, and feasibly appears the same from outside of the academy, answers many questions about why the doxa of universities often continues to be one of the ivory tower. For higher education though, the repercussions are real. Budgets are continuously cut in most countries and time and time again the politicians carrying out these acts rely and promote the notion of university extravagance and excess, and not being part of the reality of the wider community as reasons to make these cuts. As this book makes clear, the perception is far from reality for those working inside universities. Universities have responded to budget cuts by casualising their workforces and relying on contract labour. This has made securing a permanent position a hard-fought task, promotions are less readily given to those whose work deserves them, academics are forced to fight and argue for every career gain whether they deserve them or not. The corporatisation of universities also means that across most countries the sector has perfected models of restructuring and changing direction which has severely limited the power of unions and the legal protections workers possess. No longer is a permanent job in academia a permanent job, anyone can be removed with relatively little trouble (Matthies and Torka 2019). These changes not only curtail the long held academic attributes of free-speech and arguing for what is morally and socially right, it is also a system that scares academics into working harder and asking for less. Yet for all these issues, the doxa of the university reflects situations far from this reality.

The need to change the doxa of the university is at least two-fold. The first relates to how universities are thought of and spoken about in the wider public domain. The idea that often exists in the media is the glorified image of learning in a world detached from the rest of society. This is an image that perhaps understandably does not sit well with much of society during times of good economic fortune, but it causes a distinct point of contention when times are bad (Fitzgerald 2014). This book is being written in a period where COVID-19 exists, and the downturn in economy that the virus initially caused was met in most countries across the globe with university budget cuts (that only continued a trend of budget cuts over the last few decades). As funding has been reduced or models changed in many Westernised countries, time and time again, the political justification has been clear. Politicians have framed universities as almost being luxury items that are detached from society and society's needs, thus, they should fund themselves if they wish to continue. The image politicians portray exploits the doxa of higher education, and because of this, it has rarely been criticised by the media or the general public. Better understandings of exactly what life in a university is like in modern times may not result in increased funding, but informing people of the reality of academic life rather than the fictional portrayal may at least allow universities to benefit from a more informed audience.

The second reason reframing the doxa of higher education is critical is because new generations of students and academics are entering the field to study and to work, and their views are sometimes shaped by the same ideals as those discussed above. For students, it is important to note how quickly universities have changed. Not just in terms of the doxa of television and the media, but even the experience of others within the last decade. As will be discussed in forthcoming chapters, universities are being forced to run as businesses now. In some respects, this is good for students because students are viewed as customers and just like any entity trying to sell a product, a lot of time and effort goes into making sure the customers' needs and expectations are being met. However, for the university trying to attract and maintain customers, students are viewed not just as customers, but also as a commodity, and just like in mining or agriculture, universities now balance producing adequately satisfied students with the least expenditure possible; a scenario that has altered the learning experience significantly from how it was five years ago, let alone ten or more years ago (Latif et al. 2021).

For new academics the situation is much the same. Being a student, and being a doctoral student, can give many insights into life working in the university. However, the reality is, until a new academic is confronted with the demands of publication requirements, grant expectations, and teaching loads (among many other issues), the gaps in their knowledge are likely filled with generally positive understandings. Additionally, it may seem obvious to say, but academia is a profession. A doctorate and an academic position gives someone the opportunity to work as an academic, but it does not mean they will be successful at it. For example, you can have a law degree and be admitted into the bar association, but not win cases in court. You can have a business degree and get a position in a stockbrokerage or hedge fund, but not be good at predicting financial trends. Thus, it should not come as a surprise that you can gain a doctorate and a full-time job in a university, but not be 'good' at producing the capital the university often values most; research and funding.

The point could also be made that in law and business, the trope of the less successful lawyer or businessperson is equally as common as portrayals of highly successful people. In academia, this is perhaps less the case. Many portrayals of academics exist and often they might be tired, stressed, or overworked, yet, the fact they are in a university in many ways is connected to success. Ultimately, the point is that though everyone enters a profession assuming or hoping they will be successful at it, in academia the expectation for success usually seems extra high and the realisation that failure may be possible is low. This is perhaps tied to the fact that academia is an academic pursuit and those who gain doctorates have often always been towards the top of their classes. Yet, the notion of the failing, struggling, or unsuccessful academic is one that seems rarely talked about publicly or in popular culture, and yet it is a reality within the field that is sometimes only evident after someone enters the academy.

Incremental Shifts Are Lost in Translation

Universities at one time may have been a community of scholars, governed by scholars, and who were intentionally separated from the influences of businesses, governments, and communities; but this needs to be put into perspective. This structure was maintained in most countries until after World War Two. However, though universities may have changed greatly in the last few decades, it is worth noting that the original idea of scholars being intentionally separated from much of society was one that existed for almost 2500 years. Socrates and Plato both suggested that a life dedicated to the mind was one that could not fit within the life of a citizen required to complete other duties (Bloom 2012).

This is important to consider because even though universities as we know them today only began around 1000 years ago, for 950 of those years they operated in relatively the same way when it comes to their position in the community; and that method was often closer to what was happening in the classical period than what happens today. A significant difference is that for thousands of years academic study has been about mastering a topic, thus, the *master's degree.* The idea of ancient thinkers, to scholars in heavy robes reading books, to small groups of scholars discussing issues in the early twentieth century, were all aimed at mastering a topic. A master's degree was for those who had literally mastered a topic, and those with a doctorate was for those who have contributed knew knowledge. Thus, while the sciences have always had strong connections to the doctorate, the humanities (in particular) and some other areas of the social sciences were about grappling with every facet of a topic that could not (as they can today) be studied via the internet, or quickly checked via libraries with thousands of sources available online (Forsyth 2014). For those in the humanities, it was up until perhaps the end of the twentieth century or start of the twenty-first that the last of the retiring professors who rose through the ranks before the doctorate became a necessity retired from the field. Thus, the sweeping changes that have occurred in higher education have happened in only a small number of decades and are not always noticed or appreciated. The idea that not all that long ago an academic's job was to master a topic, and only contribute to knowledge when they felt they had something to offer, is virtually unfathomable in the twenty-first century where it is not unusual that students applying to doctoral programs have already written several journal articles or been part of research projects in some disciplinary fields creating new knowledge.

There is ample research about why these changes have happened that goes significantly beyond the above overview and topics discussed in this book, and some of the general suggestions are worth noting.

A primary reason for the many changes within the sector often going unnoticed is that these shifts have been incremental and occurred over several decades. In that time, some aspects, roles, and policies have also been pulled in different direction to morph into where they are now. Most changes also have repercussions, and it has been suggested that often the primary (or a primary) change might be noted, but the full repercussions across the sector, university, or role are not (Esteban 2016). These incremental shifts also have practical implications in what Bourdieu would say leads to *misrecognising* what life in the university involves (Webb et al. 2002). As an example of this, Chantler (2016) looks towards the suggestion of the ivory tower as a repercussion of the liberal university. For all the centuries of universities setting themselves apart from business and government, since perhaps the 1960s the idea of universities being anti-war, anti-capitalism, anti-establishment, and having progressive views towards most societal issues has led to the notion of universities being hotbeds of liberal thought, and thus, the 'liberal university' (Chantler 2016). However, even though the perception of the liberal university remains, the sector itself has changed to meet the global pressures of higher education; which in most cases means conforming to neoliberal and performative ideologies. Thus, many people still think of the university as the liberal university, when in practice few liberal avenues remain, and those that do, remain while universities conform to the business and capitalist pressures that most industries experience (Bourdieu 1977, 1988).

Researchers examining what goes on within universities have also found similar results. As far as administrative, research, and teaching roles are concerned, the primary issue is that the titles remain the same, even if the roles are significantly different; and the perception of what a role or job entails often remains the same. Halilem et al. (2011) conducted a study examining academic behaviours within faculties and found that an additional avenue of why the doxa of the ivory tower persists is that many academics still portray the image of a researcher purely dedicated to the pursuit of knowledge and creating and disseminating research through their teaching and publications. In this sense, their outward (and Halilem et al. 2011 suggest unintentional) portrayal mimics that of an academic conducting their work fifty, one hundred, even centuries ago. The issue with this portrayal is that it fails to acknowledge that the motivations and work happening behind the academic's outward facing appearance of creating and sharing knowledge is entirely different. There is also the fact that we should not wonder why this is the case, it is perhaps not surprising that people would not actively look behind the façade of any career. Thus, if steps are not taken to demonstrate how different a centuries old role is in the twenty-first century, there is no need for wider understandings in society to change. As we have discussed several times already in this book, the researchers make the point that the work appears the same, but it is now motivated by the need to meet research performance targets, funding expectations, and teaching metrics to improve the marketability of the institution, and government and industry funding opportunities (Halilem et al. 2011).

That universities in recent decades have had to adopt business-like practices that largely shatter the notion of the ivory tower is a topic of regular discussion within higher education research (Hickey 2015; Tuchman 2009. This information is, however, data that rarely makes it beyond a quite limited field but is the information that needs to be better known to inform audiences about how universities operate in society. The shift to mass-market higher education was pivotal to these changes. This was the shift that took universities from being a highly sought-after luxury item where supply could not meet demand, to a situation where students are a commodity, institutions must compete for enrolments, and academic talents that will result in research funding and grants (Esson and Ertl 2016). It is also important to note that in most countries, universities are not competing for a large or bountiful supply of students or funding. In most Westernised countries, even if student numbers are growing, funding per student is decreasing (Heffernan 2017). Funding models, research funds, and potential grants have also been shrinking for decades which in most cases has given rise to universities needing to aim themselves at being competitive in the market which rarely lends itself to following scholarly pursuits. Instead, they are now working to meet consumer demands and influences, designing market strategies, maintaining positions in the media, and working towards improving their positions in global university ranking tables (Heffernan and Heffernan 2018). As Pusser and Marginson (2013) argued, ranking and marketing does make a difference, and does influence student applications, academic migration, and government funding.

There has also been little debate that these changes have caused immense alterations within universities from the top-down. This means roles from vice-chancellors and university presidents to newly appointed academics, and even casual employees, are being employed on new criteria and expected to carry out actions that align with the new pressures universities face (Blackmore 2002; Pilbeam and Jamieson 2010). For university leaders, this means the shift of their employment and success is not always about their research profile and research success, or their ability to fit within a community of scholars. Instead, many researchers suggest university leaders are now being employed, promoted, and retained on the premise of their managerial experience and successes (Bosetti and Walker 2009; Gamage and Mininberg 2003; Heffernan 2020). Considering the tone of this book and the other factors that have been discussed up until this point, it may seem unsurprising that business acumen is playing a larger, and sometimes more dominant role than research or teaching ability and experience (Heffernan and Bosetti 2020a, b, 2021). However, it is the ripple effect that this requirement has on leaders that also changes the shape of universities, what they see as success, and how they are attempting to get there. Sutton (2015) highlights that it is hard, perhaps virtually impossible, for leaders to work successfully in performance driven environments and maintain the same interests and focus they once had in directing the future of their university, faculty, or school's research and teaching. When the wider changes in higher education across the globe over the last few decades has seen the shift towards the importance of funding, student enrolments and grant opportunities increase, it is difficult to follow a path towards these goals while remaining committed to the ideological practices of research and teaching objectives.

Researchers have also noted that academics are not just part of this changing process, it also alters their own actions and what guides their decisions (Ball 2012; Gibbs 2016). Academics may be more focused on research and teaching goals than university leaders, but the way their goals are achieved is also skewed towards the managerialist and corporate consequences of the systems and policies driving modern universities. In most instances this is reactive to the fact that academics are now frequently being measured on ever-increasing quantifiable targets (Ball 2012; Gibbs 2016). Of course, academics were always evaluated for the amount and quality of their work, but in recent years, this has changed as the amount and quality of work is now also about the criterion of producing certain types of work that will be recognised by certain ranking and funding agencies. This means many academics have had to change their research direction, or at least be aware of the direction they need to aim their research, to ensure that they are pursuing research directions that will result in publications in the journals that count towards university prestige, and research that is likely to be competitive in the ever-shrinking grants and funding processes (van der Vossen 2015). This has clear consequences to pursuing exploratory research or research that may be valuable to a field, but not valuable to grant committees. It also leads to research not being published in the journals or book series that are perhaps most fitting for the work, but instead, research is directed towards the most prestigious journals and book publishers where the work might fit in well enough, even if this results in a smaller audience.

Gibbs (2016) also points out that these pressures are circular. Deans and university leaders are being selected in part on their ability to manage their faculties and departments, and academics may have to alter their research course to make sure they are pursuing profitable (in terms of grants) and prestigious publishing opportunities. However, as part of their management roles, deans are also having to judge and make hiring, promotional, and firing decisions based on how well academics are fitting to these metrics.

Summary

This chapter has highlighted the shift that has occurred in higher education in recent decades and how and why these shifts are not always recognised in society. Centuries of history and portrayals in popular culture are responsible for some of these beliefs, as is the fact that universities were, for a very long time, a rather closed off field. In the twenty-first century universities are more accessible and are trying to be more accessible. Though, this still excludes many groups, and it remains difficult to bridge some of the gaps relating to cultural trajectory and successfully introducing students from different backgrounds.

As has been previously touched on, attending university does not equate to understanding what goes on in a university; just like going to school does not make one familiar with what is required to be a teacher or lead a school. All these different areas nonetheless have contributed to a perception of universities that is not always correct. Governments use these misconceptions to their advantage when they want to defund universities or raise student fees, and some universities (albeit a handful throughout the world) essentially market themselves on being exclusionary and elite which only furthers higher education's seeming disconnect from the wider community. However, this is perhaps the most important point. Universities were seen as exclusionary and isolated places that were not concerned with governments or communities because for centuries that is exactly what they were. Yet as we begin the third decade of the twenty-first century, this could not be further from the truth. Universities are unavoidably tied to government and business for funding and research opportunities, and few decisions are made without community and social good in mind.

These priorities have also changed the landscape of the university internally. The notion of the ivory tower may be all but dead in all but a few cases, and it has been replaced by decades of corporatisation and increasing dedication to producing marketable research and selling knowledge in the form of qualifications. This change should not be viewed as a negative, however, it is much more about a change of progress. The wanderlust of uninhibited research exploration in some fields has been lost, the notion of the mastery of a topic is no longer a singular objective but one that happens as an academic's production of knowledge continues. Yet, the academy has gained so much as it tries to bring in wider groups of students and embed itself more in society to make the efforts that happen behind imposing gates more accessible and visible to the community and wider society.

References

Annansingh F, Howell K, Liu S, Nunes M (2018) Academics' perception of knowledge sharing in higher education. Int J Educ Manag 32(6):1001–1015. https://doi.org/10.1108/ijem-07-2016-0153

Ball S (2012) Performativity, commodification and commitment: an I-spy guide to the Neoliberal University. Br J Educ Stud 60(1):17–28. https://doi.org/10.1080/00071005.2011.650940

References

Blackmore J (2002) Globalisation and the restructuring of higher education for new knowledge economies: new dangers or old habits troubling gender equity work in universities? High Educ Q 56(4):419–441. https://doi.org/10.1111/1468-2273.00228

Bloom A (2012) Closing of the American mind: how higher education has failed democracy and impoverished the souls of today's students. Simon & Schuster

Bosetti L, Walker K (2009) Perspectives of UK vice-chancellors on leading universities in a knowledge-based economy. High Educ Q 64(1):4–21. https://doi.org/10.1111/j.1468-2273.2009.00424.x

Bourdieu P (1977) Outline of a theory of practice (trans: Nice R). Cambridge University Press, Cambridge

Bourdieu P (1988) Homo Academicus (trans: Collier P). Polity.

Chantler A (2016) The ivory tower revisited. Discourse Stud Cult Polit Educ 37(2);215–229. https://doi.org/10.1080/01596306.2014.963517

Clark L (2008) When the university went 'pop': exploring cultural studies, sociology of culture, and the rising interest in the study of popular culture. Sociol Compass 2(1):16–23. https://doi.org/10.1111/j.1751-9020.2007.00058.x

Esson J, Ertl H (2016) No point worrying? Potential undergraduates, study-related debt, and the financial allure of higher education. Stud High Educ 41(7):1265–1280. https://doi.org/10.1080/03075079.2014.968542

Esteban F (2016) Standing at a hinge of history: what today's universities can learn from past philosophies of higher education. Austr Educ Researcher 43(5):629–641. https://doi.org/10.1007/s13384-016-0217-4

Fitzgerald T (2014) Scholarly traditions and the role of the professoriate in uncertain times. J Educ Adm Hist 46(2):207–219. https://doi.org/10.1080/00220620.2014.889092

Forsyth H (2014) A history of the Modern Australian University. NewSouth Publishing, Sydney

Gamage D, Mininberg E (2003) The Australian and American higher education: Key issues of the first decade of the 21st century. High Educ 45(2):183–202. https://doi.org/10.1023/A:1022488220850

Gibbs A (2016) Improving publication: advice for busy higher education academics. Int J Acad Dev 21(3):255–258. https://doi.org/10.1080/1360144x.2015.1128436

Halilem N, Amara N, Landry R (2011) Is the academic Ivory Tower becoming a managed structure? A nested analysis of the variance in activities of researchers from natural sciences and engineering in Canada. Scientometrics 86(2):431–448. https://doi.org/10.1007/s11192-010-0278-5

Heffernan T (2017) A fair slice of the pie? Problematising the dispersal of government funds to Australian universities. J High Educ Policy Manag 39(6):658–673. https://doi.org/10.1080/1360080x.2017.1377965

Heffernan T (2020) Understanding university leadership and the increase in workplace hostility through a Bourdieusian lens. High Educ Q. https://doi.org/10.1111/hequ.12272

Heffernan T, Bosetti L (2020a) The emotional labour and toll of managerial academia on higher education leaders. J Educ Adm Hist. https://doi.org/10.1080/00220620.2020.1725741

Heffernan T, Bosetti L (2020b) University bullying and incivility towards faculty deans. Int J Educ Leadersh. https://doi.org/10.1080/13603124.2020.1850870

Heffernan T, Bosetti L (2021) Incivility: The new type of bulling in higher education. Camb J Educ. https://doi.org/10.1080/0305764X.2021.1897524

Heffernan T, Heffernan A (2018) Language games: university responses to ranking metrics. High Educ Q 72(1):29–39. https://doi.org/10.1111/hequ.12139

Hickey A (2015) The economies of engagement: The nature of university engagement in the corporate university. Soc Altern 34(2):20–26

Latif K, Bunce L, Ahmad M (2021) How can universities improve student loyalty? The roles of university social responsibility, service quality, and "customer" satisfaction and trust. Int J Educ Manag. https://doi.org/10.1108/ijem-11-2020-0524

Matthies H, Torka M (2019) Academic habitus and institutional change: comparing two generations of german scholars. Minerva 57(3):345–371. https://doi.org/10.1007/s11024-019-09370-9

Morris J (2002) The Oxford book of Oxford. Oxford University Press, Oxford
Peacock J, Covino R, Auchter J, Boyd J, Klug H, Laing C, Irvin L (2018) University faculty perceptions and utilization of popular culture in the classroom. Stud High Educ 43(4):601–613. https://doi.org/10.1080/03075079.2016.1180673
Pilbeam C, Jamieson R (2010) Beyond leadership and management: the boundary-spanning role of the pro vice-chancellor. Educ Manage Adm Leadersh 38(6):758–776. https://doi.org/10.1177/1741143210379058
Pusser B, Marginson S (2013) University rankings in critical perspective. J Higher Educ 84:544–568. https://doi.org/10.1353/jhe.2013.0022
Sin C, Tavares O, Amaral A (2019) Accepting employability as a purpose of higher education? Academics' perceptions and practices. Stud High Educ 44(6):920–931. https://doi.org/10.1080/03075079.2017.1402174
Sutton P (2015) A paradoxical academic identity: fate, utopia and critical hope. Teach High Educ 20(1):37–47. https://doi.org/10.1080/13562517.2014.957265
Teichler U, Akira A, Cummings W (2013) The Changing academic profession. Springer
Tuchman G (2009) Wannabe u: inside the corporate university. University of Chicago Press
van der Vossen B (2015) In defense of the ivory tower: Why philosophers should stay out of politics. Philos Psychol 28(7):1045–1063. https://doi.org/10.1080/09515089.2014.972353
Webb J, Schirato T, Danaher G (2002) Understanding Bourdieu. Sage, London

Chapter 7
Vice-Chancellors and Presidents: Surveying National and International Academic Markets

Abstract This chapter begins with an assessment of what the role of the university vice chancellor or president (the highest-ranking position depending on terminology and location) traditionally involved, who was selected, and what issues they had to watch out for/contend with to complete their role. The chapter uses interviews with vice chancellors from England, and university presidents from Canada, to determine what the role involves in the twenty-first century. The chapter highlights that the highest level of office which was for centuries about the senior academic of the university directing the teaching and learning to position the university amongst their peers, and attracting academics and students who would aid to these objectives. In contrast, the leaders of today speak of their role as being largely business focused, contending with media issues, predicting funding and enrolment trends, or redistributing funds to research that is likely to result in grants and contracts. These duties have not only redefined the role, but as the chapter's analysis discusses, it separates the vice-chancellors and presidents (and other executive leaders) from teaching and research practices. They might view teaching and research as a commodity, not as methods of knowledge creation and dissemination.

This book began by establishing a baseline of what Bourdieu's theories and ideas look like in a university setting. It then used these notions to dissect the social aspects of what traditionally occurred in a university (usually furthering white male privilege), with how different pressures over the last fifty or sixty years have changed how most Westernised countries approach higher education. A majority of this work has been somewhat mechanical in nature in that Bourdieu and other researchers (including myself) have then conducted research to verify and further explore these concepts. The next chapters, however, examine interview and survey data conducted by myself and my research partner, Professor Lynn Bosetti, from the University of British Columbia. The studies about vice-chancellors, presidents, and faculty deans were carried out between 2017 and 2020. Though their findings represent a diverse set of participants across multiple continents that, in part, played a strong motivating role in writing this book, the studies were not carried out for the purpose of this book. In many ways, it was that an element of these interviews and varied sets of questions across the interviews all focused on issues surrounding career progression and trajectory, changes in the sector, and expectations verse realities of careers and roles that highlighted the need for a larger assessment of life in the modern university.

Analysis of these responses provides views from the top to the bottom of the academic hierarchy of the pressures that once shaped higher education, and currently shape higher education, and how these pressures have changed social interactions and relationships within the sector. The analysis of these views provides not only examples of how and why the sector has been changing, but also how these changes can be theorised through Bourdieu's understandings and predictions of field, habitus, and capital. Finally, they provide insights into what we can anticipate the future trends of higher education will be as we approach the mid-twenty-first century.

The Changing Field of Senior Leadership

Throughout this book the reasons universities have had to change—and are changing—has become evident. A clear factor in much of this is these changes and the changes around expectations and requirements are not altering because of the choice of an individual or a small group. The changes began as repercussions and responses to the much wider changing demographics of the higher education sector which exploded in the post-WWII born era from 1945 to 1964, and continued into the earlier first-half of the next generation who attended university from 1985 to 2005 (Esson and Ertl 2016; Forsyth 2014). This period on one hand saw immense growth as universities could not be built fast enough and were lacking the required staff to operate at full capacity. However, oversupply of positions led to universities having to engage in competition and marketing, followed by financial downturn as recession spread across several parts of the Westernised world during the late-1970s through to the early-1990s. Oversupply, recession, and difficult employment figures also had strong social implications for approaches to universities. These situations directly and indirectly brought government control and influence into higher education which made it a political issue and one for debate in terms of funding and who could and did attend universities. Different political parties and campaigns might now have varying views on higher education across the globe in terms of value and funding, but the damage in many circumstances has already been done; that higher education became a topic of debate at all means questions about its worth remain in the public psyche regardless of any current trends (Forsyth 2014).

Higher education is almost certainly not alone in this regard, and it could be suggested that many governments aid in higher education's societal value teetering between a high or low benefit to society's needs to assist governments in their own needs depending on the situation. You need look no further to the almost universal approach to higher education as the COVID-19 pandemic began to see how politicians benefit from these teetering values. Across many, if not most countries, extreme downturns in student numbers through lockdowns and restricted international, national, and local movement was not met with funding support, but funding cuts. Cuts were often justified with governments being able to position higher education as a luxury item of lower social value that did not need to be a funding priority at that time. Governments are somewhat free to define their own priorities, but in some respects, they also follow protocols around what is expected by their voters. Anecdotally, I would suggest there were few times when the media, or discourses within wider society, made any major arguments against governments operating in this way. This occurred, despite the fact, that in Australia, North America, Europe, and the United Kingdom, these are industries worth tens (if not hundreds) of billions of dollars, are the base of a huge export market, and the sector's downturn resulted in tens of thousands of job losses with few governments intervening (Blackmore 2020; Eacott et al. 2020).

Researchers are still unsure of what the long-term impacts of COVID-19 will be on the higher education sector because at the time of writing this book it is still too soon to tell. As I have indicated in other sections, from my other research projects (none of which are dedicated specifically to COVID-19), the data being generated, at this point, indicates that the pandemic has in many ways amplified or increased the trajectory of trends that already existed within the sector. This may change at any moment as global pandemics are clearly impossible to predict, but for the most part, it appears from an administration, leadership, and employment standpoint that COVID-19's primary repercussions to higher education are about increasing efficiency. Fewer students means competition has increased, less tuition fees means managerial expertise has increased in capital as leaders are forced to do more with less, academics must publish more in less time because the competition has increased, and the outcomes of teaching must increase to satisfy a student/customer-base that can be more demanding as the number of students is not always matching the available positions which makes competition between institutions fierce.

As even these more extreme COVID-19-induced changes extend on developments already present in the sector, there has been little debate for several decades that these pressures have caused operational changes in university structures. Blackmore (2002), and Pilbeam and Jamieson (2010) each highlight an almost linear shift in how the roles and expectations of leaders changed to meet the evolving funding and policy changes, and societal and student expectations. Sutton (2015) also highlights this need to change to fit the current environment as being a reason that leaders, and even those with research profiles, who were selected in part because of their research profile and would like to continue with their research, are most often unable to do so. Sutton suggests this is through no fault of the leader, but is a consequence of the changing and evolving pressures of working in an increasingly metric driven environment. Despite the research intentions of leaders coming into senior roles in universities, their role prioritises the managerial aspects, and as time pressures increase it is research intentions that dwindle because in this scenario, research is the lesser priority. Leaders are thus left with systemic reasons that their research profile is unable to be maintained. This is perhaps also why it holds a decreasing amount of capital in the selection process as it is possible that committees know a research profile will likely be difficult to maintain.

As we explore the views of several vice-chancellors and presidents from the United Kingdom and Canada in this chapter, in dissecting what has happened to their roles, and examining what each of these leaders are describing (for the most part), is about the changing expectations and requirements of their role. However, they are also inadvertently explaining how and why their field was once shaped, what pressures have caused the field to change and shift its borders, and subsequently what the field looks like at the present. Theorising these data through Bourdeu's notions of field and capital allows us to see beyond the mechanics of what is taking place in universities, because what on the surface might seem unconnected or tentatively connected is, in fact, highly related and impacted by the clear forces and repercussions of fields and capital.

These data were generated as part of a wider study conducted in partnership with Lynn Bosetti surrounding the emotional toll of leadership in higher education. The study comprised of 20 one-hour, semi-structured interviews with questions that primarily revolved around working in the knowledge economy. These interviews included 10 with vice-chancellors from English universities and 10 with presidents of Canadian universities. The participants were selected via our own determination of what would provide an equal share of views from leaders ranging from large, wealthy, and internationally known universities in terms of reputations, rankings and prestige, to institutions more likely to be known nationally (rather than internationally), and smaller and regional universities that rely on more local pools of students. The participants were extremely receptive to interview requests and subsequently the group of participants included the full breadth of vice-chancellors from some of the most famous universities in the world to those leading much smaller and newer institutions which have only been in operation for several decades.

Leaders' Views of Their Roles in the Modern University

Across the different countries, and the size, wealth, and prestige of different universities, university leaders saw their primary role in a very similar way. Their role is to publicly guide the university, carry out the wishes of the executive board (or senate, or senior committee depending on country and governance methods), and make decisions or inform stakeholders of possible methods to move the university forward. The first point to note, however, is that the vice-chancellor or president is no longer left alone to contend with these decisions. This may have been the case decades (or centuries) ago when universities were much smaller rather than institutions worth billions of dollars (Forsyth 2014). However, the requirements of the modern university mean the executive structure of deputy vice-chancellors and vice-presidents is in place so these members can oversee their own portfolios and report to the vice-chancellor or president so that they can take this information and advise others of how best to move forward. Thus, what is immediately evident with these leaders regardless of their institution's characteristics, is that the defining factor in how they gauge the best methods to move forward with advancing their institution is by determining how best to position themselves around those institutions which they see as their competition.

The result of a university's foremost leader now being a role where information is passed between the senior executive (deputy vice-chancellors and vice-presidents), faculty deans, and the controlling boards of governors, trustees, or executives, is that the vice-chancellors or presidents now have less direct influence over what takes place in an institution and instead guide the work and direction of the other members. That is not at all to suggest that vice-chancellors or presidents have low levels of involvement; across the breadth of participants, it was clear that carrying out a university's most senior role often meant being in attendance of breakfast meetings to evening events five, though usually six, or sometimes seven, days per week.

In most aspects, the senior leaders thus knew it was their task to guide different levels of management and leadership to find a cohesion in all these actions. For example, vice-chancellors and presidents knew it was not their role to have an active place in what was happening in relation to research, or teaching and learning, or marketing and strategy. For all these aspects, they relied on vice-presidents, deputy vice-chancellors, and often teams underneath them collecting data, considering future directions, and determining their own strategies to move forward. This led to vice-chancellors and presidents to view their roles as taking in all this information, combining it with the direction of the trustees, board of governors, or senate, and determining the best way for the institution to advance itself considering all the collected information. This often meant defining how the university would capitalise on its strengths, while strategising to address its weaknesses, which sometimes resulted in changing direction, or abandoning current pursuits.

Vice-chancellors also play an interesting role from a Bourdieusian perspective. Though studies could be made to examine, for example, how habitus and capital form to create a vice-chancellor, and influence how successful they will be, this chapter takes a different perspective on Bourdieu's theories. Throughout this book, the notion of institutional capital has frequently been discussed, that is, the amount of capital an agent can gain from being associated with an institution (Bourdieu 1988). What we see in the coming discussion and views from vice-chancellors about their role and duties, is very much about their role in maintaining and improving their institution's capital. No interviewed vice-chancellor spoke of their role through a Bourdieusian lens, but how they describe their role is about how to improve their university's position in the sphere that is most relevant to it. For some universities, institutional capital is about being globally competitive, for others, it is about being recognised as the best in their country, while for some, any national recognition is the primary objective (Bourdieu and Waquant 1992).

For all the above reasons, in the modern university within which these leaders hold the most senior role, this meant surveying their competition, and then determining the best ways to remain and increase their competitive position. Their language is itself telling of the current pressure universities are under. They are at competition with one another for students, the best academics who will attract the most funding, and in a capitalist society, the only way these billion-dollar corporations can move to be considered successful is upwards in terms of size and profits. If a competitor gets a new building, every university they compete with needs a new building plus one more to stay ahead. It is as if teaching and research might be the end result of what a university produces, but to get to that point involves innumerable decisions being made that often have little to do with research or teaching. These views remained largely unchanged across all the participants and regardless of the size, wealth, or location of the university they lead; the only difference was that each leader was acutely aware of who their competition was, and was not, and what this meant their institution needed to achieve.

For less wealthy universities, and what research and prestige rankings might consider less 'elite' institutions in both England and Canada, these scenarios meant their competition was most often domestic neighbours. These institutions were similarly positioned in terms of rankings and size in the case of England, but also geographically close in Canada as potential students of less prestigious universities were less likely to travel across a country the physical size of Canada to complete their studies.

The leaders exhibited similar awareness when it came to issues of attracting staff as they believed that where their institution sat in terms of international rankings played a role in which academics (and their potential research outputs and funding income) would be looking to move to their university. Vice-chancellors and presidents rarely (if ever) indicated having a direct role in hiring academics, but they did indicate that they viewed part of their role as making their institution as appealing as possible to students and staff of their target markets. A pivotal aspect of this is that they knew the demographics of staff and student for which they were competing. In reference to staff, one vice-chancellor summed up this theme by stating:

> We're unlikely to attract established academics from Oxbridge, or the major Redbricks without significant promotions. Our focus is on attracting up and comers and then providing incentives [for them] to stay.

This view is perhaps one that indicates that these leaders are aware that it is not possible to simply target 'the best' students and academics because in many ways that would be a waste of resources and not end with the desired results. Instead, vice-chancellors and presidents of these institutions point their recruitment efforts towards the demographics of students and staff they know they are likely to attract.

The idea of modelling aspiration around realistic audiences continues in more internationally known institutions; the processes simply tend to scale up accordingly. A president of a major Canadian university stated that 'We're always losing staff to Harvard and Yale, but we and [names of other select Canadian institutions] can attract staff from most other colleges so that's our focus'. At the most prestigious level of targeting students and academics, a vice-chancellor from one of the most globally recognised universities, discussed their role as primarily being one shaped by the actions of the major American universitates.

> We [the university] don't have local competition. I wake up in the morning and look at what's happening with the top Ivy League schools because the students and academics we're looking for, can come to us or could go to those US institutions. We don't have their money, we don't have their endowments. They can offer salaries to staff that we can't, and they can offer

facilities to students that we can't. My job is to make [the institution] attractive on a global scale even though others can offer things we cannot.

What this brief look into university governance at the highest level demonstrates is that leaders are not focused on guiding teaching or research direction; in the twenty-first century a sub-layer of management ultimately addresses these issues. Instead, vice-chancellors and presidents have tailored themselves to their roles which means surveying the competition, and using this information to broadly shape and guide how their institution is moving forward. Thus, they have tailored themselves to what needs to be done to maintain or improve the institutional capital of their university.

While vice-chancellors and presidents spoke of having their role be about the same types of tasks, their views on the current system were shaped by their own experiences and histories. Of the twenty leaders interviewed, a significant majority were male. This was not intended, it was the consequence of selecting universities to demonstrate a spread of size, wealth, and prestige, and these leaders tended to be male (Burkinshaw and White 2017). However, their age and career progression were telling of their approaches to higher education and leadership. Though the average age of the leaders was approximately sixty-five years old, this included a spread of participants from some in their early-to-mid fifties, to some in their early seventies.

This age difference in part results in participants having sometimes entered academia in the early-1970s, to others who began in the late-1980s or early-1990s. The variation in experience altered the leaders' experiences of the university and leadership as they worked towards holding the institution's most senior position. For some, this meant beginning their careers at a time when jobs, research allocations, and opportunities were plentiful because universities were for all intents and purposes, understaffed and challenged to keep up with demand (Forsyth 2014). However, for others, this meant they entered at a time when neoliberalism, performativity, and competition were already part of the higher education landscape, even if they are trends that have increased in the decades since (Esson and Ertl 2016). The leaders' histories have not changed how they understand the requirements of their role, but it does have some influence in how much they push back against the system. For some, this means steering their university towards research objectives where possible, but for others, this means pursuing the best way forward regardless of what that looks like: it may mean furthering research or teaching priorities, or it may mean a new sports centre to attract students.

The way vice-chancellors and presidents think about these decisions can also be thought about in terms of how they have approached, and intend to exit, the university's most senior role. Traditionally, the role of vice-chancellor or president went to one of the university's most senior academics and was a position they filled before retirement (Blackmore 2002; Ma and Dolton 2003). This system was the most prudent way forward when institutions were much smaller, and advancing the university via its strengths in research and teaching was how universities were driven forward and positioned themselves. However, the change from traditional vice-chancellor to what is now closer to the CEO of the institution (Heffernan 2019) both explains why the modern role is less about skills acquired through decades of working in higher education, and also why once someone possesses these skills, the likelihood of them both starting in the position at a younger age, and being a 'career vice-chancellor or president' who moves from one institution to another is now a much more common occurrence. This shift should raise questions about a vice-chancellor's or president's priorities. If someone is filling a role and their primary objective is to use their current position as a stepping-stone to a larger or more prestigious university, it is fair to raise ethical questions about whether decisions are being made with the university's overall best interests in mind. Or, is their objective really around those priorities that the corporate university might find most appealing, primarily outputting more for less financial outlay, which is likely to lead to a more prestigious appointment; a scenario that is rarely likely to pair with research or teaching goals, or the most positive long-term outcomes for the vice-chancellor's or president's current university.

The changes in who and why a vice-chancellor or president is appointed also has connections to the history of academic movement and migration. Traditionally, it would be expected that a university's most senior leader would be selected from its staff as the role was one about being the institution's most senior academic. Understanding the attributes and internal processes of an institution was integral to this role. However, this is a process that started centuries ago when essentially every university was an elite institution. In this scenario, it is important to acknowledge that these approaches to university structures, employment, and governance are bound in history and rarely exists today. Perhaps seventy years to a century ago, the progression of an academic in a strongly male and white sector is outlined by Morris (2002). In the English context, that meant a child of privilege (with the necessary cultural means and capital) likely left home at the age of five to board at an English public school, before moving into college at Oxford, Cambridge (or any ancient or historic university) as a student, and for those that became academics, they then never left and completed their career at that institution. This system was perhaps to be expected when universities were small in number and size, equally small in the volume of people who had the capital to become potential students, and it is clear why academic migration was rare. Even as the sector began opening up, the option to move universities was minimal because if no one raised in the ultra-elite system moved universities, the opportunity for someone else to fill their position rarely arose.

In the North American system, similar situations occurred historically, but even today, the tenure system remains a strong incentive to reduce academic movement. This stands in contrast with other higher education systems (Australia, New Zealand, Great Britain) where a permanent, full-time position can be acquired from early career entry positions post and even pre-gaining of a doctoral degree, albeit a rare occurrence (Bosanquet et al. 2017). The tenure-system essentially sees an academic have to build a body of work that demonstrates their position and ability in the field, and if this body of work is deemed acceptable by the university's tenure committee, then tenure is granted. However, tenure is rarely accepted from one institution to another (Main et al. 2019). Thus, in the English/European-based system, it would be unusual for an academic with a continuing/permanent role to consider applying for a position at a different university that was not also permanent in nature. Additionally, the hiring committee would equally be aware that it was unlikely a potential candidate who was currently permanently employed would accept anything other than a permanent position (Heffernan 2020). This allows for relatively free academic migration, and therefore, as the global higher education sector expanded, some countries have very different relationships with staff moving between institutions nationally and globally than others. That the tenure-system rarely acknowledges tenure from one university to another, particularly in times of academics promoting upwards to more prestigious institutions, is why the tenure system can disincentivise academic movement within North America which acts as a point of difference to what happens in many other regions.

The above discussion around academic movement is directly relevant to how vice-chancellors and presidents were sourced in the historical sense (Heffernan and Bosetti 2020), but in other ways, it is admittedly not at all relevant to how they are sourced today. The new hiring practices are themselves evidence of how this field has changed within the sector, but also how far removed they are from their historical roots, and away from how other aspects of the university have taken shape in the twenty-first century.

Summary

As the university has slowly changed and evolved at first over centuries, but more recently, in the last few decades, the role of vice-chancellor and president is perhaps one of the roles that has changed most. From an administration standpoint, this has changed what is expected of someone fulfilling this role, and the salaries of people carrying out these positions is also a regular topic of discussion as they are seen to be more befitting of a CEO than an academic; but perhaps that is the point (Boden and Rowlands 2020). When the doxa of the university remains largely the same, the title of vice-chancellor or president remains the same, and being the public facing leader of the institution remains their most visual role, the immense changes that have taken vice-chancellors and presidents from being the university's senior academics to business leaders of institutions often worth billions of dollars can be easily overlooked.

What is clear is that the field of academic-to-leader has been divided because leaders at this level still operate in a researcher space, but for the most part, they now tend to be full time career leaders who were once academics. Perhaps the real question is, are there any field borders truly shared at all? This is highly dependent on location, type of university, and the institution's chosen administration structure, but ultimately the answer is no—there is little sense left of vice-chancellors and presidents being academics who lead academics; they are now leaders who manage the business of academia. This is in no way a criticism of the role or the people performing the role (though perhaps it is a circumstance that needs deep critical evaluation).

What this chapter highlights is that the role has completely changed and being aware of the changes, pressure, and directives that guide vice-chancellors and presidents may make clearer why some decisions that might seem counter-intuitive are made. Leading a business that may be worth billions of dollars each year, has thousands of employees (academics and professional staff) and tens of thousands of customers (students) in the most financially prudent way forward is their objective. Therefore, individual decisions around staffing, courses, student services, or infrastructure (for example) might seem wrong, poor, or negligent (and perhaps they are because there is no guarantee that the selected leader will be a good leader or is making decisions for the good of the university and its staff rather than their own resume), but it is the decision-making process of how best to lead a corporation which is the driving force behind these decisions. These are the pressures and processes which make senior leadership in the modern university entirely abstract to a role which was once about leading the research and teaching decisions of an institute that was small, adequately funded, and isolated from government, business, and social pressures.

References

Bosanquet A, Mailey A, Matthews K, Lodge J (2017) Redefining 'early career' in academia: a collective narrative approach. High Educ Res Dev 36(5):890–902. https://doi.org/10.1080/07294360.2016.1263934

Bourdieu P (1988) Homo Academicus (trans: Collier P). Polity.

Bourdieu P, Wacquant L (1992) An invitation to reflexive sociology. Polity Press, Cambridge

Blackmore J (2002) Globalisation and the restructuring of higher education for new knowledge economies: new dangers or old habits troubling gender equity work in universities? High Educ Q 56(4):419–441. https://doi.org/10.1111/1468-2273.00228

Blackmore J (2020) The carelessness of entrepreneurial universities in a world risk society: a feminist reflection on the impact of Covid-19 in Australia. High Educ Res Dev 39(7):1332–1336. https://doi.org/10.1080/07294360.2020.1825348

Boden R, Rowlands J (2020). Paying the piper: the governance of vice-chancellors' remuneration in Australian and UK universities. High Educ Res Dev, pp 1–15. https://doi.org/10.1080/07294360.2020.1841741

Burkinshaw P, White K (2017) Fixing the women or fixing universities: women in HE leadership. Adm Sci 7(3):30. https://doi.org/10.3390/admsci7030030

Eacott S, MacDonald K, Keddie A, Blackmore J, Wilkinson J (2020) COVID-19 and inequities in Australian education—insights on federalism, autonomy, and access. Int Stud Educ Adm 48(3):6–13. http://cceam.net/publications/isea/isea-2020-vol-48-no-3/

Esson J, Ertl H (2016) No point worrying? Potential undergraduates, study-related debt, and the financial allure of higher education. Stud High Educ 41(7):1265–1280. https://doi.org/10.1080/03075079.2014.968542

Forsyth H (2014) A history of the Modern Australian University. NewSouth Publishing, Sydney

Heffernan T (2019) Reporting on vice-chancellor salaries in Australia's and the United Kingdom's media in the wake of strikes, cuts and 'falling performance'. Int J Leadersh Educ, pp 1–17. https://doi.org/10.1080/13603124.2019.1631387

Heffernan T (2020) There's no career in academia without networks': academic networks and career trajectory. High Educ Res Dev. https://doi.org/10.1080/07294360.2020.1799948

References

Heffernan T, Bosetti L (2020) The emotional labour and toll of managerial academia on higher education leaders. J Educ Adm Hist. https://doi.org/10.1080/00220620.2020.1725741

Ma A, Dolton P (2003) Executive pay in the public sector: the case of CEOs in UK universities. In: Royal economic society annual conference 2003, Royal Economic Society, Warwick, UK

Main B, Prenovitz S, Ehrenberg R (2019) In Pursuit of a tenure-track faculty position: career progression and satisfaction of humanities and social sciences doctorates. Rev High Educ 42(4):1309–1336. https://doi.org/10.1353/rhe.2019.0067

Morris J (2002) The Oxford book of Oxford. Oxford University Press, Oxford

Pilbeam C, Jamieson R (2010) Beyond leadership and management: the boundary-spanning role of the pro vice-chancellor. Educ Manage Adm Leadersh 38(6):758–776. https://doi.org/10.1177/1741143210379058

Sutton P (2015) A paradoxical academic identity: fate, utopia and critical hope. Teach High Educ 20(1):37–47. https://doi.org/10.1080/13562517.2014.957265

Chapter 8
Deans: The Faculty's New Managers

Abstract This chapter uses interviews with faculty deans to assess what they anticipated their role would involve, for many this was primarily guiding teaching and research, compared to what their role entails. The chapter explores how deans see their role primarily as managers tasked with reaching KPIs set by those above them, and also contending with the personal issues that come with running a team. Indeed, as majority of deans see their work as being financial managers, their traditional role of leading the faculty's research and teaching direction is now often left to those below them. The change in the dean's role has been severe for those in the position long-term and who have been a part of the field's change, but it has also meant that new deans (having already held senior academic positions) are entering the position knowing this is the case. While the fact that deans are now managers has also increased the opportunity for people with little academic experience to successfully become deans due to their management skills. This change not only sees an increased managerial aspect to universities as again, success is being measured on performance metrics, but the title and doxa of 'dean' remains the same, when the role has few aspects left of what was traditionally part of the role.

The changing roles of university management and expectations of what is required has taken people far from what the role traditionally looked like, and they are now operating in significantly new fields with newly-defined borders. In this chapter, interviews with deans are used to understand what deans anticipated their role would involve (for many this was primarily guiding teaching and research) compared to what their role entails. This chapter explores how deans see their role largely as managers tasked with reaching KPIs (key performance indicators) set by those above them, and also contending with the personal issues that come with running a team. Indeed, as the majority of deans see their work as being financial managers, their traditional role of leading the faculty's research and teaching direction is now often left to those below them. However, despite the fact that it is deans carrying out managerial work with the associated pressures and consequences on relationships, they are still tasked with being the orchestrators of a positive and welcoming faculty culture. These two objectives can sometimes fit together rather poorly.

The change in the dean's role has been significant for those in the position long-term, but it has also meant that new deans (having already held senior academic positions) are entering the position knowing this is the case. The fact that deans are now managers has also increased the opportunity for people with little to no academic experience to successfully become deans due to their management skills. This change sees an increased managerial aspect to universities, as again, success is being measured on performance metrics, but the title and doxa of 'dean' remains the same.

The change to a dean's role also provides some key differences from the previous examination of vice-chancellors and presidents, and the forthcoming discussion around academics in the next chapter. Primarily these changes are around the fact that deans do not have the power dynamic advantage (in terms of the academic hierarchy) of a vice-chancellor or president; though that is not to suggest that they are still not in a position of significant influence. At the same time, an argument could be made that, as in the previous chapter, it is the dean's role to facilitate the 'institutional capital' of the faculty, and that is certainly true. Yet, without the elevated hierarchical position held by vice-chancellors, this chapter (and indeed this book as it explores the changing world of the university) outlines how deans are considerably more in need of habitus and capital within the field to aid in their promotion to dean, their success in the role, and their likelihood of being promoted to a more prestigious faculty. It is also necessary to consider that the capital that leads to someone becoming, maintaining, and promoting to more prestigious institutions as dean is changing as management expertise becomes more valuable than research or teaching experience. However, the capital valued within a faculty (research profile and teaching expertise) remains the same. The nature, and changing nature, of a dean's work is explored in this chapter, but it is the later chapters that further explores the juxtaposition of university leadership requiring and valuing management skills, in a field whose hierarchy is traditional ordered by research and teaching success.

A dean's position is also not always as solid as it once may have been. Being asked to govern as instructed by senior university leaders, while also being expected to create positive workplace cultures, places a significant volume of emotional labour on leaders at the dean level. Emotional labour may have always been part of leadership roles, though with the growing and shifting dean's role, the interviews that Lynn Bosetti and I conducted that inform this chapter suggest more tasks have been added rather than taken away; creating a particularly difficult, and often hostile, environment for leaders to navigate.

This chapter takes Bourdieu's notions and builds on existing research from several angles. Challenges of the role concerning emotional labour have been assessed (Lester 2013; Oplatka and Arar 2018), but less so in terms of the consequence of why these changes are happening due to the changing face of the university. For example, it is within the new shape of the university that deans are reporting high levels of bullying towards themselves which is resulting in regular wellbeing and mental health issues (Heffernan and Bosetti 2020a, b, 2021; Hollis 2015). At the same time, Hodgins and Mannix McNamara (2017) highlight that deans are also regularly now exposed to acts of incivility (contending with staff who are generally hostile, argumentative, or participating in indirect acts of aggression such as spreading rumours or undermining the dean's authority where possible). This chapter explores these new and evolving phenomena of the modern university as it helps demonstrate the complexities of higher education, but it also aids in showing what is happening behind closed office doors. Potentially, it is very easy to assume that someone's pressure reduces as they climb the leadership ladder, or that with higher salaries comes a higher level of autonomy or control over one's career. However, this chapter shows that as the traditional structures of the university have shifted to a corporate model, the need for every aspect to be managed and controlled has led to increased pressures.

The Pressures of Being Dean

Existing studies of the modern role of deans focus on the pressures and repercussions of performing their role. A majority of these pressures extend from bullying, incivility, personal attacks, or being put in untenable positions. As becomes clear in the deans' own words, their role as middle-management sees them consistently being at odds with those above them orchestrating the corporate and managerialist directives (which are often made without regard for the human element of delivering and executing these instructions), while working with their staff who are being directed into new ways of working (yet have little regard for the business-strategies required in the modern university).

The pressures are not new, they have been evolving, and the same is true of the repercussions to those working in these environments. That faculties can be difficult places to work is not new information, and so for decades people have studied what all employees (including deans) have experienced due to the negative aspects of their employment. Some have argued that the higher education sector as a whole is having difficulty contending with these negative issues (Kahn and Kahn 2012). The regularly discussed impacts include anxiety, fatigue, low self-esteem, and depression, and all of which can in extreme cases manifest into risk of suicide (Balducci et al. 2011; Cooper et al. 2004; Hallberg and Strandmark 2006; Hogh et al. 2011; Niedhammer et al. 2006) and health conditions (Hollis 2015). The studies focused on incivility within faculties, or the impact of negative behaviours whose impact accrue over time, also found similar issues impacting on deans' mental health (Cortina et al. 2001; Lim et al. 2008), burnout and subsequent hostility, hospitalisation (Einarsen and Mikkelsen 2003), and post-traumatic stress disorder (Matthiesen and Einarsen 2004).

The way deans' roles have changed also needs to be considered regarding how their role as leaders of faculty cultures has grown at a time when the faculty itself has also changed substantially towards a corporate model. The notion of faculty culture following the growth of mass market higher education was viewed as quite straightforward up until the early-2000s. Faculty culture was based around the idea of leading a faculty that was collegial and low on personal hostility, and yet competition and success (primarily in research and grants) which set the order of the faculty's field hierarchy and shaped the faculty's culture was present (Berquist and Pawlak 2007). What this finding indicates is a theme relevant to many areas of this book. When the academy was based around a hierarchy that itself was shaped heavily by research profile and success, and these factors shaped both the hierarchy and leadership structure of faculties and universities more widely, there were far fewer primary fields that agents were operating within. It was almost as if in past decades that every academic was in the field of being a researcher and teacher, and their success both gave them their position on the academic ladder, but also gave them the option to consider (or perhaps be encouraged into) taking on leadership roles.

There are myriad reasons why this is not the case anymore which primarily relate to the size and purpose of the university. However, the changes are not always evident to those not within the field. This can lead to employees, potential employees, students, and society holding onto impressions of universities formed by popular culture rather than the business-orientated process and culture that confronts most people in the modern university.

Bergquist and Pawlak (2007) point out that these past iterations of the university were set by men and valued priorities associated with masculinity such as competition and domination; in many ways quite similar to the finance and law industry that evolved globally throughout the Westernised world during the 1980s and 1990s. The researchers argue that during this time, even as women and some people of colour and those from marginalised groups entered and were successful in the higher education sector, this success came via succeeding at a white male-dominated and shaped sector rather than shaping the sector to meet the needs of new agents entering the field. However, Bergquist and Pawlak (2007) argue that the cultural change in higher education leadership is now one that much more strongly follows what could be considered traditionally-feminine values of collaboration, care, and support. This suggestion is one shared by Hollis (2015) and Hodgins and Mannix McNamara (2017) who see leadership and managerialism in the modern university as following very clearly defined, human resource friendly, policies and procedures.

Even as this issue on one hand is being rectified in ways to try and repair the masculine-focused priorities of the past, this is a process still in progress because currently many deans find themselves being tasked with directives from their superiors that are diametrically opposed. On one hand, is the issue of deans having to shape the culture of their faculty. Hecht et al. (1999) and Angelo (2000) argued at the turn of the century that there was enough correlation between faculty satisfaction and performance to make it clear to hiring panels that part of a dean's role should be about their ability to lead cultural change as they were the natural leaders to perform this task and improve the faculty's performance. Bystydzienski and Bird (2006) notes more recently that these earlier ideas are now followed so closely that deans are seen by senior university management as the pivotal component of shaping a faculty and guiding it in clear and equitable directions. The culmination of deans holding this role, and administrators aligning an increase in faculty performance with positive faculty culture, is that Wergin (2003) and Honan et al. (2013) note the beginning and increasing trend of deans being valued for other aspects, such as being seen as respectful and good listeners in an effort to help facilitate staff and faculty goals.

In some respects, these steps in dean-selection are positive and take the academy away from the competition, domination, and hierarchy of traditional white, middle-class male filled universities. However, this line of expectations of a dean and their role is only half of the situation. As has been made clear throughout this book, the managerialist and neoliberal transformation of the university sector has not occurred overnight, and it has not occurred due to a small number of individual choices and decisions. In many ways, the change in the university sector occurred as a result of attempts to expand the sector to include more people and to make it more accessible, and it was this that started competition for enrolments, the need for growth, and the need for funds. Thus, for every directive deans receive regarding building faculty culture, they are at the same time issued instructions that are common to any business or corporation. Operations need to be streamlined, less profitable products need to be made profitable or replaced with more profitable offerings, and customer satisfaction matters. These tasks are in complete contrast to skills such as culture building and being a good listener, and in fact, one could argue are more closely aligned to competition, domination, and hierarchy than ever before (Tuchman 2009). It could be argued that in reality, the only people to receive the idealised view of a dean as a leader of culture and equity are those that fit within the faculty's requirements of publishing, bringing in money, and receiving good teaching scores in subjects that are profitable to the faculty.

The complete juxtaposition of these objectives is in part what has made the role of dean become increasingly difficult. The participants in this study were primarily asked about the emotional labour of the role, but what we found were people's whose role often placed them in difficult positions. The deans were being given multiple directives from the university's senior leadership team, while at the same time leading teams of academics who have come to realise that they are not being led or having their research or teaching guided, they are being managed. The consequences to academics are discussed in the next chapter, but that so many deans reported this as an issue highlights the need for this book because it demonstrates how the slow changes in university administration can go unnoticed even to those already in the sector. For deans, however, their position as subordinate to those above them and leader to those below them (in an industry that it could be argued sometimes feigns equity, care, and inclusion), was a noted source of poor mental wellbeing, and psychological and physical stress.

This chapter's data was generated from interviews with 20 faculty deans working in Australian universities. The study used semi-structured interviews and later thematic analysis of the transcripts to evaluate the data (Braun and Clarke 2006; Clarke and Braun 2017) as this method enabled an examination of the participants' experiences (Creswell 2013); in this case, relating to operating within their role as dean. The deans were from various locations around the country and worked across eight universities that were selected to represent the size, wealth, type, and position on the research and reputation rankings. The deans were also selected from faculties that tend to be in all institutions such as business, education, humanities, and science, rather than areas such as medicine or fine arts which are not offered across all universities. This project generated data from deans working in a wide range of faculty and university settings which is reflective of many global higher education settings prevalent in developed countries (Heffernan 2018a, 2019; b) including North America, Great Britain, and many throughout Asia (Knight 2013).

Only three deans from the twenty participants interviewed said they felt they were not currently under any form of undue stress or wellbeing issues. For the three deans currently finding themselves in what they viewed as fortunate positions, they knew this was not about their leadership skills. It was, as one dean framed it, about 'the ebbs and flows' of the faculty and university, and the fact that the interview was conducted at a time when their institution was in a 'flow' rather than an 'ebb'.

The three deans who found themselves in positive positions were adamant that being in an optimistic position was less about their leadership, but further investigation of these beliefs highlight to what extent deans feel they have very little control over their faculties, and instead are the people in the position of carrying out the wishes of the university's executive management (Sing and Yaqiong 2018; Thornton et al. 2018). For example, one dean spoke of coming into their role after their faculty had carried out a major restructure which was prompted by the university providing less money to the faculty.

> We lost 20% of all academics the year before I got here. […] They chopped the 20% out really quickly, which for my arrival was fantastic because I didn't have to do it.

Coming into the faculty following the restructure allowed the dean to enter and carry out the traditional role of leading their staff and as Bystydzienski and Bird (2006) suggested; creating culture, even if this occurred through rebuilding the faculty and being able to listen to the views of those who remained as the faculty was reborn. However, the dean was acutely aware (and reiterated on several occasions) that their current success was due to the timing of their arrival. At other times, they stated that they knew the requirements of leadership would result in them being a leader of distrust, fear, and anger amongst their staff (such as if staffing issues or another restructure were to arise). This acceptance is largely at odds with the traditional role of deans being in place to guide and lead their staff. Instead, they are an extension of human resource departments in place to help execute the wishes of the executive management. As Harrington et al. (2015) argued, human resource departments are at their core designed to protect the institution at the cost of employee wellbeing; deans knew they would often fall into the same category.

The other two participants who stated that they found themselves in currently positive positions also pointed towards a factor that was evident in the first example; that being that they envisaged issues would occur due to their need to manage people, not because of their need to lead people in the traditional areas of teaching and research.

One dean had been in their current role for almost a decade, and suggested that they had enjoyed a relatively positive experience because the faculty had grown significantly in student numbers and overall finances, which in turn bolstered academic numbers, publications and grants had increased, and the faculty was increasing its position in global research and prestige rankings. The dean spoke of these achievements as being a mix of metric-based and traditional (to a faculty) based achievements. However, the dean also knew that for all the goodwill, trust, and positive relationships that had been formed, some of that was soon to be eroded as they spoke of being about to begin the process of 'tidying up' the faculty. That is to say, after a decade of widespread prosperity throughout the faculty, the dean suggested that smaller issues relating to some staff underperforming had been watched but ignored for the sake of the wider-faculty's culture. Yet, the dean knew a time was approaching where this number was beginning to increase and so performance management was going to have to come into play which they knew would negatively impact on relationships and culture.

The final example comes from a dean new to their role. They spoke of operating in the 'calm before the storm' because while they spoke of their new faculty's 'great culture and great work ethic within the team', and they were excited to be 'leading a fantastic team of both experienced and relatively new people', they expected this to be short-lived as they knew restructures and increased performance metrics were coming. On this topic, the dean was both able to speak to the needs of the faculty to be managed, but also the likely repercussions.

> We are working at the moment around reimagining our research priorities. […] How do we imagine priorities that speak to our industry partners, to the public etc., but that also take into account the work that we're doing within the faculty. So the bit that keeps me awake is what happens to people's children [if they are managed out]. What happens to their research profile if we decide that we're on about a certain aspect or certain aspects of the faculty and that doesn't include particular people. So how do we manage that, and how do we manage people who we would say are non-performing in their role?

The notion that it is the need to manage people that leads to conflict becomes clearer still when looking at deans currently finding themselves in difficult situations. Several deans spoke of the difficulty of being a 'brick in the wall' of university leadership because they had academics below them who assume they were the leader and the decisions being made were their choice, when the deans felt they were simply the mouthpiece of those above them. These deans spoke of being subjected to difficult relationships with those above them. One dean stated that:

> The challenge is that you're a brick with people below you and people above you. You're trying to support everyone and please everyone, but sometimes they want different things. Sometimes it's even the case that different deputy vice-chancellors want different things and you have to balance all of this knowing they will take the issue out on you, and not the person issuing the directive they do not like.

Another dean identified similar issues, but they specifically referred to issues surrounding the changing fields of university leadership and how people are recruited to these positions and what skills are most valuable in the application process. The dean spoke of this adding an extra pressure as 'management is now "the man", they're not academics'. The dean had no solid opinion on the practice of how senior executives were recruited, and they were accepting of the fact that in the current climate this was a necessary procedure. However, the dean (and other deans in the study) did note executives without academic experience sometimes making decisions that did not work in an academic setting, or else they were overruled by others with academic experience which led to hostility and difficult work environments and relationships. This scenario could be considered a casualty of the eroding borders and priorities that fill universities and leadership in the modern university, but it also acts as a warning of the complexity of universities expanding at rates and to extents perhaps not envisaged only a few decades ago.

In terms of leading their faculty, most deans considered their role as being either about the management aspect, or the traditional teaching and research focus. What cannot be ignored is that most deans identified the management decisions as the ones that led to conflict within the faculty, but often, they no longer made decisions surrounding research or teaching (as this went to associatedeans etc.) which meant every decision the dean made was around management and thus led to conflict. One dean summed up their role by explaining what happens each time they made a decision:

> People are in two groups and are trying to lobby me. I know people are trying to convince me to join them. […] But you know when a choice is made, people will be disappointed [and that potentially leads to conflict].

The dean went on to make a statement that reflects what other deans, and vice-chancellors and presidents echoed, in that they felt they could have good and meaningful conversations with colleagues about teaching and learning, because that is the language academics speak. The communication breakdown and hostility they experienced in their role was when they had to have business-based discussions because that is a language academics do not speak, and for many academics, this is a language or consideration they have not had to be aware of for much of their careers.

Multiple participants thus spoke of the 'us versus them' culture of university leadership, which in many ways is an addition to the earlier view that 'management is now "the man"'. The 'us versus them' mentality had in interesting repercussion in the views of most deans as it soured relationships regardless of whether they were generally positive or negative. Several deans spoke of relationship issues with their academics even when their academics achieved beyond expectation and received the research time, funds, and assistance they requested (because the requests deserved to be fulfilled). Some deans even reported that academics who were regularly rewarded for their achievements were cautious around management as the academics knew they were being measured and rewarded on metrics rather than any pure research or personal connection. This is again an example of the fields separating and the sector not yet knowing how to contend with these new roles. Even if the deans were high profile researchers, or remain high profile researchers, the decisions they make are not about intellectual leadership, they are not decisions being made as the senior academic of the faculty, they are decisions being made as the faculty manager. This puts them in an entirely different field to academics, and while they clearly share many borders, I would argue those borders are shrinking while aspects of management and hierarchy are increasing.

If the new structures of the modern university have led to management models of leadership becoming the standard, it cannot be ignored that this change is beginning to have repercussions. One of which was noted by several deans as being that the notion of collegiality has been lost. One dean succinctly summed up the issue when they said 'I've found that people aren't collegial, they're interested in themselves and not the school or the university'. Collegiality is difficult to define as definitions likely change a little from one person to another, but when the sector has created new mechanisms driven by neoliberalism and performativity, which in turn has led institutions to be managed rather than led, it cannot really be a surprise that this has led to academics becoming highly competitive and not interested in collegialism if it can come at the cost of their own success.

A final insight into the changing nature of deans and their work comes from the multiple deans who have collectively led faculties and across several countries, beginning as early as 1998, as they spoke about the almost paradoxical shift in their work in the last two decades. One dean declared that in the beginning of their career in faculty leadership (in the early-2000s):

> The university told me I could employ *this* many people, and then my job was to make sure I had a staff that worked well together and whose expertise could build off of each other for the best research and teaching outcomes.

Jump forward to 2019, (when the interviews were conducted for this project) and the dean declared 'I could never have imagined my life would be waking up and dealing with budgets and spreadsheets day after day', while another dean said 'I used to be part of the research and helped shape the teaching […] now other people [associate deans] do that'. Yet the dean concluded that, even then, the associate dean's objective is to meet performance and budget targets and was not about shaping the faculty to fit the skillsets they possessed.

Summary

This chapter has focused on the realities of middle leadership in higher education two decades into the twenty-first century. Deans walk a difficult line as their superiors are focused on university growth, marketability, and student (customer) satisfaction, but they rarely contend with the customers or workers; they issue directives to people such as deans. This has completely changed the field of the faculty, and in rather predictable ways because few of these changes are new or unexpected, they are the results of continuous incremental shifts that have occurred over decades.

The result is deans who now manage the faculty, who allocate workers to produce the sellable items of teaching and research, and decide who and how much of their available resources should be spent on each pursuit. A time did exist when a dean's role was to guide teaching and research, and make the most of the people and skills within their faculty, but for centuries that meant within the confines of a sector that was highly exclusionary to all but a few privileged white men. Perhaps during the mid-to-late twentieth century this trend declined as universities expanded, student numbers grew incredibly fast, and governments around the world saw higher education as a method to produce economic growth and a profitable industry. Today, however, that is not the sector with which we are confronted. Enrolments are down, funding is down, a global pandemic has caused current and unpredictable damage to student travel, and it is through all this that deans are being asked to lead. It can be of no surprise that the capital that gets someone selected as a dean, or makes them a successful dean or leads them to be asked to move to a more prestigious university has changed. At this point, universities value a dean who can manage their staff into achieving more, while costing less. For deans, this comes at great potential risk, and as this chapter discussed, personal cost. The capital that gets them selected and defines their success, is rarely the capital valued within a faculty, and this divergence features heavily in the remainder of this book.

References

Angelo T (2000) Transforming departments into productive learning communities. In: Lucas AF, and Associates (eds) Leading academic change. Jossey-Bass, San Francisco, CA, pp 74–91

Balducci C, Fraccaroli F, Schaufeli W (2011) Workplace bullying and its relation with work characteristics, personality, and post-traumatic stress symptoms: an integrated model. Anxiety Stress Coping 24(5):499–513. https://doi.org/10.1080/10615806.2011.555533

Bergquist H, Pawlak K (2007) Engaging the six cultures of the academy: revised and expanded edition of the four cultures of the academy. Wiley

Braun V, Clarke V (2006) Using thematic analysis in psychology. Qual Res Psychol 3(2):77–101. https://doi.org/10.1191/1478088706qp063oa

Bystydzienski J, Bird S (2006) Removing barriers: women in academic science, technology, engineering and mathematics. Indiana University Press, Bloomington

Clarke V, Braun V (2017) Thematic analysis. J Posit Psychol 12(3):297–298. https://doi.org/10.1080/17439760.2016.1262613

Cooper C, Hoel H, Faragher B (2004) Bullying is detrimental to health, but all bullying behaviours are not necessarily equally damaging. Br J Guid Couns 32(3):367–387. https://doi.org/10.1080/03069880410001723594

Cortina L, Magley V, Hunter-Williams J, Langhout R (2001) Incivility in the workplace: incidence and impact. J Occup Health Psychol 6:64–80. https://doi.org/10.1037/1076-8998.6.1.64

Creswell J (2013) Research design: qualitative, quantitative and mixed method approaches. SAGE

Einarsen S, Mikkelsen E (2003) Individual effects of exposure to bullying at work. In: Einarsen S, Hoel H, Zapf D, Cooper C (eds) Bullying and emotional abuse in the workplace. Taylor and Francis, pp 127–144

Hallberg L, Strandmark M (2006) Health consequences of workplace bullying: experiences from the perspective of employees in the public service sector. J Qual Stud Health Well-being 1(2). https://doi.org/10.3402/qhw.v1i2.4923

Harrington S, Warren S, Rayner C (2015) Human resource management practitioners' responses to workplace bullying: cycles of symbolic violence. Organization 22(3):368–389. https://doi.org/10.1177/1350508413516175

Hecht J, Higgerson M, Gmelch W, Tucker A (1999) The department chair as academic leader. Orys Press, Phoenix, AZ

References

Heffernan T (2018) Using university rankings as a potential indicator of student experiences in American higher education. Perspect Policy Pract High Educ. https://doi.org/10.1080/13603108.2018.1517108

Heffernan T (2018) Approaches to career development and support for sessional academics in higher education. Int J Acad Dev. https://doi.org/10.1080/1360144X.2018.1510406

Heffernan T, Bosetti L (2020) University bullying and incivility towards faculty deans. Int J Educ Leadersh. https://doi.org/10.1080/13603124.2020.1850870

Heffernan T, Bosetti L (2020) The emotional labour and toll of managerial academia on higher education leaders. J Educ Adm Hist. https://doi.org/10.1080/00220620.2020.1725741

Heffernan T, Bosetti L (2021) Incivility: the new type of bulling in Higher Education. Camb J Educ. https://doi.org/10.1080/0305764X.2021.1897524

Heffernan T (2019) Reporting on vice-chancellor salaries in Australia's and the United Kingdom's media in the wake of strikes, cuts and 'falling performance'. Int J Leadersh Educ, pp 1–17. https://doi.org/10.1080/13603124.2019.1631387

Hodgins M, Mannix McNamara P (2017) Bullying and incivility in higher education workplaces: micropolitics and the abuse of power. Qual Res Organ Manage Int J 12(3):190–206. https://doi.org/10.1108/QROM-03-2017-1508

Hogh A, Mikklesen E, Hansen A (2011) Individual consequences of workplace bullying/ mobbing. In: Einarsen S, Hoel H, Zapf D, Cooper C (eds) Bullying and harassment in the workplace. Taylor and Francis, pp 107–128

Hollis L (2015) Bully university? The cost of workplace bullying and employee disengagement in American higher education. SAGE Open 5(2):1–11. https://doi.org/10.1177/2158244015589997

Honan J, Westermoreland A, Tew M (2013) Creating a culture of appreciation for faculty development. New Dir Teach Learn 133:33–45. https://doi.org/10.1002/tl.20044

Kahn A, Khan R (2012) Understanding and managing workplace bullying. Ind Commer Train 44(2):85–89. https://doi.org/10.1108/00197851211202911

Knight J (2013) The changing landscape of higher education internationalisation—for better or worse? Perspect Policy Pract High Educ, 17(3):84–90. https://doi.org/10.1080/13603108.2012.753957

Lester J (2013) Work-life balance and cultural change: a narrative of eligibility. Rev High Educ 36(4):463–488. https://doi.org/10.1353/rhe.2013.0037

Lim S, Cortina L, Magley V (2008) Personal and workgroup incivility: impact on work and health outcomes. J Appl Psychol 93(1):95–107. https://doi.org/10.1037/0021-9010.93.1.95

Matthiesen S, Einarsen S (2004) Psychiatric distress and symptoms of PTSD among victims of bullying at work. Br J Guid Couns 32(3):335–356. https://doi.org/10.1080/03069880410001723558

Niedhammer I, David S, Degioanni S (2006) Association between workplace bullying and depressive symptoms in the French working population. J Psychosom Res 61(2):251–259. https://doi.org/10.1016/j.jpsychores.2006.03.051

Oplatka I, Arar K (2018) Increasing teacher and leader professionalism through emotion management and engagement. J Prof Capital Community 3(3):138–141. https://doi.org/10.1108/jpcc-07-2018-036

Sing Y, Yaqiong J (2018) The relationship between leadership behaviors of university middle-level managers and faculty engagement. J Manage Train Ind 5(2):1–13. https://doi.org/10.12792/jmti5.2.1

Thornton K, Walton J, Wilson M, Jones L (2018) Middle leadership roles in universities: Holy Grail or poisoned chalice. High Educ Policy Manage 40(3):208–223. https://doi.org/10.1080/1360080x.2018.1462435

Tuchman G (2009) Wannabe u: inside the corporate university. University of Chicago Press

Wergin J (2003) Departments that work: building and sustaining cultures of excellence in academic programs. Anker/Jossey-Bass, San Francisco, CA

Chapter 9
Academics: The Business of Teaching and Research

Abstract This chapter discusses how surveys with academics paint a picture of existing academics who have had to change their practices as they are now teaching students with more consumer like demands, while also having to conduct research that is likely to be published in higher 'quality' journals, and more likely to lead to funding opportunities. At the same time, academics report promotion and job success taking new shapes as networks play an increasing role in these activities; much like ample research suggests is the case in the business world. Shrinking funding is also heightening the competitiveness even at the lowest levels of the academic hierarchy as participants indicate feeling that no amount of their efforts or success is enough and that they can always do more. The chapter also makes clear how habitus and capital in the field of the academy influence who is successful at securing an academic role, and what role it plays in their overall career trajectory and success.

This chapter discusses the findings of empirical research into how the nature of academic work is changing. It explores how academics have had to change their practices as they are now teaching students with more consumer like demands, while also having to conduct research that is likely to be published in higher 'quality' journals, and more likely to lead to funding opportunities. At the same time, academics report promotion and job success taking new shapes as networks play an increasing role in these activities; much like ample research suggests is the case in the business world (Hadani et al. 2012; Williamson and Cable 2003). Shrinking funding is also heightening the competitiveness even at the lowest levels of the academic hierarchy as academics indicate feeling that no amount of their efforts or success is enough and that they can always do more.

This chapter and its discussion about academic work must also be considered amongst the other chapters that preceded it, examining different levels of university leadership. We have seen how vice-chancellors and presidents have had to become CEOs of their institution. They are no longer the unquestioned leader of the institution, they are the appointed face of university boards, senates, governors, and trustees. Their role is to consider the university amongst its competition, contend with changing levels of funding and funding models, and use their resources of deputy vice-chancellors or vice-presidents to determine how to succeed in a competitive market that increasingly receives less, and yet the sector's students ('customers') demand more, and have more options than ever before. As the COVID-19 pandemic took hold in 2020, researchers (Blackmore 2020; Eacott et al. 2020) have been highly critical of university leaders seemingly discarding academic jobs and students in the interest of money; and any criticism of university leaders also leads to discussions around salary. Researchers are right to be critical of executive university leaders, do they deserve exorbitant salaries when it is now becoming clear that many built their previous success around the unsustainable house of cards of ever-growing student numbers? Rebecca Boden, Jill Blackmore, Julie Rowlands and even myself, among many others, have examined these issues and two points are quite clear. On one hand, executive leaders are not business owners who can make final and widespread decisions, they are leaders put into positions that have many controlling factors guiding what they can and cannot carry out. However, on the other hand, this cannot excuse the power people in these positions have obtained. If a vice-chancellor or university president cannot fight against job cuts or negative working conditions for academics and other staff within their institution, what chance to people with significantly less capital and voice hold?

Many of these same attributes are true of middle leaders in universities such as faculty deans. As the previous chapter explored, these leaders are tasked with carrying out directives that originate from the vice-chancellor or president, and an entire sub-layer of management comprising deputy-vice chancellors, vice-presidents, and committees focused on improving student experience and research direction. As became clear, however, a primary issue for deans is their close and personal relationships with academic staff. Academics who think deans will act in the interest of research, in the interest of academic integrity, in the pursuit of teaching excellence, are often disappointed to discover this is not always the case. Today, deans are not teaching and research leaders, they are management who are, to quote one of the interviewed deans, 'bricks in the wall' who are tasked with managing a faculty in a way that ultimately benefits the university from a corporate standpoint. Sometimes, these tasks do not reflect what an academic might view as good faculty leadership.

So where does this leave academics in the modern university? Bourdieu, decades of research, and this book's examination of both avenues make it clear who higher education is set up to advantage, what type of people are most likely to succeed in this environment, and what changes are being made to make universities more inclusive places. One challenge is that solutions to exclusionary practices have been slow, and are often reactionary. That is to say, the problem has to occur, be identified, and then measures put in place to counter the original problem. This process takes time, and while universities appear to be expediting these processes and looking for as many paths to solutions as possible, the landscape has been changing around them often at a very fast pace. Thus, new issues are arising as or before old problems are dealt with, and COVID-19 significantly changed the field on top of these scenarios.

A primary focus of this chapter is around employment: partly *gaining* employment, but also what it takes to be competitive for promotion and career progression once employment (regardless of type, for example, precarious, contract, continuing/tenured) has been obtained. What is clear about what has happened in academia is that as the market has tightened, and finances or funding have decreased, aspects of successful careers and employment have placed the emphasis on the individual academic being hired or promoted. This has had the clear impact of making measures put in place to increase inclusion and diversity less successful, and sees a return of cultural trajectory, privilege, and capital as the primary keys enabling success.

This chapter draws on data I have generated from a major study around precarious employment, networking in academia, and academic career trajectories. This study used a survey of seven demographic questions, followed by thirteen open-ended questions around employment history, experience, and intention. The survey was completed by 168 academics, primarily from Australia, New Zealand, North America, and the United Kingdom with 109 participants being currently employed academics in a full-time/permanent/tenured capacity, with the remainder being precariously employed academics or those who have left the industry within the last five years. The survey generated over 82,000 words of raw data and has been the basis of numerous journal articles and conference presentations. However, a brief note must be made regarding COVID-19. As has been mentioned previously in this book, when we are looking at higher education, COVID-19's impact has changed the sector in significant ways, but that is not to say that these changes were unpredictable or unforeseen. COVID-19 occurring or its financial impact could not be anticipated. However, the repercussions of what financial instability and issues surrounding student numbers, and particularly international student numbers in many countries was, and continues to be, extremely predictable. In so many instances, COVID-19 has only exacerbated trends and occurrences that have already been witnessed in higher education for several years, and in other instances have been happening for decades (Blackmore 2020). From an academic standpoint, this ensures that what has and is happening in universities because of COVID-19 is easily assessable. In most instances, COVID-19 has furthered what was already happening in universities in terms of shifts to the importance of careful management, need for sourcing funds outside of government-led funding bodies, and how these changes have impacted on the roles of those working within the sector. Yet the transitions COVID-19 has caused also play another scholarly role. Much of this book, Bourdieu's own notions, and existing research of the higher education sector is concerned with trends, trajectories, repercussions, and incremental shifts. Throughout all this research, those conducting the work have been making predictions, recommendations, and warnings against the direction in which the sector was heading, and in an unfortunate twist of events, COVID-19 has shown that their predictions were correct. Ultimately, in higher education, COVID-19 has been about lower funding and issues surrounding student numbers. At the same time, issues around funding and student enrolment have been the catalyst to changes, albeit it to varying degrees in different universities and locations, for many years, and COVID-19 has only added to these concerns.

Academic Work in the Modern University

Time and time again, the data generated from academics shows that academia is an occupation that is getting increasingly difficult to 'break into', as it is taking longer for people to gain secure employment or promotion, and any misstep can lead to consequences that are difficult to overcome. These are topics already touched on at different points throughout this book, because higher education is so layered with one action often having consequences throughout the sector's hierarchy. However, it is still worth discussing these issues in isolation to examine what we can learn about life in the modern university with the aid of Bourdieu's concepts and ideas.

Breaking into the field has been largely redefined by how the field's borders have been changing to accommodate other issues in the sector. The history of students becoming academics has perhaps only had a few broad changes in centuries of history. In the elite history of higher education this process was guided by cultural trajectory as private tutors who themselves studied at university, or later England's public schools (or private and grammar schools in other locations), had a primary role of preparing the male children of already well-to-do professionals for a university education and professional career; one of which was academia (Heffernan 2020b; Soria et al. 2013). Depending on country, and highly dependent on discipline, women also entered the field through the nineteenth century in increasing numbers though they were a minority, and whiteness, wealth, and capital was still often of paramount importance.

World War, and particularly after the second World War, was when universities truly began to open as potential employers for larger numbers of more diverse members of the population. Universities had to grow as more professions became professionalised; for example, education, engineering, and accountancy became occupations with professional standards that could largely only be met with a university led or aided education much like happened with law and medicine in the centuries before. At the same time, as nations were rebuilding after two wars and depression, governments saw the financial benefits of a more highly educated population that could gain easier employment, and potentially make and spend more money. As was touched on in the previous chapters, this led to massive university growth throughout many Westernised nations and made university employment possible for a much wider group of people, as universities could not grow fast enough to meet the increasing student numbers and academics were in short supply. In different nations and in different institutions, this rapid growth existed anywhere from the mid-1970s until the early-1990s. The primary reasons this growth was interrupted was various recessions which were triggered by different causes depending on location. However, recessions meant job losses in most industries, and much of the positive ground gained by the university sector's expansion was lost as the notion that a university education did not always result in employment damaged the sector's appeal. Furthermore, this occurred at a time when higher education had only recently stepped away from its elitist roots (Forsyth 2014).

The mid-to-late 1990s is when a slight shift also began to take place as the plausibility of academia as a career altered on several fronts. Firstly, this period marks the shift where more people began gaining doctorates each year than there were positions available either by university growth, or via the natural transitions of people leaving the profession either through retirement or moving to other employment opportunities (Larson et al. 2014). More graduates than jobs might be negative in terms of employment opportunities, but it must also be considered in the context of higher education employment. The growth that occurred from the late-1970s until that point was ultimately unsustainable. The growth in the sector occurred because of societal reasons and while the expansion of mass market higher education was immense (Esson and Ertl 2016), it was still a standout period of two decades of growth in an industry with clear links stretching back almost 1000 years; thus, twenty years of rapid development was unlikely to ever be sustainable. The 'decline' in the sector was also not an immediate drop-off of employment opportunities, it was that statistically year-on-year expansion began to slow as newly conferred doctoral students continued to graduate in ever-increasing numbers.

For academics, this initially meant employment became slightly more difficult. As this book has discussed on several occasions thanks to the work of Hannah Forsyth, Tanya Fitzgerald, James Esson, and Hubert Ertl (among many others), the growth of the sector led to universities being understaffed and employment and promotion being relatively easy to acquire for a larger group of people. The end of this growth did not occur overnight or make employment or promotion instantly more difficult; it often just delayed the processes. For example, the rate of doctoral students gaining employment before completing their degree or going into full-time employment immediately after gaining their degree only slowed, it did not stop. This occurrence shifted a group of people into teaching assistant, research assistant, and postdoctoral work before gaining full-time employment, and people may have remained in these positions for slightly longer. Thus, at least in the beginning, this was about a delay in careers rather than significant increases in difficulty in beginning or continuing a career. However, the late-1990s into the 2000s still saw universities (which are generally viewed as progressive workplaces) grow in their acceptance of varied members of society and as their funding remained relatively high, scholarships and opportunities for people for who academia may not have sat in their cultural trajectory, still allowed universities to grow in terms of inclusion and diversity.

This period leading into the 2020s (even before the consequences of COVID-19) simultaneously saw two things happen in academia which are in many ways in stark contrast to each other, but also highlight the importance of Bourdieu as he can help shine a spotlight on what is happening behind the façade of university declarations and statements.

The first is that universities became aware of equal opportunity, equity, and the importance of inclusion and diversity not just as a social practice, but also to aid in reducing the view of universities as elitist institutions that excluded some (as they had for centuries before). This has been touched on throughout this book, but the vital point is that universities had expanded the cultural trajectory of who attends university as part of the turn to mass market higher education. In a global sense, this meant that white middle-class men and women who may have chosen to immediately enter the workforce following compulsory education, or may have elected to pursue learning a trade, were instead choosing to attend universities. The important factor to note is the notion of 'choice'. Members of these groups could have chosen one of several pathways, but increasingly more chose to attend university.

Increasing inclusion and diversity meant making university a viable option for those who may not necessarily have previously had the option to 'choose' this pathway, or 'desire' this pathway (Percival et al. 2016). These issues were discussed earlier in relation to cultural trajectory and some students electing to not attend more prestigious institutions for fear of not possessing the right social capital to fit into these environments. Albeit to varying levels of success, universities have made strong efforts over the last two decades in trying to make institutions more approachable for those from working/labouring-class backgrounds, immigrant backgrounds, those with non-white heritage, those from the myriad other marginalised backgrounds, and increasing gender diversity in subjects that were traditionally male-dominated (McKenzie and Schweitzer 2001; Smit 2012).

How successful these programs have been at getting students into universities that have then gone onto pursuing academic careers is debatable. Sometimes admitting new groups still is not enough to overcome the dominant culture of an institution, at other times, having people succeed academically but without middle class capital and connections behind them is still not enough to lead to success (McKenzie and Schweitzer 2001; Smit 2012). So, while universities have tried to increase diversity (and this success is very much dictated in part by location, type of university in terms of size, wealth, background, prestige, and disciplinary area), efforts have been made to encourage and increase the diversity and inclusion of the university workforce.

However, while the last two decades has seen efforts to diversify the university workforce increase, changes in workforce expectations and pathways to success during some of this time, but perhaps particularly during the last five years (let alone after the implications of COVID-19 began to be felt) have largely worked in contrast to these efforts.

As universities and faculties have had to become more cautious of their spending, methods have been put into place to reduce 'waste', but in many ways these decisions also reduce opportunity. Researchers have noted the shift from academics regularly holding teaching and research positions, to a shift of academics with research credentials and experience being given increased research loads, while those with unproven research skills, or those who have been given research opportunities but failed to meet the targets, having their teaching and administration duties increased (Ryan et al. 2013). From a purely administrative or business-focused perspective, there is clear logic to why they would adopt this process. If one considers the university as a production line, then it only makes sense that people are streamlined into where they excel most. The problem with this method, however, is that it has quickly become not so much about the academic's choice, but rather their choice is determined for them by their opportunity which is heavily related to their cultural trajectory, and social and economic capital.

The primary issue with this system is that research time is allocated on pre-existing success, but how does someone gain research experience and success? This was a topic explored regularly in my work with precariously employed academics, early career researchers, and discussions around career progression. In terms of how a career unfolds, this potentially starts with someone during their masters or doctoral study, and the opportunity to be involved in the research being conducted by their supervisor or their supervisor's immediate circle. This may be casual work, it may even be unpaid work that is nonetheless a good opportunity for career advancement, but these opportunities in the opening stages of someone's academic career can have significant repercussions later in their career trajectory. Thus, even at this early stage of career advancement, who has the opportunity to carry out this work?

An academic can be supervising any number of masters or doctoral students at a time; I have seen ten be a common number, more than 20 is also not surprising depending on disciplinary area. This means these initial selections of masters and doctoral students to assist with research projects (and subsequently the students gain research experience and publications) is not based on merit, because little to no opportunity to demonstrate skills above other doctoral students has occurred. Instead, these initial decisions are based on cultural capital, who is able to immediately connect with their supervisor, who shares the same interests, has had the same experiences, and uses the same language (Bourdieu 1988). Thus, having capital that matches that of the supervisor or research project lead is what begins this opportunity. It is also very clear that this is not a secret or a mystery; it is very clear that academics at all stages know a factor of success is having strong academic networks (Heffernan 2020a).

In the early stages of a career, however, being able to create strong and immediate networks with those in a position to foster an early career academic's research profile is only the first step. Economic capital also plays a role in who, and how successfully, these opportunities can be leveraged. The first question is around economics and time, in so much as who has time to build relationships with their colleagues and those higher up the research chain when they are not employed or being paid by the university. This scenario has a lot to do with location, traditions, and disciplinary area, but it is nonetheless a situation that makes a significant difference. In some areas (perhaps the sciences and the arts) it is not uncommon for students to leave high school, enter university and complete their undergraduate degree before immediately going into post-graduate and higher degree research. This group of people is thus potentially only in their early to mid-20s as they complete their honours or master's degree before completing their doctorate. While this is a generalisation, as an example, these researchers due to their age are perhaps less likely to have financial dependants, not have financial obligations like mortgages and loans, they might still live on campus, they might live in shared accommodation, and they might even still be receiving financial support from their parents. This situation is not at all to say that this person will not work or will not have obligations, but here is a selection of circumstances that potentially allow them the opportunity to build rapport with those in their field by going to public lectures, or having the time to help out with small tasks that might turn into larger research opportunities (Gaertner 2009). Thus, there is a greater chance of someone from this group having the opportunity to move their schedule around to be on campus or available to be on campus more than is necessary to complete their degree.

Consider this scenario against the circumstances of someone in a field where often the standard process is that an individual does not enter doctoral research until they have had some years in the professional field. Education is a good example of this because most people completing undergraduate education degrees are doing so to become teachers rather than academics, which tends to lead people into schools before they begin their post-graduate and higher degree research work. Being that this situation can lead to people entering their doctoral degrees at older ages, also increases the likelihood that they have dependents, have mortgages, have partners, are financially independent, and might still work in the school/education system while they complete their postdoctoral and research degrees. These are various scenarios in which it becomes potentially more difficult in some disciplinary areas than others for students to have the free time to build relationships. However, disciplinary area aside, the fact remains that economic capital is a pathway to potential early career success.

Whether it be from family, a partner, or earlier career and life planning, for those who do not have to maintain full-time employment in a different career while completing their postdoctoral and research degrees, this allows them to be on campus more, go to lectures, go to meetings, and interact with the student and academic body on more occasions. Additionally, should this lead to opportunities (paid casually, via contract, or unpaid), it is those with economic capital who can carry out this work as the financial aspect is not as crucial, but it is also those with time available who can carry out this work on top of their degree work and other obligations.

The above discussion is about the very first steps someone might take into an academic career. However, as employment has become more competitive, let alone as COVID-19 has increased the need for managerialist and corporate approaches, how capital has altered employment prospects has also changed.

The previous chapters discussing the university from the view of the vice-chancellor or president and deans has shown how the university has had to shift and adapt to society. In the meantime, however, it has grown from a large educational institution to an entity that in a growing number of cases is also worth billions of dollars each year, employs thousands of people, and has tens of thousands of students enrolled. Universities have never been about waste, but chance, opportunity, and time were once significantly more part of how they operated than they are today. Academics were hired on promise and potential, and then they were given time to 'find their feet' both in terms of research and teaching. In the modern university, and certainly post COVID-19, the time for academics to find their feet is shrinking as people are increasingly streamed into research *or* teaching roles rather than teaching *and* research roles. There is also the question of who is getting streamed into research because it is often one based on capital and privilege. At the same time, the chances of someone being streamed into teaching ever being able to transition into a higher research workload allocation is slim (Barrett and Barrett 2011; Dobele et al. 2014; Guarino and Borden 2017; O'Meara et al. 2017).

Any shift away from academics being given time to find their feet and prove themselves is almost inevitably replaced by a system where potential is replaced by performance. In academia, performance (particularly early performance) is often connected to opportunity. This circumstance also has potential long-term career impacts which sees the seeds of the chance to pursue research success planted during the doctoral and postdoctoral years. The previous section highlighted how social and economic capital could lead certain demographics of students getting their first opportunities to research, publish, and collaborate. However, when moving into a career, these scenarios also mean that when this group of people secure full-time employment, they are the ones who already have research profiles and will be likely given larger research workloads and streamlined into research roles. For those people who, for example, did not have the opportunity to publish with their supervisor, or who worked full-time during their doctoral studies, or had family or carer duties which prevented them for doing extra or unpaid work during their doctoral candidature; when this group secures an academic position, they are the ones likely to be streamed into higher teaching and administrative workloads. It could also be argued that once someone has a heavy teaching load, the opportunities for them to publish are limited (Byers and Tani 2014; Crimmins 2017). Thus, essentially the only way to gain a larger research load is to rely on personal time to ensure that publications are produced while their teaching and administration obligations are being met—duties I would suggest can rarely be completed within the time allocated in most situations.

What these scenarios mean is that an increased level of pre-determinedness exists for those both entering, and already within, the higher education sector. More often than not, this means that trajectories are already set in place, including cultural trajectories largely determined from birth, and are having an increasing impact on who gets to choose what success looks like in their academic career.

A primary implication with these circumstances, however, is how they fit with diversity and inclusion. Universities may be taking steps forward to ensure diverse and inclusive workforces. Yet, as the financial pressures on faculties grow as the need for performance to increase also becomes an issue, diversity and inclusion may happen statistically. However, this chapter's discussion has shown how these measures may be equitable in getting people into the sector, but we would be right to question how equitable this is if people from non-traditional backgrounds are then subjected to structures which appear merit-based, but in fact, are largely already determined, are destined to prevent academics from non-traditional backgrounds having the ability to choose their career path, and most likely be unable to pursue one that focuses heavily on research.

Figure 9.1 shows what this looks like in practice. Universities once had more funding, could be less financially performance driven, and could allow people time to find their feet and demonstrate their research potential. During this time, the hope was that diversity and inclusion programs aided in seeing people from various social classes or cultural trajectories being given the opportunity to enter higher education, gain the skills, produce the work, and diversify the institution. Eventually, this would lead to people from different backgrounds being a part of the university hierarchy and changing the traditionally white, middle-class nature of higher education.

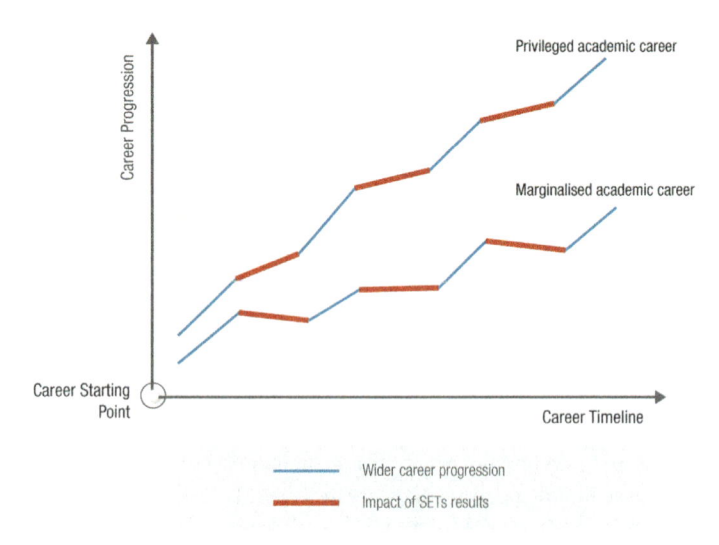

Fig. 9.1 Example of how SETs can impact on marginalised academics

In the current climate, however, the system is often failing because the systems and transparent processes that lead to university appointments, which themselves are flawed because there is little semblance of merit in education (Bourdieu 1977, 1988), are enabling academics from diverse and marginalised backgrounds to enter higher education and this should be celebrated. However, as Fig. 9.1 demonstrates, creating pathways into the field becomes less meaningful if the field is then determined by performance and factors that are increasingly influenced by social and economic capital, and often which is connected to cultural trajectory that can be set decades before someone enters a university as a student or as an academic. Ultimately, inclusion and diversity measures enable people from different backgrounds to enter academic life where everyone was on a similar career trajectory. However, now that there are increasingly two career trajectories, it cannot be ignored that academics from non-traditional backgrounds are more likely to be streamlined into only one of those career trajectories.

Networks and Success

For the purpose of getting onto the research trajectory, getting a casual or contract position, turning that into a continuing position, or even increasing someone's research allocation to help change their trajectory; relying on academic networks are regularly seen as the keyway to enable these processes. The role networks play in academia are not new, it is arguably simply a case that they are less hidden now than they once were, and this has enabled more people to see how clear they are and subsequently how they work.

Researchers know networks can have an overriding impact when compared to publication record or the prestige of where an early career researcher graduated (Burris 2004; Hadani et al. 2012). Bedeian et al. (2010) have also made the argument that networks are often used to subvert any form of merit-based approach to job hires and instead represent a process that is only carried out to appoint the hiring panel's pre-selected candidate. The above occurrences are perhaps not a surprise in an environment that is increasingly corporatised, and this notion has led several researchers to point out that hiring patterns in Standard & Poor's 500 index of firms position networked candidates above merit-based candidates, and we should not expect academia to be any different (Hadani et al. 2012; Williamson and Cable 2003). What is important to note, however, is that these findings all relate back to Bourdieu's notion of reproduction. These networks are working to get their selected candidate hired, but the candidate must still have the capacity and ability to carry out the role and subsequently help build the network's influence (Bourdieu 2000).

The work I have completed about precarious employment, career progression, and how to develop academic careers has regularly pointed to academics viewing networks as their method of success, or otherwise they follow the trend of one of my study's participants who said that networking 'gives me hope that it is possible for me to continue in academia'. The notion that someone is relying on 'hope' to enable them to continue in academia may seem extreme, but this is possibly less surprising when we consider what people are gaining from their networks. Perhaps the pinnacle of a network is employment, and my smaller-scale qualitative studies have found that people are hoping to gain employment and promotions through their network activity. Employment via networks is happening. This occurrence has only been noted by around 10–15% of participants in each study, and includes those who gained employment (including continuing full-time employment) with no interview process. Or in other instances, the candidates were informed they would be the successful candidate prior to the recruitment and interview process beginning.

A much more common scenario, in approximately 45–55% of participants depending on the study and who was being interviewed (early career researcher, mid-career researcher, late-career researcher) is that networks are used to create the capital that makes someone more employable in an academic setting. Primarily these include publishing opportunities via special issues of journals and book chapters, co-authoring publications with other network members, and being invited to present keynote addresses or present findings at conferences either on their own or with other members of the network. In these scenarios, the network allows someone who otherwise might have been trying to achieve their goals on their own to share in the network's capital and capacity to produce more work, using the shared resources of the network in terms of research quality, but also regarding the option to disseminate the research to the widest audience possible.

That networks work this way is clear to those on the inside. One participant declared of their network-based successes that they 'will do similar for those [in my network] in the future'. Other participants accepted this was the way forward as another stated 'They say it's who you know, and I think that this is especially important in a fluid sector like tertiary education', which led 30–40% of academics in the study feeling that they are hindered by their lack of network as they 'feel at a disadvantage compared to peers that have easily found a postdoc job […] thanks to the connections of their promoter'.

Summary

This brief examination of what networks can achieve and why people rely on them has reflected topics of discussion that have regularly occurred throughout this book. Networks do work, people are getting and are more likely to get opportunities and employment because of them, and this is because a network is capital, but you also need capital to get into a network. This notion again circles back to one covered extensively in this work. Capital in academia is not distributed fairly, and for all the methods of increasing inclusion and diversity, these systems are often unable to combat the advantage of capital which continues to begin and accrue from cultural trajectories that fit with what the higher education sector values most. Thus, it could be argued that methods aimed at subverting the benefits of privilege and capital in academia will unlikely be hugely successful when what the university values remains those aspects most easily gained via privilege and advantage. Changing this system is about changing the benefit and capital associated with systemic advantage, but that is unlikely to occur in a heavily and increasingly corporatised environment that is feeling the long-term impact of funding reductions and the need to produce more sellable items for less financial input.

References

Barrett L, Barrett P (2011) Women and academic workloads: career slow lane or Cul-de-Sac? High Educ 61(2):141–155. https://doi.org/10.1007/s10734-010-9329-3

Bedeian A, Cavazos D, Hunt J, Jauch L (2010) Doctoral degree prestige and the academic marketplace: a study of career mobility within the management discipline. Acad Manag Learn Educ 9(1):11–25. https://doi.org/10.5465/amle.2010.48661188

Blackmore J (2020) The carelessness of entrepreneurial universities in a world risk society: a feminist reflection on the impact of Covid-19 in Australia. High Educ Res Dev 39(7):1332–1336. https://doi.org/10.1080/07294360.2020.1825348

Bourdieu P (1977) Outline of a theory of practice (trans: Nice R). Cambridge University Press, Cambridge

Bourdieu P (1988) Homo Academicus (trans: Collier P). Polity

Bourdieu P (2000) Pascalian meditations. Stanford University Press

Burris V (2004) The academic caste system: prestige hierarchies in PhD exchange networks. Am Sociol Rev 69(2):239–264. https://doi.org/10.1177/000312240406900205

Byers P, Tani M (2014) Engaging or training sessional staff. Aust Universities' Rev 56(1):13–21

References

Crimmins G (2017) Feedback from the coal-face: how the lived experience of women casual academics can inform human resources and academic development policy and practice. Int J Acad Dev 22(1):7–18. https://doi.org/10.1080/1360144x.2016.1261353

Dobele A, Rundle-Thiele S, Kopanidis F (2014) The cracked glass ceiling: equal work but unequal status. High Educ Res Dev 33(3):456–468. https://doi.org/10.1080/07294360.2013.841654

Eacott S, MacDonald K, Keddie A, Blackmore J, Wilkinson J (2020) COVID-19 and inequities in Australian education—insights on federalism, autonomy, and access. Int Stud Educ Adm 48(3):6–13. http://cceam.net/publications/isea/isea-2020-vol-48-no-3/

Esson J, Ertl H (2016) No point worrying? Potential undergraduates, study-related debt, and the financial allure of higher education. Stud High Educ 41(7):1265–1280. https://doi.org/10.1080/03075079.2014.968542

Forsyth H (2014) A history of the modern Australian University. NewSouth Publishing, Sydney

Gaertner D (2009) Labour as gift: gift economies in the Neoliberal University. Engl Stud Can 35(4):15–18. https://doi.org/10.1353/esc.2009.0046

Guarino C, Borden V (2017) Faculty service loads and gender: are women taking care of the academic family? Res High Educ 58(6):672–694. https://doi.org/10.1007/s11162-017-9454-2

Hadani M, Coombes S, Das D, Jalajasi D (2012) Finding a good job: Academic network centrality and early occupational outcomes in management academia. J Organ Behav 33:723–739. https://doi.org/10.1002/job.788

Heffernan T (2020) There's no career in academia without networks': academic networks and career trajectory. High Educ Res Dev. https://doi.org/10.1080/07294360.2020.1799948

Heffernan T (2020) Understanding university leadership and the increase in workplace hostility through a Bourdieusian lens. High Educ Q. https://doi.org/10.1111/hequ.12272

Larson R, Ghaffarzadegan N, Xue Y (2014) Too many PhD graduates or too few academic job openings: the basic reproductive number in academia. Syst Res Behav Sci 31(6):745–750. https://doi.org/10.1002/sres.2210

McKenzie K, Schweitzer R (2001) Who succeeds at University? Factors predicting academic performance in first year Australian university students. High Educ Res Dev 20(1):21–33. https://doi.org/10.1080/07924360120043621

O'Meara K, Kuvaeva A, Nyunt G, Waugaman C, Jackson R (2017) Asked more often: gender differences in faculty workload in research universities and the work interactions that shape them. Am Educ Res J 54(6):1154–1186. https://doi.org/10.3102/0002831217716767

Percival J, DiGiuseppe M, Goodman B, LeSage A, Longo F, De La Rocha A, Hinch R, Samis J, Sanchez O, Augusto Rodrigues A, Raby P (2016) Exploring factors facilitating and hindering college-university pathway program completion. Int J Educ Manag 30(1):20–42. https://doi.org/10.1108/ijem-04-2014-0051

Ryan S, Burgess J, Connell J, Groen E (2013) Casual academic staff in an Australian university: marginalised and excluded. Tert Educ Manag 19(2):161–175. https://doi.org/10.1080/13583883.2013.783617

Smit R (2012) Towards a clearer understanding of student disadvantage in higher education: problematising deficit thinking. High Educ Res Dev 31(3):369–380. https://doi.org/10.1080/07294360.2011.634383

Soria K, Stebleton M, Huesman R (2013) Class counts: exploring differences in academic and social integration between working-class and middle/upper-class students at large, public research universities. J College Student Retention Res Theory Pract 15(2):215–242. https://doi.org/10.2190/cs.15.2.e

Williamson I, Cable D (2003) Predicting early career research productivity: the case of management faculty. J Organ Behav 24(1):25–44. https://doi.org/10.1002/job.178

Chapter 10
Shifting Borders in the Modern University

Abstract This chapter draws together to examine the key themes within the book, and highlights how as individual roles within the university have changed, they have also changed the relationship between people and structures within the institution. This chapter is primarily concerned with Bourdieu's notion of fields and how they relate to each other in a university. The chapter highlights that in past decades, let alone centuries, the roles of academics and leaders within an institution was hierarchical, but research and teaching remained the primary motivator. Thus, even if agents were doing different things, a lot of what they did nonetheless put them in similar fields to others. This chapter accordingly highlights how with vice-chancellors, deans, and academics now having to address their own specific roles such as vice-chancellors and deans taking on tasks much more closely related to management than research or teaching, the connections that once still kept the hierarchy of the university relatable to each other is now lost as vice-chancellors and deans are increasing hired on their management expertise, and increasingly smaller regard for their research profiles, because that is not the criteria for their success. This inevitably causes disconnectedness along the university hierarchy as people employed for specific roles, rarely understand the pressures other people face.

The previous chapters have provided a brief overview of how the university has changed in the last few centuries and outlined how the impact of the corporatisation of education has forced universities and those within them around the world to operate in new ways. This chapter examines what this has done to the traditional fields and their borders in higher education. As has been touched on throughout this book, the university is changing, the roles within it are changing, and the expectations of those working within universities are changing. From the outside, though, much of what happens in a university appears to be the same as it was decades ago. The titles of leaders and academics are no different, and the overall objectives of these parties is often still largely the same, but how those objectives are being met is new, and these processes are changing the fields of higher education, their borders, and their hierarchies.

This chapter looks at how fields have changed because the new expectations of leaders and academics has created new fault lines in institutional hierarchies that are impacting on intra-faculty relationships as each group adjusts to the changing expectations placed on everyone within the higher education sector. On the surface, this issue perhaps looks straightforward. Many people within the sector must take on slightly different responsibilities and have new objectives to satisfy their role requirements. However, Bourdieu's tools let us examine what the repercussions are of fields that are having their borders shifted and altering the hierarchies inside. When we think about universities as traditionally being a community of scholars which was also led by scholars, every party still had a primary vision of creating and disseminating research; some parties led these movements and other parties carried out the work. However, everyone involved was a scholar and leadership roles were attributed to senior academics rather than people with management expertise.

Why Shifting Borders Matter

These changes have caused a shift in what people in universities are being asked to do from the highest role of vice-chancellor and presidents, to faculty deans, to the staff carrying out research and teaching duties. These changes are not just about vice-chancellors and presidents having to survey their competition, deans being recruited and measured on managerial experience, or academics knowing that their work is quantifiable and that their success will be gauged on publications and grants. The previous chapters have examined what these new work expectations can look like, but this chapter examines why these new roles can be causes of tension when these changes are rarely addressed and yet have altered the fields of the university. It is the shift in dynamics that can be a cause of tension because even with all the changes, at the end of the day, research is still what drives universities forward; but this happens in a very different way to how it once did.

When leaders at different levels of the hierarchy are now managing that research, but not contributing to the research themselves, we are left with a situation where (to borrow Bourdieu's regular use of sports metaphors), a team's coach once also played the game. Leaders were once senior academics; they were leaders because they were the best player in the faculty or had a research profile that warranted being the leader. Nowadays though, that is quickly changing. As we saw in chapter nine, leaders are coaches who have sometimes played successfully, but sometimes have not played successfully, and sometimes they are coaches who have never played the game before. Add to this the fact that the role players are being asked to take on is also changing. There was a time when essentially most players were given an opportunity to teach, but sometimes also try their hand at research. This was a period of time where research skills could be honed; it was not guaranteed that research excellence would follow, but the opportunity to try was given to them. In the modern university, the stakes are increasingly too high for coaches to give potential researchers what is now often seen as the luxury of research time if results are not guaranteed. As the previous chapter highlighted, this means academics who hope to gain significant research components in their workload essentially need to enter the field as already successful players who are focusing on areas which will be published in the right journals, and will likely lead to regular and fruitful grant opportunities. This is another example of how the fields of higher education are changing constantly, but nonetheless still focus on the central goal of research.

Where these situations often lead us in the modern university, and increasingly so as budgets continue to be constrained as funding shrinks, is that the workforce is being divided as roles are becoming more defined. No longer are faculties and universities filled with researchers who teach, and those at the top of the field may also lead. Nowadays, leaders are being recruited to just lead and manage their faculty, department, or school. Some academics are being funnelled into research roles, and others are being directed towards teaching positions. It could be argued that in some instances this is leading to tension and difficult relationships (Heffernan and Bosetti 2020a, b; 2021), but even if the relationships are not difficult, these changing fields have shifted the career path of what many academics envisaged their academic career might look like, and in fact often still do for new academics entering the academy who had not anticipated the many field changes that have occurred (Heffernan and Heffernan 2018). For most, the academic expectation is to research and teach, but it is the creation and dissemination of knowledge that is the primary goal. For people being given leadership roles (and leadership salaries) the shift away from the traditional roles of research and teaching may be a worthwhile trade off. However, it cannot be denied that for academics coming into their first roles, few likely aspire (or pictured) going into heavily teaching-focused or teaching-only roles. These roles may be enjoyed by an increasing number of people as it removes some of the ample pressure to publish and receive grant funding, but I would suggest it was not the expectation of most people as they entered the profession (Benbow and Lee 2019).

Who Does (and Does not) Benefit from These Shifting Borders?

A brief consideration before discussing the implications of the changing fields, however, is to examine who gains access to these opportunities, particularly at the entry level. Even though some leaders in the earlier chapters spoke of largely being coerced into leadership positions, to suggest they had no power in the matter is in most cases a poor explanation of the situation. They may have felt compelled to take these positions, they may have felt some obligation to the faculty, or their supervisors, but choice was still an element. Choice is rarely an element to someone entering the field at an academic level and being streamlined into a role and what guides this lack of choice is important.

As we have touched on, a sizeable aspect of how research time is allocated is determined by statistical information such as number of publications, prestige of journals the publications have appeared in, and the prestige of co-authors and their affiliated institutions. The issue is that these parameters all seem very objective and fair, but they completely ignore the invisible hurdles faced by some members of society, but not others, as discussed above. Primarily this system puts women in a negative situation as the primary caregivers in the home when it comes to children or other carer duties such as those concerning elderly parents (Ward and Wolf-Wendel 2017). This is important because often research profiles are starting to be built as doctorates are written; this may be the case more in some disciplines than others, but it is a growing trend. This means, the first step towards a research career can begin while a doctorate is being completed which ensures someone is likely to be completing it while working full or part-time (a sizeable double-act on its own), but then women are also likely to have family responsibilities whereas men often have the opportunity to use this time to complete the extra work that leads to publications. At the same time, men are completing this work, but are also known to use their networks for career advancement rather than career support, so even from the doctoral stages, men are more likely building themselves research profiles (Heffernan 2020a).

These trends continue in the early career researcher stage after gaining a doctorate. To begin with, the doctoral trends are only amplified. Those who were able to get their research career started with several publications will already be in a better position to secure more research time. However, even for researchers essentially starting a fresh (as is common when people worked in other careers while completing their doctorate) a group of new academics might be given the same amount of teaching and research, but more often than not, it is the men in the group who can find additional time on top of their work duties to further increase their research outputs while women provide care and perform domestic duties. Which means in the second year, and in subsequent years, those without carer or domestic responsibilities quickly increase their research profiles.

The same is true of any researcher starting out from more financially challenging situations. Part of being a successful researcher is about skills, which many people can have and refine, but the equally important factor is time which tends to go alongside privilege. Not having financial means has repercussions in several ways. It can mean the doctoral students from poorer backgrounds may not have a choice in their working options. This might see them working several jobs while completing their doctorate which reduces their opportunities for research or having the option to 'gift' time to other academics/projects that would result in publications. For the early career researcher, this might look like taking on any and every casual position/contract offered to them, which, for many reasons all outlined in this book, are very unlikely related to research and are much more likely related to teaching. Thus, this scenario might be beneficial in getting someone known within a faculty and could lead to their longer-term or even permanent employment. However, it will likely be steered towards teaching because they have not had the opportunity to build their research profile in their own time and survive on their own/family's financial resources.

When time becomes the resource that is integral to starting a research career, any factor that can impact on that resource is one that detracts from the likelihood of success for some groups, while fostering it for others. Thus, disabilities around sight, hearing, or movement (or anything that impacts on someone's processes as they work) might have the same impact as someone with carer responsibilities because the result is likely that the work being produced is occurring at a slower rate (Waterfield et al. 2018).

The results of these processes are at least two-fold. The first is that many of these prejudices are hidden by the apparent merit of the selection process. If the first step of a post-doctoral opportunity or continuing position (for example) is to rank candidates on their research achievements, the spreadsheet of these results will completely extinguish individual circumstances including domestic obligations, financial constraints, or disability. This perhaps should not come as a surprise because this is yet another example of merit in education being a myth (Bourdieu 1977, 1988). As is so often the case, however, a primary issue is that the doxa of this process remains around merit, but it is a merit that only a very small and privileged group will possess. It is the type of merit that is curated by economic and cultural capital, and a very particular cultural trajectory.

The second scenario these situations cause is what universities get out of these performative and ever-increasing demands. This is not to suggest that higher education systems are responding with notions of exploitation, it is more that as a business system, impacted by decreased funding and increased customer choice, they will inevitably feel the impact of market results. For academics, however, the results are still the same.

There is the flow-on effect of some people from the onset of their career being put in advantageous research positions, meaning those in less fortunate positions must use their own time to make up the difference. Academics will be familiar with the discourses that valorise overwork and emphasise that the extra/unpaid work is what gives someone an edge on these metrics. This type of thinking is all part of a vicious cycle; the more people engage in this practice, the more additional work becomes normalised, and so the more additional work people must do and so on. The university is of course not entirely innocent in all of this. For example, targets for promotion and grants could be set at a minimum standard to qualify someone past an initial round before their project or research-fit becomes the primary factor. However, for the most part, universities have chosen not to do anything. Instead, the implication of meritocracy is that the best person does the best job and will have the most publications and citations of their work. Which, it cannot be ignored, leads a lot of universities to getting a lot of free labour while they leave the outstretched carrot of incremental promotions and the possibility of grant funding which itself has ever-decreasing success rates.

As these processes continue and the pressure to conduct work on one's own time continues, there are of course health, family, and social implications to academics knowing no amount of work is likely to be enough, regardless of what they get paid. However, each time these pressures increase, the group of people who can meet the demands shrinks even further, and most often, the group to benefit are middle-class men because they have the financial stability to find the extra time, and then have the networks, connections, and confidence to leverage their extra time into higher research allocations which only puts them further ahead.

Shifting Borders in a Context of Change

An element of the discussion around shifting borders is that they have led, and are leading, to tension. Even if these changes are not leading to a tension within a faculty, there is nonetheless a temporal shift which ensures staff are now being defined and viewed differently, and new staff (or people aspiring to enter the academy) may also benefit from being aware of these changes. On one hand, we do not need Bourdieu to get an idea of why shifting borders is problematic.

The simple answer is that for centuries most people in the academy were researchers, and the people leading institutions and faculties were researchers who had to make leadership decisions. Nowadays, academics do not want to be managed by people who are not researchers, or who have been hired due to managerial experience and success rather than research abilities. At the same time, the people taking on these roles, who are increasingly only being hired because of their management performance, often speak of being at a loss as to why they are experiencing pushback from academics (Heffernan and Bosetti 2020a). The notion that academics do not want to be led by non-academics, while managers are only doing the role they were employed to do might seem oversimplified, but the existing research and studies that have contributed to this book all point to a version of this thinking being part of the shifting roles of the modern university. However, this is where Bourdieu's theories come into play because his work allows us to dissect the social dynamics behind these relationships, make sense of why the hostility is present, and explore the difficulties with reconciling these groups.

The reasons why these changes have needed to happen (that being, taking a business approach to higher education) have been well established throughout this book. Funding cuts and changes to funding models and the increased competition of the mass-market higher education system forced consumer-driving practices onto the sector. In turn, institutions have had to reply through marketing strategies and promoting themselves through the research and reputations standings because these rankings do matter in the twenty-first century and can play a role in the allocation of resources (Pusser and Marginson 2013). This has led to at least two decades of higher education researchers noting that these changes have caused shifts in the qualities being sought out for those filling leadership roles that retain traditional outlooks and doxas (Blackmore 2002; Bosetti and Walker 2009). These qualities usually relate to performance surrounding people meeting the ever-increasing accountabilities of the new higher education sector as targets and success are frequently defined by quantifiable objectives of achievement rather than more subjective appraisals of research success (Ball 2012; Gibbs 2016).

The subsequent shift in workplace relationships as traditional roles and expectations have changed has also been noted by researchers (Jameson 2018; Watson 2000). Primarily, researchers have focused on the extremes of what these shifts have caused. For example, Smith and Rae Coel (2018) investigated the increase in institutional bullying alongside the pressures of universities now being coerced into operating via quantifiable targets relating to research and teaching performance between academics. These expectations having to be managed by leaders has inadvertently created environments across universities and faculties that encourage aggressiveness, reward competition, and focus on short-term achievements—aspects that breed hostility.

It is amongst these changing expectations and roles that the shifting fields within universities begin to take shape. For all the falsehoods that exist within the current doxa around higher education and the modern university, universities are still about research and the most 'famous' exports are research profiles which are built on publications, grants, and media engagements; not faculty leadership or university management prowess. This provides an example, albeit it an extreme example to prove the point, of how shifting borders in the traditional fields of higher education can be blurred. If universities are still places of intellectual debate, and no longer is everyone involved from a leadership perspective being hired on their intellectual research and standing, then this exposes a line of separation between academics and management with academics still possessing the most valued skills. Smith and Rae Coel (2018) also point out that this is the perfect breeding ground for hostility. Universities are places of intellectual debate, and the standard act of engaging someone in an intellectual conversation can be done with criticism and humiliation as the primary objective of the academic over the manager; and this can be done in a seemingly innocent way.

The above is a purposely simplified example to demonstrate the point, but these are the scenarios of the modern university where the academic workforce and leadership is changing to a new system where academia has become increasingly competitive, and the academic profile of leaders sometimes less important. Misawa (2015) also identified that the shifting fields of higher education are increasingly breeding grounds for new relationship dynamics, power dynamics, and hostilities which have not been tested because they are so new after centuries of the dynamics changing very little. The research that informed this book has also pointed to similar findings with faculty deans reporting higher numbers of incidents of hostility from their academics. Deans' routinely pointed to hostility and difficulty in communication coming from academics relating to management issues. The hostility was rarely about a faculty's research and teaching objectives because they are the discussions and topics academics understood.

The Fields of the Modern University

The previous chapters have outlined how the major roles associated with leading, research, and teaching are viewed today, and often this has included discussions and examinations of previous research of how these roles have appeared in past years or decades. The data generated that formed this chapter included a mix of interviews and surveys. Rarely did any group talk about their changing role from a Bourdieusian perspective and explicitly name the changing borders of their field, or the sub-fields within which they worked; yet analysis of the data showed that was what was taking place.

Bourdieu is thus the key to demonstrating why what might be considered even minor role changes of some positions within the context of the entire higher education sector appear small, but they all have repercussions. Every movement changes the field, every movement changes the hierarchy, and every movement leads to shifting and overlapping borders changing positions. It is important to note that these changes can both alter existing fields and borders, or create new ones. Much of this book has focused on issues within the faculty, and the faculty again provides clear examples of Bourdieu's notions at work in this circumstance.

In the original notion of the faculty, researchers have for decades noted that faculties were led by the senior academics (Fitzgerald 2014; Forsyth 2014). These leaders have also had an established or noted research profile which led them to leadership roles in their faculty. In that traditional form of faculty, the fields may have appeared such as those in Fig. 10.1 which demonstrates an example of how and why a growing teaching and research profile would qualify someone for a faculty leadership role.

What is clear about the traditional faculty is that research profile and expertise remain a primary factor in the field's hierarchy. In this instance, research profile provides structure to the hierarchy. A dean's research profile may not be the biggest in the faculty and their research outputs and teaching roles will very likely decrease after they take on the responsibility of leading the faculty, but in the traditional form of the faculty, the overall values of the faculty, the university, and higher education (that being creating and disseminating research) are maintained. For those within the faculty, it is ultimately the respect gained from research and teaching excellence that legitimises someone as a leader and brings credibility to their decisions.

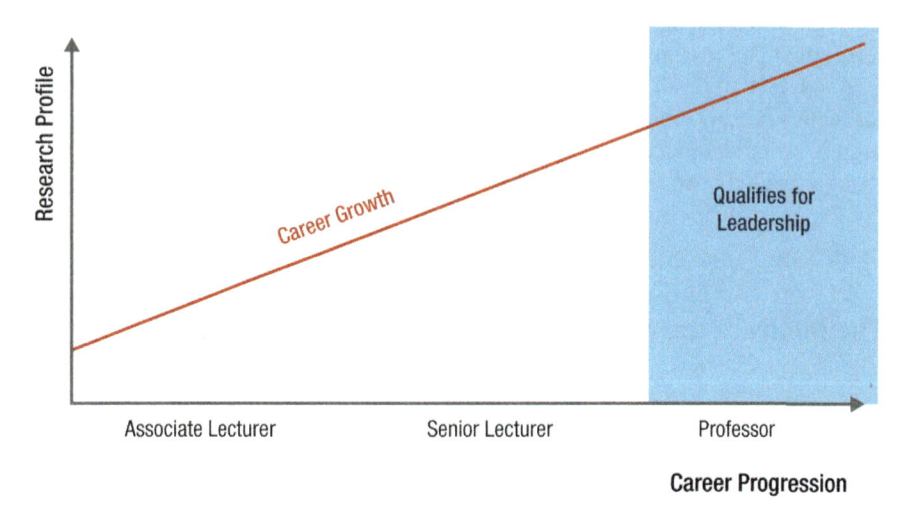

Fig. 10.1 Leadership in traditional faculty fields

However, that was in the traditional faculty; a version of the faculty and university that is only a reflection of what it once was today. Business acumen and corporate strategies are now part of the university; and they must be while funding is shrinking, funding models are changing, and there is competition for students. Figure 10.1 shows an example of what a faculty might look like after decades of neoliberalism. That is not to say this is how the fields are set in every faculty of every university in every country. However, it is how the situation is playing out in many faculties with participants across numerous studies that I and Lynn Bosetti have conducted all pointing to this becoming a growing trend, and Fig. 10.2 is also representative of how and why many fields within the university are changing.

Figure 10.2 demonstrates that the dean is separated from the field of research. On one hand the result is somewhat clear. The dean is appointed to, and is expected to, lead the faculty through times of budget-conscious course delivery and research growth, and ensuring that the research that takes place has some likelihood of attracting attention or funding. Few participants in the studies that contributed to this work question this fact. Many participants might be highly against the fact higher education is now influenced by such procedures which, for example, stops research being conducted in some areas because they are not areas likely to attract funding or large numbers of students, however, most accept that for now, these systems are here. Where the tension or issues can rise, is that the hierarchy of research has been broken. No longer is the dean who leads the faculty always high on the research ladder, they can be anywhere of varying research profile from high to not at all.

Figure 10.3 next gives an overview of what some major fields in the current university system might look like in an average university setting. I say 'major fields' because it is difficult to predict just how many smaller fields and sub-fields would exist in a university. However, the fact that Fig. 10.3 represents an extremely basic

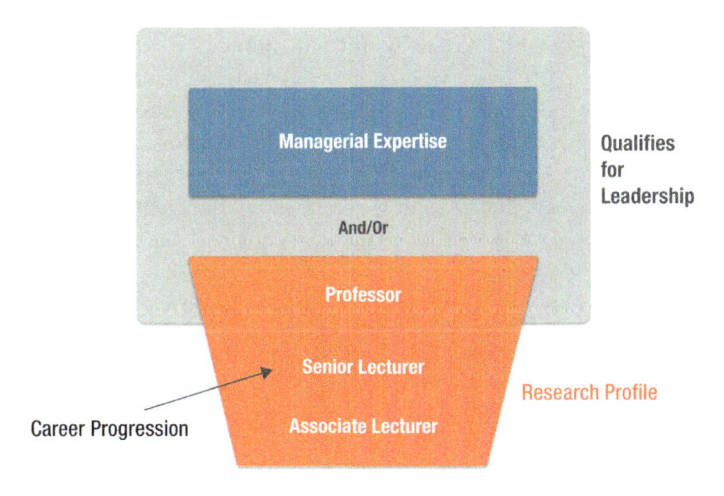

Fig. 10.2 Faculty fields with the onset of managerialism

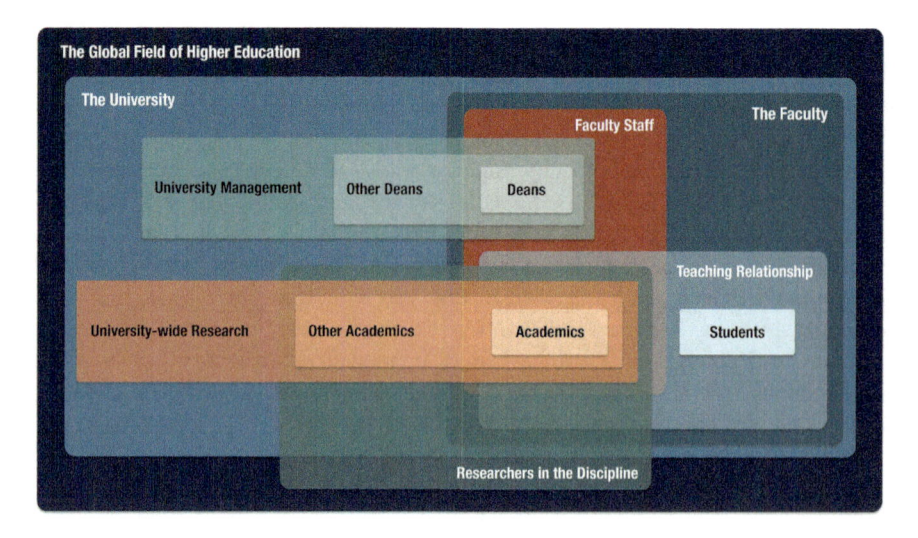

Fig. 10.3 Field map of deans and academics in universities and the sector

field map should provide some indication of how quickly a field map of a major organisation could expand.

Take for example the single field of 'Academics', in Fig. 10.3 this is one field, however, one could easily expand that by creating fields according to academic level (lecturer, senior lecturer, professor etc.). Fields could also be made according to academics being teaching focused, research focused, or having a mix of teaching and research duties, and fields could be made according to disciplinary area (early childhood, primary, secondary, tertiary, vocational education etc.). Even these basic examples are ways fields could be expanded on that would easily see a field of one (in Fig. 10.3's example) converted to a field of twenty or more. However, dividing fields to such extremes is only relevant when doing so provides data needed for analysis. For the purpose of this discussion, the most prudent information is that even basic representations of fields in universities are significant, many smaller fields and sub-fields exist if one chooses to identify them, but in all cases, every change to any field hierarchy or border will have a flow-on impact in how neighbouring fields are impacted.

This examination of deans and academics with the assistance of Figs. 10.1, 10.2, and 10.3 make several points clear. The first is to highlight that at the centre of all that is going on, deans and academics are in separate fields, even if many of their interests and experiences cross-over in other areas. Deans and academics work in the same disciplinary field, might have published on the same topics, and might know the same people within the disciplinary field, but at the core of these events, a dean's primary role is different to an academic. This is also important to note because while researchers have highlighted this difference as a cause of tension and even bullying in some situations (Heffernan and Bosetti 2020a, b) there are many cases where these differences cause no issues and the divide between academics and deans is bridged successfully, but the differences are still present.

The relationship is nonetheless where the modern university and Bourdieu's notion of fields comes into play. At the centre of many field maps around university management, there are several reasons that deans and academics from their faculty will find themselves grouped together in similar fields. In fact, in many fields outside the university that relate to a disciplinary area, academics and their dean will continue to find themselves in similar fields and this is where the tension, or at least the differences in fields is noted when deans may not be employed based on research profile, and equally, academics are often being measured on quantifiable targets of outputs produced, grant money received, and teaching results.

Despite these similarities and differences, a major issue is that the fields academics and deans are being pulled into today, are not the fields they were being drawn into in previous decades or centuries, and they are being drawn into these new fields at different levels. As university leadership and executives grow, some deans may find themselves part of a growing leadership field that includes members from marketing, planning and recruitment, and takes them away from their faculty and a dean's traditional role. At the same time, particularly in larger faculties, the duties a dean once oversaw (such as teaching and research direction) are now overseen by a new level of associate or deputy deans which again, further removes deans from their traditional duties.

The many fields within a faculty, and the other fields those within the faculty find themselves in, is also a demonstration of how the changes in higher education can be attributed to different reasons such as funding cuts or changes, mass-market education, or the need for universities to adopt business-like methods. However, what this has really resulted in is a shift in processes, and it is these shifting and new processes that begin to define life in the modern university.

Where Leaders Find Themselves

Where leaders from deans to vice-chancellors and presidents find themselves today is in a relatively distant position to where most spoke of themselves thinking they would be only a few years ago, let alone those at the end of their career who have been in higher education for several decades.

This shift in expectation is primarily two-fold. The first is that universities might still be places of research and teaching, and research and grant success might be the commodity valued most as that is what contributes to research and reputation rankings which are important in the current climate (Pusser and Marginson 2013). However, for higher education's leaders, they are no longer part of the process. The notion of a community of scholars led by scholars has largely ended (Fitzgerald 2014) but this should not be a surprise. A single university can be home to tens of thousands of students, thousands of academics and professional staff members, and must manage and account for multiple billions of dollars of grants, funding, and revenue travelling in and out of the institution each year. Researchers may debate if, or to what extent, universities are businesses, but in the twenty-first century what is not in question is the logistics of the operations of any structure that size.

With such immense factors a part of the university, it becomes clearer why research profiles have become, or must become, less of a priority in selecting people to manage and lead an institution worth billions of dollars. At the same time, the expansion of the university means leaders who once would oversee multiple tasks, are now more likely to take on a role that is only one part of the equation; again, repercussions of the size of the machine.

Vice-Chancellors and Presidents Looking Outward

At no point was this clearer than when researching the work of vice-chancellors and presidents, and how they have viewed their roles in recent years. A valuable point about most vice-chancellors is that even though those interviewed had only been in their current role for a number of years, vice-chancellor is nonetheless a role that usually comes after several decades in academia. Additionally, the vice-chancellor or president is a role that usually comes, if not always comes, after several other leadership and senior leadership roles have been successfully completed. The advantage of this situation is that it means that vice-chancellors or presidents have usually been in academia for several decades and filled several other leadership roles, which in the current climate means most have witnessed, and been a part of, the seismic shift in higher education over the last two or three decades.

What vice-chancellors and presidents do today is paradoxically different to the traditional objectives of their roles. These senior positions have always been about leading the university, and it has always been about determining the best way forward for their institution. This was traditionally done by looking outwards at the competition, looking internally at the qualities of their institution, and working out how one paired with the other. Vice-chancellors and presidents were of course aided and guided in this practice by deputy vice-chancellors, and vice-presidents, and other executive leadership members, but they nonetheless had an overarching and controlling position in collecting and analysing the necessary data, and executing the best way forward.

The fields of executive leadership, even at the most senior level, are in the current environment much more diverse in number. Though perhaps more crucially, even though the vice-chancellor or president remains the outward facing persona of university leadership, the way they speak about leadership is one where they are increasingly guided by statistics, marketing, the advice of others, and they must react to outside pressures.

Certainly, the most common discussion point amongst vice-chancellors and presidents was their need to react to outside pressures. This primarily related to universities having to react to the decisions, successes, and failures, of the universities that each institution saw as their competition. This is necessary to consider because it shows that universities are no longer bound by the field of location, but by the field of their competition which may, or may not, be about location. Ultimately, this scenario means considering if and what specific universities are likely to compete for each other's student base and academics. Education is now a global commodity, some universities can attract students from all over the world; sometimes because the student-base feels the offerings in their own countries is lacking, sometimes they want a new experience, but sometimes the prestige of an institution is enough to lure students across the globe. At the same time, academic migration is a very real consideration. For decades, the notion of the 'brain drain' has plagued some countries that have not supported research and higher education, and this led some academics to search overseas for more lucrative options; and if they have the ability, there are often institutions looking for their skills (Siekierski et al. 2018).

The COVID-19 pandemic provides many good examples of what the role of the vice-chancellor and president is in the modern university. The pandemic and its associated international and national travel restrictions (depending on location) severely limited student movement. Mostly this is assumed to be a case of students not being able, or being willing, to travel overseas for their studies because they either cannot leave their home country, or they can leave their home country but cannot risk not being able to return when desired. At the same time, however, COVID-19 has caused global economic downturn which has also reduced the number of students, both international and domestic, with the financial capacity to complete university degrees. These are all problems with which vice-chancellors and presidents ultimately must contend with, however, this is only the beginning.

Student downturn means economic downturn, many governments are also reducing university funding which is leading many institutions across the globe to have to reduce their staff numbers; a move that is predictably wildly unpopular with university staff. These varied reductions also mean a reduction in grants and funding opportunities being present which in turn places increased value in successful researchers, but only those at the extreme pinnacle of their field which, as Bourdieu and this book attests, often means those that have had extremely privileged academic experiences. Budget cuts for funding and reductions in grants essentially means the exploration to find new researchers, and opportunity of new researchers to prove themselves has been eliminated. When finances are tight, the ability to gamble on someone's success reduces which for academics means being pushed into more research if that is how they are viewed, or heavier teaching loads if their research does not meet the level of success needed during times of financial strain.

This incredibly diverse set of circumstances is why the role of the vice-chancellor and president today in no way reflects what the role entailed in previous decades and centuries. For hundreds of years in England and Europe, a few centuries ago in America, and less than a century ago in Australia and New Zealand, universities were incredibly small (Forsyth 2014) with entire student populations smaller than a large high school in the twenty-first century. Therefore, the field was once a field where vice-chancellors and presidents found themselves with largely unparalleled influence; it was their task to lead in an environment which was not large enough for them to have multiple levels of support structures to cover every aspect of the university.

For vice-chancellors and presidents, this is where the major field changes have evolved in recent decades. Student recruitment is handled by a deputy vice-chancellor or a vice-president, as is marketing, research teaching, and every other detailed aspect of a university's existence. However, even then, it is not necessarily the role of the vice-chancellor or president to manage what is done with this information and what direction each deputy or vice-leader takes this information. Vice-chancellors and presidents are not the elected leader, rather, they are the figurehead of (depending on location and institution) university executive boards, senates, or boards of trustees. It is thus the ability to manage across a large portfolio of issues that can impact on tens of thousands of staff and students and hundreds of millions of dollars, if not billions, each year which sees vice-chancellors and presidents in completely different circumstances to how they were when their role and responsibilities were originally envisaged.

The New Fields of Deans

Looking at the new fields and work of vice-chancellors and presidents tells us a lot about how even when titles of roles and their duties remain the same or appear not all that different to how they have always been, can nonetheless be severely limiting in understanding how a field has changed. However, looking at senior management still distorts this information much of the time because even though a vice-chancellor or president is performing a very different role than they were only a few decades ago, the fields and hierarchy of this level of leadership have largely remained. That is to say, vice-chancellors and presidents are not in regular contact with academics, and when they are, the power dynamics of that relationship are heavily in favour of the more senior member.

The dynamic changes in fields between deans and academics is a much more detailed area. This assessment better highlights how evolving roles, changing field hierarchies, and changing field borders can combine to demonstrate how streamlined hierarchies in the past have been replaced by new hierarchies today. These new systems can cause tensions not just with deans and academics, but with much of the middle-management layer who regularly work with academics, and these managers are increasingly not judged on their academic performance. However, unlike senior managers, this middle-management layer cannot rely on the heavily weighted power dynamic that executive management possesses as a method of maintaining harmony when overseeing the operational aspects of academics' day-to-day university lives.

We need look no further than deans operating in their own field, such as a conference or meeting of deans from a single faculty type (for example, a meeting of deans of business faculties) to see how the changes of expectations and roles can change a field even without regard to other fields.

In a meeting of faculty deans, the factor that is most likely to provide the base-hierarchy of the attendees is the institution from which they are affiliated, and more specifically, their home institution's prestige, wealth, and rankings performance. Though that will likely be how the deans are ordered without other details being known. The more shared knowledge a group of field members have about each other, the more refined a field's hierarchy will become as some members can (and other members less so) rely on other factors to bolster their position in the field. The changes will be more about minute changes rather than sweeping variations in the field's order. For example, it would be exceptionally rare that a dean from a teaching-focused rural or regional faculty would possess the means to create enough capital to be positioned near the deans of faculties that are globally renowned for their research success. However, many smaller factors in any field will be considered and lead to smaller adjustments within a field hierarchy; some of these may even lead to deans subverting the order of sub-fields to a larger than expected degree which again, might also help make small improvements in their own position in the primary field of deans of business faculties.

Bourdieu (1977) was aware of all the games people played to improve their position in a field, as he also was about the fact that everybody in most fields would take steps to improve their positions; though he conceded some would go to greater lengths than others. Bourdieu discussed many areas that can form someone's capital in an educational institution in *Homo Academicus* (1988). Though he did not specifically discuss capital relating to deans, that he knew what the doxa of higher education was (even if some aspects of it are no longer relevant), this nonetheless provides a foundation for what aspects guide the hierarchical order of most people in most fields. As pointed out previously, these factors primarily relate to the prestige of the institution of which the faculty is a part, and also the wealth and size of the faculty itself. What shifting borders and changing fields tells us, however, is how new expectations can alter the field hierarchy.

In a field of deans, two deans from institutions from similar sizes and wealth will still be ordered in the field and their personal profile will then likely be the deciding factor. In a standard situation, if one person has a strong research profile and the other was selected based more on their business acumen, than the dean with the research profile will likely be ranked higher as they will be seen as having contributed more to the field. This is because at its core, faculty deans are still part of the field of higher education where the doxa remains that a primary function is the creation of knowledge; thus, a dean can use this profile to bolster their position. This is of course a very basic example that does not include the almost infinite number of other factors that could contribute to one dean being ranked above another, however, basic examples help prove the point of what is shaping fields. As was stated earlier, a dean from a moderately ranked university with a good research profile is unlikely to be ranked above a dean from a very prestigious university without a research profile because the prestige of the institution holds such a great value in this field. Yet, if the dean of a faculty in a moderate university was a former politician, a former minister of education, or their partner was a vice-chancellor or noted public figure, these are examples that though rare, do sometimes occur and have a significant impact on field rankings. Bourdieu (1984) knew this and suggested that though factors affecting field position are difficult to predict and often hard to quantify, they nonetheless do make a difference and alter where someone is positioned within a field.

The earlier chapters of this book and this chapter's discussion surrounding field combine to build upon points that have started to be discussed in the existing literature. That is, deans being hired for management expertise is so vital in how the current higher education sector has been shaped by internal and external forces, that the practice is not restricted to any discipline, or prestige, wealth, or size of a university (Misawa 2015). However, as far as deans (and many other situations in the modern university) are concerned, the impact of making these changes to how staffing has been selected has never been addressed, they were simply changes that occurred over time, or without consideration to their larger impact. These points both highlight the need for this book's use of Bourdieu's social theories to help understand why these changes matter.

Academics in Their Own Field

An examination of how academics might be assessed in their own field also helps bring together Bourdieu's notions of field and capital not only to distinguish what aspects are valued in higher education and for academics, but what it looks like within the field as these aspects are changing. A point that has been made many times before in this book is that for some time in higher education, research excellence was the primary indicator of someone's success. It helped place them within fields that were small and quite restricted (such as academics in a highly specific disciplinary area at a defined career stage) to much broader terms such as within a faculty or within the subject area on a global stage. The power and influence research excellence once held should also be considered as that was what led to academic promotion (lecturer to senior lecturer to professor etc.) but also led people from academic roles to more senior roles such as dean, deputy vice-chancellor, and vice-chancellor) because this was a time when universities were a community of scholars governed by scholars (Fitzgerald 2014).

This topic is also an interesting crossroads for Bourdieusian scholars to consider because it represents an area where Bourdieu set out the reason and theories in his own work, and then applied those theories to demonstrate their effectiveness. However, his reasoning and theories might have been correct during the 1980s and as he examined the elite French system of universities (Harker et al. 1990). Yet four decades later his reasoning remains correct, but the higher education sector has changed across the globe to such an extent that the examinations of his work nowadays often provides examples of how to apply his theories, but they can no longer be directly applied because the higher education fields he worked with are so different to the fields of today. This scenario provides researchers interested in Bourdieu with immense opportunities to take his work, and apply his theories to understand new situations, or aid in breaking down changes by using comparative analyses of the old and new.

Where academics are concerned, the primary measure of their successful placement within a field was research excellence. As difficult as that is to quantify, and Bourdieu (1984) knew most forms of capital other than academic were difficult to quantify, academics were thus largely working towards one ultimate goal of research profile. As we have discussed at length in this book, and Bourdieu (1988) knew, this meant academics being ordered (for example) via the number of publications they have produced, the prestige of the journals they have published in, the people they have worked with, the institutions they are affiliated with, and the grants they have received. This is, however, where changing fields have changed the priorities.

Fundamentally, the notion of all academics aspiring to have the strongest research profile possible is why research excellence guided the field's order. Similarly, that deans were often respected researchers in their field aided in their gravitas when making leadership decisions. The shift in university structures and functions predictably caused changes to fields and borders surrounding academics and how they were ranked. This was all about research which started in elite institutions, and those institutions making their selections from the available candidates (Fitzgerald 2014), but continued into the expansion of the higher education sector which took shape as the 'baby boomer' generation reached university age during the 1960s and 1970s. This marked a distinct shift in higher education as teaching became a larger part of what was often primarily (or only) a research pursuit. This shift nonetheless happened at a time when universities were growing at a pace which meant suitably qualified researchers (though teachers is what they needed) with doctoral degrees were low in number which meant academic positions were easy to attain and promotions through the academic ranks quick to be achieved (Forsyth 2014). A secondary implication of a growing sector that was understaffed occurring at the same time as research institutions became teaching institutions (it was teaching that was leading to the growth after all), was that the shift to teaching from research was incremental so that research could be continued even as teaching increased.

For perhaps fifty-years or more, this has led to the notion of academics having teaching and research positions. This would of course change if grants or fellowships were part of the equation, but for most academics in universities, they were allocated a portion of research time, a portion of time to teach, and a portion of time to carry out other duties in service of the university. Thus, it was because everyone started on a somewhat level playing field and were working towards the same goals that meant research profile could be (and was) used to measure field hierarchy. However, funding changes have started to transform this situation over the last five to ten years.

These changes have been touched on earlier in this work, though, higher education's usually clear trajectory also makes it apparent in what directions some aspects had to change. One could suggest that the last decade has seen two negative areas of higher education come to a head at relatively the same time; funding cuts, combined with an oversupply of academics. These two factors have completely changed the field in a very short time, and it has changed the field in an amount of time that means people who ascended the academic hierarchy before these changes are still very much in the academy in (often) associate professor, professor, or leadership roles.

The earlier chapter on academics in the modern university outlined what these changes look like in practice. In the modern system, however, universities do not have the funds they once did for promotions, growth has slowed (and is sometimes declining following the COVID-19 pandemic), and there is an oversupply of academics to fill a limited number of positions. The first step for any new academic is thus the struggle to gain employment. The issues with precarious employment are well documented (Crimmins 2017), but a system that once saw people commonly go from doctoral studies to continuing employment, or into a post-doctoral position until permanent or tenure-track employment was secured, is now becoming much rarer. Existing studies, and the studies and participants I have worked with in generating this book's data commonly describe being in precarious employment for multiple years or multiple postdoctoral positions, and even then, the path out of precarious employment usually relates to network rather than merit; conclusions that fit firmly with Bourdieu's (1988) understanding of networks and education.

Once employment is secured, the run up the academic ladder is now also increasingly difficult. The targets needing to be met for each academic level have increased year upon year relating to publication targets, teaching performance, number of doctoral students completed, and funding secured. Additionally, it is no longer about meeting or exceeding someone's current targets to secure promotion. Instead, it is about proving, usually over several years, that someone can meet or exceed the targets of the level they are applying, to increase the likelihood of a successful promotion application. Therefore, what we see today is not academics being promoted for doing their current job well; there is no suggestion that someone will now be promoted on potential. Nowadays, promotion comes by proving that you can work at (or beyond) the level to which you are applying.

Studies have also repeatedly suggested (Darnon et al. 2009; Heffernan and Heffernan 2018) that universities rarely set binary targets (that could lead to transactional promotions, aka, meeting a set level ensures promotion) and instead institutions set benchmarks that are largely unattainable, but make it known that meeting a number of targets, but not necessarily all of them, may be enough for promotion. However, which of these targets need to be met or acceded, and by how much, is almost always not advertised and at the discretion of the promotion committee. Academics find this incredibly frustrating because they view any situation where personal choice of their superiors or a promotional panel is one that is destined to benefit some over others depending on their social capital with those groups (Heffernan 2019, 2020a).

From a management standpoint, this may not be the intention of the current system. However, it cannot be denied that it results in prompting academics to work and achieve far beyond their paygrade in the hope of promotion, and encourages employees to take on duties that they perhaps otherwise would not normally do so at their current level. Thus, this system of promotion can also be a cost saving measure as it encourages extra work to be carried out that may, or may not, be rewarded.

This discussion is another where the timing of this book has become relevant as it draws on studies that have been carried out pre-COVID-19, or as the impact of COVID-19 has started to be felt. In higher education, it seems as though in most aspects relating to administration and the systems within the university, COVID-19 has not necessarily created new issues, but has sped-up the trajectory of current trends. The reduction in funds due to COVID-19 regardless of it being because of a country's budget cuts, changes to funding models, or reduction in student numbers is that competition has increased. Supply and demand of course mean expectations of performance are now likely higher for successful promotion applicants because the money to fund additional salaries is stagnant or in decline.

At the same time, however, applying for promotion at least means someone is already in secure employment. The consequences of COVID-19 and the expectations of gaining employment are too early (at this point) to be known through solid data but predictions and anecdotal evidence can be used to make solid estimates. Essentially, the result of COVID-19 was that tens of thousands of jobs were lost throughout the sector and across many countries. These were not limited to entry-level positions, and often they did not relate to performance but often about universities focusing on their larger and most profitable degrees and research streams. At the same time, many people not on permanent or tenure track positions such as those completing postdoctoral work or research fellowships have had their employment cancelled. In many cases, this has occurred not because they were underperforming, but because universities have prioritised retaining permanent/tenured staff over contract staff. The ethics of this decision may be debatable, but the implication to those who have lost their employment is very real.

Nonetheless, what COVID-19 has done, in many cases, is caused hiring pauses, at the same time as the quality and size of the applicant pool has been pushed to extraordinarily high proportions compared to what positions are available. This scenario is a difficult one to assess because in many situations the successful applicant will be one hired on the merit of their performance, but also have contacts in the university (Heffernan 2020a). However, this means people who are essentially mid-career, people who are and have been working at senior lecturer/assistant professor/reader level, are now competing for entry level and early-career positions. In this scenario, the university benefits purely from a supply and demand standpoint, and the most qualified applicant will likely be successful, but the likely candidate will likely be bordering on, if not, a mid-career academic filling a position that pre-COVID-19 would have gone to an early-career researcher; perhaps a year or two out from completing their doctorate.

So where does this leave academics about to complete their doctorate or who have just completed their doctorate? Again, the research is not yet available, but this is a book about life in the modern university and this is what is happening right now. It could be suggested that a 'positive' aspect of what is taking place is that it is not happening behind closed doors. It is well documented. Most people within the field of higher education know this is a difficult situation. It appears that for the most part, prospective academic employees know the next few years will unlikely lead to solid employment and sessional/contract/casual employment is realistically the most likely work opportunities they are to receive. For some, this means they need to step away from academia and into more solid employment options in other fields, for others, they are willing to wait and piece together work opportunities in the hope of being in a good position when continuing/full-time employment becomes more readily available. This situation is nonetheless highly predictable regarding the privilege with which people have entered higher education and their likely success. It is likely to reflect the elitist history of universities and undo much of the work the sector has engaged with over the last few decades to make universities more inclusive and diverse workplaces.

What many taking their first steps into academia have found, and will continue to find in the current environment, is that the path from doctoral degree to secure academic career has increased in the time it takes to go from completing a doctoral degree to gaining full-time employment, let alone continuing/tenured employment. Thus, long-term success is about who can 'weather the storm' between these two points. Therefore, this is not about who has access to the system, or how welcoming the system might be, this is purely about aspiring academics needing to consider their own life and financial position before deciding if they have the option of remaining in a system that may not offer secure employment for an extended period. This circumstance does not benefit those with the best ideas, those with the best research results, or those with the highest number of teaching prizes. It benefits those with the financial resources to survive in precarious employment, or without employment, as they build their research profile to a point that they become competitive in the high-stakes competition of academic employment.

Even once employed, however, the evidence is growing (much of it as this book is being written) that the shape of faculties and what is expected of academics is also changing, which again, alters the field and field hierarchy. Shrinking funding and more competition for grants may be responsible for the trend of academics being directed more towards research or teaching (rather than everyone operating on the same research and teaching allocation). This is also a process that started before COVID-19 amplified the potential need for this situation to continue. It is the current downturn in economics and student numbers that has reiterated that students are not just a resource that universities have competed over for the last several decades. Students have reappeared as proving themselves as invaluable in aiding in institutional growth and providing financial steppingstones to enabling research. The re-emergence of the value students play has also paired with a new focus on student satisfaction, and ensuring quality teaching. This is not at all to suggest these issues were not important in previous years, or decades, but even Bourdieu (1988) knew that teaching awards and performance helped shaped someone's position in a field, but these forms of capital were secondary to those around research. Bourdieu may have been correct then, and he may have been correct in many Westernised nations until the mid-2010s, but the incredibly high competition for students in the current setting has raised the profile and capital associated with teaching significantly.

However, it has (or will) be another divide between academics. As academics shift towards being viewed as researchers and teachers, and teaching and leadership in course design and direction become viable career and promotional paths, the field of teachers and researchers will become a field of researchers and a field of teachers. The two will overlap highly, but it is a cause of division and a split of direction.

Summary

Examining the shifting borders of the university demonstrates why changes that appear minimal, and on the surface are sometimes so small they may appear as if they rarely warrant changes in position titles, can have significant implications for the operation of, and working life within, universities. What can be seen from several decades of slower change, more rapid changes in the last decade, and an escalation of many of these events during and post-COVID-19, however, is a splintering of the core focus of academic staff and leaders throughout the university hierarchy. It is this splintering of focus, roles, and purpose that has significantly altered what life in the modern university looks like as we approach the mid-twenty-first century.

References

Ball S (2012) Performativity, commodification and commitment: an I-spy guide to the Neoliberal University. Br J Educ Stud 60(1):17–28. https://doi.org/10.1080/00071005.2011.650940

Benbow R, Lee C (2019) Teaching-focused social networks among college faculty: exploring conditions for the development of social capital. High Educ 78(1):67–89. https://doi.org/10.1007/s10734-018-0331-5

Blackmore J (2002) Globalisation and the restructuring of higher education for new knowledge economies: new dangers or old habits troubling gender equity work in universities? High Educ Q 56(4):419–441. https://doi.org/10.1111/1468-2273.00228

Bosetti L, Walker K (2009) Perspectives of UK Vice-Chancellors on leading universities in a knowledge-based economy. High Educ Q 64(1):4–21. https://doi.org/10.1111/j.1468-2273.2009.00424.x

Bourdieu P (1977) Outline of a theory of practice (trans: Nice R). Cambridge University Press, Cambridge

Bourdieu P (1984) Distinction: a social critique of the judgment of taste (trans: Nice R). Harvard University Press, Boston

Bourdieu P (1988) Homo Academicus (trans: Collier P). Polity

Crimmins G (2017) Feedback from the coal-face: how the lived experience of women casual academics can inform human resources and academic development policy and practice. Int J Acad Dev 22(1):7–18. https://doi.org/10.1080/1360144x.2016.1261353

Darnon C, Dompnier B, Delmas F, Pulfrey C, Butera F (2009) Achievement goal promotion at university: social desirability and social utility of mastery and performance goals. J Pers Soc Psychol 96(1):119–134. https://doi.org/10.1037/a0012824

Fitzgerald T (2014) Scholarly traditions and the role of the professoriate in uncertain times. J Educ Adm Hist 46(2):207–219. https://doi.org/10.1080/00220620.2014.889092

Forsyth H (2014) A history of the modern Australian University. NewSouth Publishing, Sydney

Gibbs A (2016) Improving publication: advice for busy higher education academics. Int J Acad Dev 21(3):255–258. https://doi.org/10.1080/1360144x.2015.1128436

Harker R, Mahar C, Wilkes C (eds) (1990) An Introduction to the Work of Pierre Bourdieu. Macmillan

Heffernan T (2018) Approaches to career development and support for sessional academics in higher education. Int J Acad Dev. https://doi.org/10.1080/1360144X.2018.1510406

Heffernan T (2020) Understanding university leadership and the increase in workplace hostility through a Bourdieusian lens. High Educ Q. https://doi.org/10.1111/hequ.12272

Heffernan T (2020) There's no career in academia without networks': academic networks and career trajectory. High Educ Res Dev. https://doi.org/10.1080/07294360.2020.1799948

Heffernan T, Bosetti L (2020) The emotional labour and toll of managerial academia on higher education leaders. J Educ Adm Hist. https://doi.org/10.1080/00220620.2020.1725741

Heffernan T, Bosetti L (2020) University bullying and incivility towards faculty deans. Int J Educ Leadersh. https://doi.org/10.1080/13603124.2020.1850870

Heffernan T, Bosetti L (2021) Incivility: the new type of bulling in higher education. Camb J Educ. https://doi.org/10.1080/0305764X.2021.1897524

Heffernan T, Heffernan A (2018) The academic exodus: the role of institutional support in academics leaving universities and the academy. Prof Dev Educ. https://doi.org/10.1080/19415257.2018.1474491

Heffernan T (2019) Reporting on vice-chancellor salaries in Australia's and the United Kingdom's media in the wake of strikes, cuts and 'falling performance'. Int J Leadersh Educ, pp 1–17. https://doi.org/10.1080/13603124.2019.1631387

Jameson J (2018) Critical corridor talk: just gossip or stoic resistance? Unrecognised informal higher education leadership. High Educ Q 72(4):375–389. https://doi.org/10.1111/hequ.12174

Misawa M (2015) Cuts and bruises caused by arrows, sticks, and stones in academia. Adult Learn 26(1):6–13. https://doi.org/10.1177/1045159514558413

Pusser B, Marginson S (2013) University rankings in critical perspective. J Higher Educ 84:544–568. https://doi.org/10.1353/jhe.2013.0022

Siekierski P, Correia Lima M, Mendes Borini F (2018) International mobility of academics: brain drain and brain gain. Eur Manag Rev 15(3):329–339. https://doi.org/10.1111/emre.12170

Smith F, Rae Coel C (2018) Workplace bullying policies, higher education and the First amendment: building bridges not walls. First Amendment Stud 52(1):96–111. https://doi.org/10.1080/21689725.2018.1495094

Ward K, Wolf-Wendel L (2017) "Good" places to work: women faculty, community colleges, academic work, and family integration. New Dir Commun Col 179:47–58. https://doi.org/10.1002/cc.20261

Waterfield B, Beagan B, Weinberg M (2018) Disabled academics: a case study in Canadian universities. Disabil Soc 33(3):327–348. https://doi.org/10.1080/09687599.2017.1411251

Watson D (2000) Managing in higher education: the 'Wicked Issues.' High Educ Q 54(1):5–21. https://doi.org/10.1111/1468-2273.00142

Conclusion New Directions in the Modern University

Abstract This chapter brings together the major points and conclusions of the book. The chapter illustrates what the new university looks like, may look like in the future, and why stakeholders, and society in general, need to be aware that the notion of the ivory tower is now all but lost. Universities are no longer communities of scholars intentionally separated from government and business, and are now in fact major corporations, operated for profit, selling knowledge and skills for dissemination in the form of teaching, creating knowledge for external buyers in the form of grants and consultancy, and creating knowledge that may result in future funding.

Across the breadth of the university hierarchy, the reshaping of roles and new focus of different positions and tasks has created a modern university that in many ways is a significant augmentation of how universities looked a decade ago, let alone during the late-twentieth century.

The changes may be the result of shifting funding structures and the need for universities to meet the demands of a changing society. However, the impact from the top down has been different across the spectrum of university positions. Even a brief assessment of what vice-chancellors and presidents are now required to do makes it clear that being selected or asked to fill the role of vice-chancellor or president was once the sign of an academic with excellent leadership skills around the areas of research and teaching. Today, the primary role of the vice-chancellor and president is to be the spokesperson of the senior executive, board of trustees/governors/directors, and lead the university as it navigates the best ways forward regarding the competition with universities vying for the same students and academics; whether they are geographically-close universities, or institutions similar in prestige and rank. For all these changes, the change in the vice-chancellor's and president's role more than most other fields in the university depicts a role that has changed and alters who is being selected, what they are required to do, and what makes them successful. However, this field is so much higher in terms of power and influence than any other field in the university. They sit at the top of the field.

At the dean and academic level is where shifting borders becomes more complex, but also more telling of potential current and future workplace tensions as the higher education sector is modernising while still holding onto many of its traditional values. For deans, in a field comprised of other deans, their order will be tied strongly to institutional capital and this will make the size, wealth, and prestige of the faculty and affiliated institution a primary factor in how the field is ordered. Again, as we see with vice-chancellors and presidents, research profile may have some bearing in altering the order, but it will not be significant. However, it does still play a role because while some deans might be appointed more on their managerial skills than their research profile, and this trend may be growing, many currently serving deans were (and will continue to be) selected with their research profile carrying varying degrees of capital with the selection committee. It is because of this variation of some deans having their research profile carrying some weight in their appointment and selection that research plays some role in the hierarchy of deans.

Studies have suggested (Heffernan and Bosetti 2020a, b) that for vice-chancellors and presidents, research is significant in how they have climbed the leadership hierarchy, because in previous years research profile was more influential. However, once someone reaches the level of vice-chancellor, research profile becomes significantly less important to their capital as a leader; perhaps because few people expect someone with the time pressures of the senior university leader to still be research active. For deans, the situation is amplified but also a little different. Deans have been appointed to their positions with research profile playing a varied amount of significance depending on the research focus of their institution and faculty. In many ways, how research impacts on deans is how research impacts on the careers of the burgeoning field of teaching-focused academics. The primary capital that shapes teaching-focused academics in the field of a faculty is their skills around course design and implementation, knowledge of student voice, values, and priorities. In these circumstances, research success may alter the field's hierarchy to some degree. However, as I have discussed throughout this book the impact of this capital is minimal, as it is not the primary capital being measured to shape the field's hierarchy.

This all changes when research becomes the primary capital being measured. This can occur in set fields where it is expected that research profile will be the primary capital measured, such as an academic conference. It also has an impact in the faculty, and these instances are about how power dynamics are shaped. At an academic conference, it was once the case that deans would have solid research profiles and it was in part their research profile that led them to the position of dean. However, now that the requirement to fulfil the role of dean has changed, in a field where research profile is key, some deans may find themselves far from the top of the field's hierarchy because their position as dean, rather than their research profile, positions them in the hierarchy. The position of dean still carries significant capital, but it will not be enough to alone ascend the research hierarchy.

This issue becomes more complicated for deans whose faculties also include one of, or some of, a field's leading scholars. In any given discipline, the true leaders of that field (in terms of publications, citations, grant success, and perhaps more importantly in this context, global profile) are likely very few. One could suggest there are far fewer global leaders in the field than there are deans. This scenario gives academics at the top of their field incredible power and allows them to set much of their own agenda in ways lower ranked academics cannot.

This scenario highlights a fundamental shift in structure with how roles are changing in the academy. When research profile was still a guiding factor in all positions, it was as if the dean of the faculty, was (to return to Bourdieu's sports metaphor) the coach of the team, and at the same time, also a high-profile player. As trends continue towards professional career deans, the management skills are increasing, but they are no longer players. Thus, deans are becoming managers with required and valued skills, but these skills are used to help deploy academics in the best possible ways. This can result in some deans having less influence within the disciplinary field itself, compared to what they once may have held. In many instances, this may not matter because research is no longer their function, yet, deans with little or no research may also find themselves feeling like 'fish out of water' (Bourdieu 1990) in some settings because they do not have the skills to play the game, that is, to examine and evaluate particular ideas, or being aware of the latest research. This is not a criticism. Rather, it is a reflection of a system that is prioritising management skills in a particular role. When academia is increasingly performative and measured via quantifiable and accountable targets, interpreting and working with those data becomes the priority and can be done without specialist knowledge of the field.

Deans, however, still have a position of power. It is also necessary to consider the changes to the internal structures of universities, when some groups do not have power. Once the focus shifts to academics, and in particular academics' research profiles, how they are ordered in a field, and thus the capital and influence they possess, becomes very distorted. Much like deans, for a long time in university history, the academic hierarchy was primarily ordered by research success; the higher number of publications and more prestigious journals that published those articles, the more quickly and higher someone ascended through the academic ranks. Therefore, in a field that in its widest sense is about the creation and dissemination of knowledge, the primary capital that shaped an academic's position was research and closely associated achievements like grants and fellowships. Teaching of course played a role in this too, but it was not one of the primary forms of capital that contributed to someone's position in the hierarchy. The conclusion of this system was that in a faculty, research was the primary factor that ordered academics, at a conference, institutional capital played a significant role, and position (senior lecturer, professor etc.) was indicative of research performance.

The consolidation of funding, changes to funding models, and increase in competition for students has, however, made teaching more of a focal point in many faculties and quality teaching (though arguments could be made about what constitutes quality teaching) a valued skill and one that can lead to promotion and influence within some faculties. This circumstance shares many characteristics with deans being appointed via their managerial expertise; in a field traditionally dominated by research performance, characteristics outside of the capital that has been most valued for centuries can influence and shape someone's career. These shifts in borders and the changes these shifts can create nonetheless cause some, or has the potential to cause, tension in yet unexplored ways.

Much like the appointment of deans, these issues are very university and faculty dependant; that is to say, being promoted and valued on teaching expertise may be limited and need to be assessed on a faculty-to-faculty basis. In faculties where it is present, we need to be aware that these changes are happening, and will result in long-term impacts which have not yet run their course. Some of the issues that need to be considered include the fact that two academics can be at the same level, but one could be there because of research excellence, and the other because of teaching excellence; but who is higher in the faculty hierarchy? That answer would largely lay with the composition of the faculty, but it is nonetheless a question that needs to be answered because one person will be ranked above another. Perhaps at the extreme, is also questions of what happens if one form of expertise is significantly higher valued than the other. If academic levels are not tied to the same requirements, does a lecturer focusing on research rank higher than a senior lecturer focusing on teaching, or vice versa if that is what the faculty prefers?

This dynamic is shaped by the field so the choices of individual faculties or universities to place different amounts of capital on teaching or research will be a defining factor. However, outside of the faculty or university, in the wider sphere of higher education, the determining value of capital will be what the field prioritises most. Bourdieu (1988) knew this meant teaching will be respected, but the capital that matters is publication number and prestige, the number and value of grants received, and noted accolades within the field. This results in rather predictable consequences. In the field of a conference, for example, research profile is the prioritised capital. Thus, in this field, being 'known' is perhaps the greatest contributor to capital, and being known is likely to fall to those with research profiles rather than those employed due to their teaching excellence.

The field of a conference is perhaps most reflective of approaches to a disciplinary field in a national sense, let alone an international sense. Faculties and universities can make choices, and these choices may be common within a specific geographical area or with comparatively sized/wealthy/prestigious universities, but this is rarely enough to make a large-scale impact on the national or global approach to a field or doxa within a field. Therefore, we see changes that are impacting on the field, but are not making large enough impacts (at this point) to change the field's primary measures of capital and influence.

As much of this book has pointed out, there have been decades of changing policies and reasons that universities have had to change their administration and operational stances and approaches to academic work, research, and teaching. Many of these changes have been about funding, student expectations, but also what purpose the university serves in different societies. It is also the case that some of these pressures to change are global, or happen to have occurred in multiple geographic locations, while others have been in response to national or local demographic changes or funding changes.

In amongst these changes, life in the university has in some cases stayed the same, but in other ways it is completely different. Or perhaps worse, because these changes appear invisible, things appear the same but are controlled by new pressures. It is because of these pressures that we see the splintering of the workforce and roles. For centuries, almost every decision within the university was guided by priorities around research and teaching. Promotion, career advancement, and leadership were components based strongly on research performance; in these scenarios, research was the capital that guided most staffing decisions. However, in the modern university, the role research plays in these decisions is shrinking. In some areas, research plays little to no role in how decisions are being made because management and corporate decisions are taking priority as a matter of survival. It is crucial that we acknowledge what these changes mean moving forward because we are moving towards unexplored territory and the better the information administrators, policymakers, leaders, and academics have about these new ways of working, the better prepared we can all be to contend with them.

Bourdieu told us decades ago that education was what the middle and upper-classes used to maintain and increase their privilege via a method that appeared merit-based and led to the notion that people succeeded because they tried hard and excelled at their schooling (Bourdieu 1977). What we have seen in this book is that this transition of privilege begins perhaps before birth, is evident through compulsory schooling and into university, and continues with those who choose academia as a career path because cultural trajectory and capital leads to networks which increases capital, and the system repeats. For centuries, this created a system that excluded many from higher education both as a student and as an academic, but it was the need for mass-market higher education paired with a time of enlightening, progressive, and liberal thought filling universities from the 1960s onwards that allowed so many to enter these fields. Bourdieu's work around field and field hierarchy shows us how there is, nonetheless, a difference between being admitted to a field, and having the opportunity to improve someone's position in the field order. The field order in academia is still highly dependent on capital, even if merit and objective-looking processes guide those decisions. In reality, these are processes that value capital which itself is merit-based, but the methods to accrue this capital are highly influenced by cultural trajectory and privilege.

The system is not impenetrable, there will always be exceptions to the rule and a central point of much of Bourdieu's work was that he knew his transformation from a poor farming village to revered academic was one such transformation. However, he knew his experience was atypical, and in fact only aided in the negative issues surrounding merit and achievement because he could be used as an example of people working hard and achieving their goals. When in fact, people without capital are working in systems that at almost every turn favour those with capital. To borrow an idea from the opening chapters; this book has made clear how and why academia, even in the twenty-first century, is still a space where some people will have the gates to opportunity, employment, and promotion opened for them at every barrier. However, those without capital will have to navigate around closed gates and borders which makes the journey longer, more difficult, and less likely to be successful. Universities were not unaware of this and have tried to increase diversity and inclusion through varied processes and methods which have been successful to differing degrees. Some researchers would say these attempts were never successful, and certainly depending on their focus area they are likely correct, though I would hope some areas have been more successful than others. However, what has become evident over the last decade as managerialism and corporatisation increased across the university sector, is that as financial pressures have grown, universities and faculties became less able to take chances on people, people are increasingly employed and promoted on proven skills rather than potential, but proven skills often go together with privilege and begins in the earliest days of people entering universities as students. Thus, I would also question if any system has been successful if an unexpected issue (such as a financial downturn) causes a sector to return to its default mode; and that default mode remains being one that benefits the economically and socially privileged.

As we enter the first stages of the mid-twenty-first century, Bourdieu has shown us that the university sector and those within it must stop looking for methods that increase diversity and inclusivity for students and staff by opening one or two gates of an otherwise closed off field that essentially only allows people to enter and then be ordered by capital and privilege. As it has been several decades since Bourdieu's death, we have the advantage of seeing more than twenty years of efforts in trying to rectify some of the issues he identified with class and privilege in the higher education space, but in reality, many of these efforts have occurred alongside and in contrast to the financial pressure universities are facing. Undoing centuries of traditions that have focused on privilege is a daunting task, but Bourdieu and many researchers since have shown audiences around the globe what the problems are and why the impact is so severe. It is now time for the wider higher education sector to take this information and aim to build a better future aimed at including new structures that are no longer at their core centred around cultural trajectory, capital, and privilege.

References

Bourdieu P (1977) Outline of a theory of practice (trans: Nice R). Cambridge University Press, Cambridge

Bourdieu P (1988) Homo Academicus (trans: Collier P). Polity

Bourdieu P (1990) In other words: essays towards a reflexive sociology. Stanford University Press, Stanford

Heffernan T, Bosetti L (2020) The emotional labour and toll of managerial academia on higher education leaders. J Educ Adm Hist. https://doi.org/10.1080/00220620.2020.1725741

Heffernan T, Bosetti L (2020) University bullying and incivility towards faculty deans. Int J Educ Leadersh. https://doi.org/10.1080/13603124.2020.1850870

Ma A, Dolton P (2003) Executive pay in the public sector: the case of CEOs in UK universities. In: Royal economic society annual conference 2003. Royal Economic Society, Warwick, UK

Printed in Great Britain
by Amazon

Bourdieu and Higher Education